Study Commentary on Job

A Study Commentary
on
Job

Hywel R. Jones

 EVANGELICAL PRESS

EVANGELICAL PRESS
Faverdale North, Darlington, DL3 0PH, England

e-mail: sales@evangelicalpress.org

Evangelical Press USA
P. O. Box 825, Webster, New York 14580, USA

e-mail: usa.sales@evangelicalpress.org

web: http://www.evangelicalpress.org

First published 2007

British Library Cataloguing in Publication Data available

ISBN-13 978 085234 664 8   ISBN 0 85234 664 6

Printed and bound by Gutenberg Press, Malta.

Contents

Author's preface and dedication

The book of Job has been highly spoken of by many[1] whose aim has not been to hold a brief for the Christian church. Literary giants who have ransacked language in order to depict life's dignity and agony have all praised it — for example, Dante, Milton, Shakespeare, Goethe and Dostoevsky.

Thomas Carlyle, the nineteenth-century man of letters, wrote of it, 'I call it, apart from all theories about it, one of the grandest things ever written with pen. One feels, indeed, as if it were not Hebrew; such a noble universality, different from noble patriotism or noble sectarianism, reigns in it. A noble Book; all men's Book! It is our first, oldest statement of the never-ending Problem — man's destiny, and God's way with him here in this earth. And all in such free flowing outlines; grand in its sincerity, in its simplicity; in its epic melody, and repose of reconcilement... Sublime sorrow, sublime reconciliation; oldest choral music as of the heart of mankind — so soft, and great; as the summer midnight, as the world with its seas and stars! There is nothing written, I think, in the Bible or out of it, of equal literary merit.'[2]

Welcome as such commendations are in an age when the Bible is no longer regarded as highly as it ought to be, it should be remembered that Job belongs primarily to the Christian church. Martin Luther described it as 'magnificent and sublime as no other book of Scripture', and as such it is imbued with a far higher inspiration than any one of the world's great classics. By it, God aims to instruct and encourage his people in their earthly pilgrimage towards heaven, just as he does in all the other books of the Bible.

But the breadth of its appeal should not be forgotten. Set outside the life of Israel, the book of Job provides a ready-made point of contact with unchurched people. There are now so many who have lost their way, either because they do not ask the big questions about life, or because they are swamped by the fact that there seem to be no real answers to them. By its presentation of both the grim realities of human existence *and* the wonder of divine grace, the book has something to say to any who would consult it seriously. It therefore supplies excellent material for lively and relevant preaching to people of every culture, not only by way of edification, but also evangelism. This study is written partly in the hope that such preaching will take place.

The English Standard Version is the translation that is most often used in this commentary.[3] Selected verses which highlight the focus of the exposition are printed out for easy reference, but the relevant sections of the Bible text should be read in full in advance of the comment on them. It might suit some readers of this book to pass by the first part of the introduction, dealing with matters of a scholarly nature. Whenever the name *Job* is italicized, this is to indicate that the reference is to the book and not to the person.

I have derived help from so many who have written on *Job*, but a decision has been made in the interests of length not to include quotations from their works. Some of these are listed in the select bibliography.[4] There is, however, one which I must mention because in many ways it was the catalyst for this study. It is *The Argument of the Book of Job Unfolded* by William Henry Green, who taught at Princeton in the latter half of the nineteenth century. The copy that I saw was on a conference bookstall in Felixstowe, England. It was in a rather crumpled condition but its title caught my eye. It was *The Triumph of Job over Satan*, and those words by themselves had the effect of putting *Job* back in my Bible after an academic course of study of its text.[5]

Much of this material has been taught and preached over the years in too many places to mention. It has been revised many times and I am grateful to be able to satisfy the requests (and to silence the reminders!) that it should be put into printed form. The trustees of Westminster Seminary, California, kindly granted me a sabbatical in 2003 and my faculty colleagues have encouraged me in the task, especially President W. Robert Godfrey and the late Dr Robert G. den Dulk.

I am grateful for the supervisory eye of Dr John Currid, the editorial skill of Anne Williamson and the goodwill of Evangelical Press in accepting this material for publication. The fact that it does not correspond in all respects to the usual format of their Study Commentary series is due to the distinctive literary character of the book of Job.

As always I am indebted to Nansi for her patience in reading this material after having listened to it over the years and for her enthusiastic support with regard to this project. In one way or another, the book of Job has figured in our life together since our student days in the late 1950s and we are equally glad that it has come to this completion. That being so, I am glad to dedicate this to our generation following:

Gruffydd and Amanda, Johanna and Lowri
Elinor and David, Angharad and Dilys
Gareth and Sarah, and Hannah.

Hywel R. Jones
Westminster Seminary California, 2007

Introductory matters

Considerable attention has been given to the book of Job in the last hundred years or so. This is largely due to two factors. On the one hand, the horror of two World Wars, which dealt a severe blow to the optimism with which the twentieth century had begun, brought to the fore the reality of suffering and the mystery of evil which culminated with Hiroshima and the Jewish holocaust. On the other, serious attention began to be given to what had been a somewhat neglected field in the scholarly study of the Old Testament, namely its wisdom literature. *Job* stood at the confluence of those two streams of reflection and, consequently, a spate of material on it of all kinds has appeared.[1]

As the aim of this volume is to present the teaching of this book for the Christian church, I will adopt the perspective of the New Testament about it (see James 5:10-11). It is my conviction that nothing like justice can be done to the book as a whole, or indeed to its parts, in any other way. Taking this route, however, does not entail ignoring the challenges of the text, because *Job* does present real verbal difficulties and such a rich variety of sub-themes. The only presupposition it requires is a rejection of the notion that the book is incoherent, and that is in keeping with today's scholarly consensus, which is to work with text as we have it. Even so, it would be naïve to think that there is no hangover from that earlier approach which sought the history of the

book's successive editions and expressed considerable doubt about its harmony.[2] This came to a focus
in connection with the identity of the 'real' Job. Is it
the 'patient' Job of the prose chapters, or the petu-
lant Job of the poetical sections?

James, the Lord's brother, provides a more than
satisfactory answer to this question, if we will have it.
By directing attention to the 'steadfastness', or 'endurance', of Job he shows that there are not 'two Jobs'
but one. By that single stroke he also provides the key
to the whole book, although many particular difficulties do remain. [3]

The title of the book

Some orientation to *Job* is needed because our study
of the content of the book will be pursued along
pastoral rather than academic lines. For this purpose
we shall take as our starting-point the traditional title
of the book in the English Bible in the hope that this
will encourage any that are eager to become involved
with the text itself to read these pages of introduction
to it. After all, the title of a book should say something
helpful about its character and content.

The origin of the title 'The book of Job' is difficult
to identify. It is not a translation of its title in either
the Hebrew, the Septuagint (Greek) or the Vulgate
(Latin) versions. What appears in all of those is just
'Job'. The longer form of the title seems to have made
its first appearance in the Authorized or King James
Version of 1611. This uncertainty should not have an
unsettling effect because all the books of the Bible
were given titles subsequent to their completion,[4]
with the first word of the book, or the first important
term in the opening sentence, often being chosen for
that purpose. Each title has therefore the value of an
ancient tradition, but no more, and in the case in

hand there is not that much difference between 'Job' and 'The book of Job'. What is more, the thinking behind the latter is obvious. By it the reader's attention is being directed to a book and to a person, or to a book about a person. Those are the two categories that we shall use as the main headings for this introduction.

The book

Both Jews and Christians accepted *Job* unhesitatingly as worthy of inclusion in their lists of sacred books, in spite of the fact that there was no unanimity about its authorship or date. It would, of course, be useful to have had such information provided (much time and fruitless effort would have been saved), but it so happens that the book can be studied and appreciated without it. However, in the course of seeking answers to those questions, other, more pressing, concerns have come to light.[5] These relate to the book as a piece of literature, to its integrity and to its genre. We shall focus on these and refer to the other matters as appropriate.

Integrity and authorship

A single book is what is referred to by way of the traditional English title 'The book of Job'. But should it be thought that the Hebrew text that we have was originally a single whole? Or was it enlarged over the years by editorial activity? Several things should be noted here.

1. It has to be admitted that growth of the text is not impossible because the book has no named author and no firm date of composition (see below), and editorial activity is not absent from other Old Testament books, for example

the account of the death of Moses in Deuteron-omy 34.[6]

2. It should be acknowledged that the book has all the features of a completed text. Al-though it does not begin with an account of Job's birth, something which is alluded to later, his death is recorded at the end.

3. There is no shorter or otherwise-ordered *Hebrew* text of *Job* extant.[7]

4. While so many redactions of the text have been proposed, none has commanded general acceptance.[8]

Given these facts, an assumption in favour of the text's integrity is not unscholarly and that is in prac-tice the approach that many now profess to adopt, although they have not given up the idea of its being a composite text on the basis of stylistic and thematic considerations.[9] We therefore have a state of affairs that resembles the old four-source theory of the composition of the Pentateuch, which is now being played down but not being explicitly repudiated.

I regard the book of Job as we know it as being an original unity and its parts as being inseparably bound together. In my opinion the composite view is more than satisfactorily refuted by showing that the several parts of our text of Job do cohere, especially those whose status as original has been challenged. That is what I shall attempt to demonstrate in the course of our treatment of the text.

What then of its authorship?

The unity that is being claimed for the book points inevitably in the direction of its having had just one author — whoever he might have been.[10] The mention of Job in our title should not be taken as a pointer to his identity. *Job* is anonymous and, currently, there is no way of knowing who the author was, or when he wrote it. There is, however, a reference in the

Jewish Talmud to Moses as the author,[11] but that is
of a late date and has to be balanced by the fact that
the book was placed in the third section of the Hebrew Bible because of its acknowledged anonymity.[12]
Even so, the idea of Mosaic authorship was widely
held until the early twentieth century — and there is
nothing impossible in that, seeing that Moses wrote
the books of the Pentateuch. Taking this view would
place the composition of the book around 1500 BC.

No claim for the Mosaic authorship of *Job* is being
advanced in these pages, however, but it would be
interesting to have all the objections to such a possibility set out so that they could be evaluated. What is
being argued for here is that our book is the work of
a *single* author. This is much more likely than that it
is the final product of many hands, which, although
they are said to 'make light work', do not generally
produce 'great work(s)' of any kind!

Genre[13] and date

Up to the middle of the last century the prevailing
view about the genre of *Job* was that it belonged to
the wisdom literature of the Old Testament, along
with Proverbs, Ecclesiastes and the Song of Songs.
This categorization was not only due to the presence
in the book of a poem on wisdom (see Job 28) but
also, as we shall see in the course of our exposition,
because it contains questions about life of the type
that wisdom literature is renowned for.

'Wisdom' was one of the ways that God used to
make known his saving truth (Jer. 18:18). It existed
in the ancient Near East and in Israel before the
reign of Solomon, when it flourished, just as it continued into New Testament times.[14] It has therefore
been suggested that *Job* is best dated in the tenth
century BC, when Solomon was on the throne. E. J.

Young adopted this dating as the one that had the least objections to face. It is credible and I incline to it.

But much later dates have also been advanced for the book. These are based on the fact that it contains an account of a crisis of faith, something that is identified with the sixth-century Babylonian exile or the influx of Hellenism in the wake of the conquests of Alexander the Great in the fourth century BC. To make either connection overlooks the fact that Job's crisis of faith was individual, not national, and that, more importantly, it was not punishment for sin. We can therefore set these associations aside, while at the same time being aware that there are features in *Job*, such as loan words from other languages and the mention of Satan, which are regarded as pointing to the Persian era, although there are no Persian words in *Job* at all.

Job could therefore be the latest or the earliest book in the Old Testament, but for reasons given (and for another that will be mentioned later) we shall adopt a tenth-century dating. In doing so it must be stressed that this does not mean either that the events recorded in the book are regarded as having taken place at that time, or that this commentary endorses the theory of how wisdom thinking is supposed to have developed over the years. The first point hardly needs to be stated; the second needs a little explanation. There is a general notion that runs like this: Proverbs presents wisdom as that which enables the pious to prosper, while Ecclesiastes sees the pursuit of all that the world has to offer as vanity. These are contrasting but complementary windows on life in a fallen world. But *Job* deals with piety *in* adversity. Such a perspective on life, it is argued, requires a period of time to elapse in order for reflection to take place, and so the conclusion is drawn that *Job* must therefore be much later than either Proverbs or Ecclesiastes.

There is a difficulty with this reasoning. It seems to rest on Hegel's theory of how ideas develop.[15] While the pattern outlined above supplies interesting but not unassailable perspectives on these three canonical books,[16] the question may be raised as to why the movement might not go the other way. After all, Abraham was prosperous but experienced famine. Could piety deprived of prosperity in *Job* not give rise to a focusing on prosperity with piety in Proverbs, and the emptiness of prosperity without piety in Ecclesiastes?

The question can therefore be asked as to whether *Job* could not date from earlier than the tenth century BC. There are a couple of considerations that favour this view, but they do need to be weighed.

Firstly, there are several indications in the narrative that Job lived in (pre-?)patriarchal times, for example the fact that he acted as priest in his own household. Consequently, there is something very natural about an early date for the book, and such a dating would reduce the difficulty of the time-gap between the events and their being recorded in writing — an interval that otherwise has to be accounted for in terms of the remarkable reliability of oral tradition in the ancient Orient.

Secondly, other pieces of literature have come to light from Egypt and Mesopotamia that resemble *Job* in format and theme, and they are all dated before 1000 BC — some from well before that date.[17]

But, as a counterweight to the possibility of an early date, the fact that there are many words in *Job* of either Aramaic or Arabic origin has been referred to as supporting, or even necessitating, a late date. (At one time it was thought that the original text was in one or other of these languages.) Certainly, there are many rare words in *Job* and difficult syntactical features, giving rise to difficulties in translation, but it must be remembered that Aramaic was widely used long before the Babylonian exile.

My conclusion, therefore, is that it does not seem outlandish to assign an earlier, rather than a later, date to the book, and even to regard it as the oldest piece of literature in the Old Testament. But I would prefer to think of some incredibly gifted littérateur living in Solomon's times, who, having heard the story of Job by way of oral transmission and being greatly impressed by it, was divinely assisted in writing it up.

But to return to the question of genre, our adoption in this commentary of the wisdom category is not intended to suggest that there is no other way in which *Job* could be regarded. There are many that have been suggested and there is something of worth in each of them, with the exception of the idea that the book is a drama.

There was no tradition of drama in the ancient Near East. That came with the Greeks in the fourth century, and a late date for the book would make this a possibility. Some have therefore inclined to this view of it, using both the genres of tragedy and comedy to describe *Job*. However, even allowing for the possibility of a late date, it seems to me that these categories are unsuitable for it — comedy[18] because of the book's content (even if we think of Shakespeare rather than the music hall), and tragedy[19] because the book has a positive message of hope. This does not mean that the dramatic character of the narrative is being called into question — and that should become obvious as we proceed — but just that the book was not written with the stage in view. Interestingly, attempts to present it as a drama have not met with success.[20]

Recently, another genre has been suggested, namely that of 'parody'.[21] This is not really very different from the idea of 'comedy' (albeit of a black kind), but it would seem preferable to regard it as wisdom having taken a different turn in order to debunk the empty notion that piety always leads to prosperity.

There is yet another perspective on *Job* — one that more than merits attention and that may be gaining strength. Using form-critical methods, but in a way that is more sensitive to the traditional perspective on the book, this approach sees *Job* as law-court literature. There are many parallels to this in ancient Near-Eastern culture and also in the Old Testament. Adopting this view entails more than a recognition that legal terms are present in the book.[22] It requires accepting that its very structure conforms to the pattern of a lawsuit.

Following pioneering work in this area written in German,[23] several doctoral dissertations were completed in the 1970s on this subject. Some of the most useful excerpts from two of these appear in the symposium listed in the bibliography.[24]

One of them is by Sylvia Scholnick, who examined the meaning and uses of the common Hebrew term *mishpat* (judgement/justice) in *Job* and has shown that *mishpat* can mean either a judge's verdict or a ruler's edict. In the light of this helpful distinction it can be seen that Job and his friends operate with the law-court frame of mind, whereas God confronts all with his right and capacity to rule. Interestingly, Elihu paves the way for this by his dual use of the word. Scholnick writes, '... the author of the book is trying to expand the understanding of the nature of God to include a realization that He is King of the universe ... the prologue enables the reader to understand that God is acting as Ruler to test his subject, not as judge to punish him for wrongdoing.'[25] To this I would only add that 'God' does all this as 'Jehovah' (see comment on 1:6 and also 38:1 onwards).[26]

There is no denying that the book of Job records a trial. It has a prosecutor, a defendant and a judge. In fact it operates like this on more than one level, as Meredith Kline has shown,[27] for in addition to Job's desire to call God to account, there is also God's dispute with Job — not to mention Satan's with each of them, and vice versa. It must be recorded that Kline pinpoints a major weakness of this approach, in that all too often its advocates treat 'the Satan' as only a literary device — a mythical antagonist rather than an actual prosecutor.

In this volume we shall work with the view that *Job* is wisdom literature with elements from law-court literature. Whether this is acceptable to all or not, it is as well to recall Pfeiffer's words at this point: 'If your poet ranks with the greatest writers of mankind, as can hardly be doubted, his creative genius did not of necessity rely on earlier models for the general structure of his work and for the working out of its details. Admitting at the outset that there is no close parallel to his poem, in form and substance, we may regard it as one of the most original works in the poetry of mankind. So original in fact that it does not fit into any of the standard categories devised by literary criticism ... unless the poem is cut down to fit a particular category... Even the more comprehensive characterizations ... fail to do justice to the scope of the work.'[28]

Job

In concentrating now on Job, the man, we come closer to the content of this book because he is its principal human character. It covers a lengthy period in his life but also a stage of Jehovah's dealings with him. The book is therefore both biographical and theological. It records human history and redemptive history and therefore has a messianic focus. We shall consider each of those aspects, the biographical and the theological, and, as a subset of both, the messianic.

The biographical aspect

The opening verses of our text present a historical figure, and the fact that they are written in prose, as is almost the whole of the first two chapters, strengthens that viewpoint. In addition, the narrative in the book is plainly set in the age of the patriarchs, as can be seen by the following:

- Job's wealth is measured in terms of flocks and herds (1:3).
- He is head of, and priest for, his family and household (1:5).
- His offerings are of the earliest form (1:5).
- The names for God (*El/Eloah*) are generally pre-Mosaic.
- Job's age compares with that of Jacob, who lived 130 years less than Isaac (see 42:16; Gen. 47:9).

- There is no reference to the Sinai revelation,
  but Adam and the Fall are referred to in 31:33
  (see ESV footnote), and there may be an allusion to the murder of Abel in 16:18.

There are also references to Job in other books of
the Bible. In Ezekiel 14:14,20, Job is mentioned
along with Noah and Daniel[29] as a man of prayer, and
that is in keeping with his description in the book
that bears his name. All three are referred to as
intercessors, and Job's praying for others is mentioned in the opening and closing chapters of the
book.

He is also referred to in the New Testament (see
James 5:7-11), a section which we have already seen
to be all-important for interpreting the book of Job.
There, in a context that also refers to praying, another aspect of his life is brought to view which it is
vital to note. After reminding Jewish Christians that
godly people have been oppressed but have nevertheless persevered (v. 6), James urges them to wait
patiently for the Lord's coming. He then refers to the
prophets 'who spoke in the name of the Lord' as
examples of that very perseverance (vv. 10-11) and
concludes with the words: 'Behold, we consider those
blessed who remained steadfast.' It is at that point
that he reminds them that they had 'heard' of 'the
steadfastness of Job' and had 'seen the purpose of
the Lord' (emphasis added). Where and how, we
might wonder, had they heard and seen these
things? Well, supremely in the book that bears Job's
name and doubtless in teaching and preaching from
it.

Here, therefore, is the New Testament perspective
on *Job*. James refers to 'the prophets'. Is Job also
among them, we might ask? Is he 'speaking the word
of the Lord' in some sense? He is. And what is he
saying? He is speaking about 'steadfastness', or

'endurance', leading up to 'the purpose of the Lord' and, like Abel, Job 'through his faith, though he died ... still speaks' (Heb. 11:4).

James therefore understands Job's biography as a study in steadfastness, or endurance (*hypomene*), before the Lord's appearing. *Hypomene* is a word for the soldier's courage and bravery. The 'patience', or 'perseverance', of Job is therefore his valiant endurance in his suffering of affliction until the 'purpose [literally, "end" (*telos*)] of the Lord' is accomplished by his appearing (*parousia*) in abundant compassion and tender mercy, with all that it entails. As we shall see, this is what the book is about on one level. It depicts an individual believer undergoing trial, triumphing over it and being gloriously honoured. By extension, it is a book about the perseverance of the saints, of the church militant, and about the day of glory when Christ returns. Job on the ash-heap in Uz is an Old Testament counterpart of John in prison on the Isle of Patmos.

The theological aspect

In what has just been said we have already moved beyond a consideration of the book on a factual and human level to reflecting on it on a theological level — something that is not often done. It should be viewed in this way, however, because Job is only the chief *human* actor in the book; God, the sovereign Jehovah (see comments on 1:6) is the one who is central and in control.

In her study of Calvin's sermons on *Job*[30] Susan Schreiner surveys the ways the book has been studied down through the ages of the church. She points out that prior to the rise of 'higher criticism' in the eighteenth century, it was treated as both history and theology. Thereafter, it came to be considered largely along linguistic-textual lines, in comparison with Near-Eastern parallels and in terms of the process by which the text is thought to have achieved its final form. While that method had real importance and usefulness (and still does),[31] it came to be regarded as an end in itself and so failed to do justice to the grandeur of the book and to its message. (This was also the case with other books of the Bible, with the result that the people of God were deprived of truth that edifies and large tracts of the church were devastated.)

More recent studies of *Job* treat the work more empathetically from the standpoints of religious as well as literary appreciation,[32] and that is to be welcomed. Schreiner, however, in a chapter entitled 'Modern Readings of Job',[33] shows what is lacking even in this more holistic approach. She writes, 'Modern exegetes do not work with a metaphysic of hierarchy; for the twentieth-century scholar, reality has been made thoroughly historical. Moreover, no contemporary interpreter finds in Job any message of detached transcendence or any belief in the beneficial or curative power of suffering.'[34]

And later she is even more specific with regard to these twentieth-century studies. She points to the absence of theological principle, saying, 'Crucial differences divide these modern readings from the earlier tradition [Calvin]. The assumptions about suffering, revelation, nature and moral justice have changed in the intervening centuries.'[35]

In studying *Job*, therefore, the older, pre-higher-critical, approach associated with John Calvin[36] and Joseph Caryl[37] is the path to follow.[38] These men saw that the book dealt with God and Satan; with providence and suffering — the former mysterious and the latter awful; with believing, doubting and questioning and with resigning oneself to God, but also with the richness and the wonder of the divine compassion. These sets of truths enable one to descend with Job into his *angst* (which is what his three friends ceased to do), to note God's gracious purpose towards him (which also extends to the people of God in every age and place), and so to rise with him in renewed strength.

These are the perspectives that are essential for understanding and deriving benefit from this book, which is not about the problem of human suffering in the world at large, but about the suffering of the godly in a fallen world over which God yet reigns supreme.

The messianic aspect

Job is an essential part of the unfolding of saving truth in Holy Scripture. It therefore has a messianic focus. It anticipates the coming of Jesus Christ, the seed of the woman (and of Abraham and David). How is that seen in the book of Job?

We must not only read *Job* in its social era (the patriarchal) but also its redemptive-historical setting. In particular, Satan's assault on Job points to his enmity against the woman and her seed (see Gen. 3:15; Rev. 12:17). Genesis 1 – 3 and Revelation 12 must be borne in mind as we proceed through this book.

We have noted that James presents Job as someone who has something to say to new-covenant believers as they wait for the Lord's return in the midst of their afflictions (James 5:7-8). There is therefore something in *Job* which represents that, and it is of course the appearing of Jehovah at the end of the book. Those chapters therefore acquire a messianic dimension. Seen from a New Testament perspective, they are the equivalent of the 'day of the LORD' in other parts of the Old Testament.

But there is also something else to note. It is that
Jehovah six times identifies Job as 'my servant Job'.
This is done twice in the Prologue and four times in
the Epilogue (see 1:8; 2:3; 42:7-8), but more significant than the number of occurrences of this description is their distribution in the narrative, their place
in the book. Job is not described in this way in the
opening verses of the book, or the concluding ones —
that is, before he attracts the attention of Satan or
after he is restored by the Lord. 'My servant Job' is
always used in connection with his suffering. Job the
man is therefore not just a servant of Jehovah but a
suffering servant; in other words, he is a type of 'the
Suffering Servant of the LORD'.

John Hartley has noted the correspondences
between *Job* and Isaiah in a section of his most
painstaking and useful commentary.[39] On this matter
of the righteous sufferer he writes, 'Because the
people consider him to be smitten of God (Isa. 53:4;
cf. Job 19:21), they despise him (Isa. 53:3; cf. Job
19:18), spit on him (Isa. 50:6; cf. Job 30:10), and
then desert him (Isa. 53:3; cf. Job 19:14). The Servant's suffering equals or surpasses Job's [most
certainly the latter!], even though he too is innocent,
never having done violence or spoken deceit (Isa.
53:7,9; cf. 50:5; Job 6:30; 16:17). Both sufferers rest
their cases with God (Isa. 49:4; 50:8-9; Job 13:15;
16:19).'

With regard to vicarious suffering, Hartley writes
that it is 'merely hinted at in the book of Job, e.g.
when God instructs Job to pray for his comforters
when they offer up burnt offerings (42:7-9; cf.
22:30).' I would go so far as to say that the adverb
'merely' could well be omitted and in the same way
would argue that Job's restoration is typical too.
Hartley contrasts the Servant and Job at this point
and writes, 'In Isaiah God brings the Servant back to
life after his cruel death (Isa. 53:10-11) and awards

him the spoils of victory (v. 12) ... [whereas] Job finds
no possibility that an individual could rise from the
grave (14:7-17).' One wonders why a connection is
not made at this point between the Servant's exaltation after suffering (see Isa. 53:10-12) and Job's
restoration. Both are given to 'see descendants' and
both have their 'days lengthened'. However, we can
agree with Hartley's conclusion that the thought of
victory over death is developed further in Isaiah than
it is in Job and also that Job could have provided the
model for Isaiah's depiction of 'the servant of the
LORD' who is Jesus Christ.

Two interrelated matters remain to be considered
by way of introduction. They are important because
they concern what is actually said about God and
also by him in the book. They relate to the fact of
human perception and to the use of Canaanite mythology. More will be said on these as we proceed
through the text, but a few comments by way of
orientation will be helpful.

The reality of human perception

As *Job* is part of divinely inspired Scripture it is to be
received from God as wholly trustworthy. But it
contains statements that are not true. It tells us that
itself. Job says things about God, and his friends say
things about him that are not correct. They are all
indicted on that score, first by Elihu (32:2-3) and
then by God himself (40:2; 42:3,7-8).

In our study of the book we must therefore be
prepared to recognize the presence of what is not true.
This applies particularly to parts of chapters 3 – 31,
but we are introduced to it in the opening chapters,
where we have two levels of reality and two active
agents. We have conversations in the heavenly court
about what has transpired on earth, held between one

who cannot lie and the other who cannot tell the truth. Very diverse viewpoints are expressed in these exchanges. If in that supernatural realm truth about what has transpired on earth is contradicted by untruth, then it is not to be wondered at that the one can so easily be confused with the other by those who are involved in that same conflict when it takes place on earth. In addition, that conflict is not just about events and their meaning, but also about motives — human, divine and satanic. God, who has given Job life by his truth, is being opposed by Satan, who is once again intent on murder by deception, just as he was in Eden. Job is unaware of what has transpired in the heavenly court and therefore has to fight blind-fold, in the darkness of the divine providence. It is therefore easy for mistakes to be made — and they are, both by Job and by his friends. In her book Schreiner describes this as 'a perceptual nightmare'.[40]

To say that there are 'wrong' statements in the book does not mean, however, that they are *wholly* inaccurate. Some distinctions have to be made be-tween levels of truth in connection with them. First, no statement is wrong in the sense that it does not correspond with what was said. We can be sure that the speaker said what the author wrote. In that sense, such statements are to be received as true without a moment's hesitation. The same holds good for the words of the narrator in the prose sections, and that includes 32:1-6, a vital section for the harmony of the book and its message.

But words do not only have content; they have intent. This means that the speaker has a particular purpose in saying what he says. Here is where what is true at one level is not true on another.[41] What Job is recorded as saying about God, and about how God was dealing with him, Job indeed said. But it was not true of God. (Often what Job said would be remark-ably accurate if it were applied to Satan. It is as if

Job has put the wrong address on his letter!) Similarly, what the friends are recorded as saying about
Job, and how he had dealt with God, and how,
consequently, God had dealt with him, they also
indeed said. But these things were true neither of
Job nor of God. This interplay, which is part and
parcel of real dialogue, is present at the beginning
and throughout the book. It is largely resolved at the
end, but not entirely even then, for God does not
explain himself either to Job or to his friends.
Enough is said, however, for God to be honoured and
for them to be restored to fellowship with him; on the
other hand, Satan, the real liar, gains nothing!

There is one further distinction to be made on this
point. It is that content can sometimes be separated
from intent, so that what is said can be true in itself
but without the payload intended. For example,
Eliphaz says, 'He catches the wise in their own crafti-
ness' (5:13) and he means that God has caught 'crafty'
Job. While that was not true of God vis-à-vis Job, it is
true of how God deals with the worldly-wise with
regard to their thinking. The apostle Paul uses these
words in this way in 1 Corinthians 3:19,[42] where he is
thinking of how God 'defeats' the attempts of the
world's wisdom to solve its problems (in other words,
to save itself) by means of the death of Christ. The
statement can therefore be preached in this way.

We need to bear in mind these levels of meaning in
our study and continually be asking questions like:
'Why is this being said? What is being thought? Who
is being described?' Supremely, we need to ask,
'What did Job say that was right and what did his
friends say that was wrong?' (42:7-8).

The use of Canaanite mythology

Archaeological discoveries have made such an important contribution to nineteenth and twentieth-century biblical studies. By their confirmation of the general picture presented in the Old Testament, especially of the patriarchal narratives, they have shown how prejudiced textual study was in the heyday of higher criticism. A particular benefit recouped from their finds is the light cast on the religious environment of Israel by way of information about the beliefs and customs of several of her neighbours, from Egypt to Babylon.

In 1928 discoveries were made in Syria, Israel's nearest neighbour. The ancient city of Ugarit was excavated and tablets were found, the language of which resembled Hebrew. They contained information about Canaanite culture and religion and exhibited similarities with details in the Old Testament text. In particular, they contained references to gods like Leviathan and Yamm, whose names are found in *Job*[43] and also elsewhere in the Old Testament (see some psalms and Isaiah).[44]

What view are we to take with regard to these in general, and particularly as they occur in *Job*? First, we must reject the view that sees them as indicators of Israel's early religion, as if monotheism only came at the end of a long process. By contrast, it is far safer to assume that some degree of disapproval, or even outright polemic, is present in the text when mythological allusions occur in it.

Two general points need to be made about the presence of mythology in the Bible.

First, we must not treat it from our standpoint, as if it were just unreality. A myth is a story about something important, like the origin of life. It therefore had meaning for those who believed it — and also power. It bound communities together. It should therefore never be treated dismissively just because it is fictional.

Secondly, and more ominously, myths are often connected with polytheism, and therefore with idolatry. When that is so, a myth has more influence than something that is just man-made which generates social cohesion. It is connected with sin and Satan. In principle, this is exactly the same as we find in the New Testament Gentile world where, though an idol is 'nothing', there is a power behind it (1 Cor. 8:4-5; 10:19-20).

Coming now to mythological references in *Job*, it is not adequate to regard them merely as word pictures (mythopoetic language) and pass them by. They have some meaning in themselves, and that meaning should be sought. But the all-important question is what the person who used them meant by incorporating them in whatever he was saying. At this point careful exegesis is called for and a hesitant conclusion! An example of the point that is being made might be helpful. The one that is often used concerns Matthew 12:27. There the Lord Jesus refers to the devil as 'Beelzebul', or Baal-Zebub. The question is, did he believe what was current about Baal-Zebub, or was he just using a term because of its familiarity to his audience? Or, to take a secular and contemporary example, are we declaring our belief in the god Woden when we use the term Wednesday?

Elmer B. Smick has written two useful articles on the mythology of the book of Job.[45] He examines many passages in which such terms appear and shows that they are used of the elements of nature, cosmic creatures and cosmography. The first and last-named are clearly in chapter 26 and elsewhere, and the reference to cosmic creatures is in chapters 38-40. These passages will be considered at the appropriate points in the commentary. Helpfully, Smick highlights Job 3:8 as providing the only other category of use of such terms — namely that of heathen *practices*. He points out that this is the only occasion in Job where anything like this is referred to and that Job expressly declares in 31:26-27 that he had not participated in such activities. Mythological terms are used, but most of them are metaphorical.

Now let us think of Job in Edom. As he was not of the line of Abraham, he lacked the divine revelation which Abraham received. But revelation had been given to Adam about God and his law, Satan and his power, and God and his grace in the woman's promised seed. This was not only passed on in the generations of Adam, Seth and Enoch, but also of Cain and his descendants where it became corrupted by the unchecked power of sin. This is the setting in which the alternative accounts of creation and the flood are to be located and also the gods invented in connection with them. Fyall recognizes this pagan dimension, but he also includes C. S. Lewis' comment that such myths are 'good dreams' sent by God in preparation for the gospel.[46] That is hardly in keeping with Romans 1:19-23.

What then about such references in *Job*? First, they should not surprise us because Job lived in a polytheistic environment in Edom. So, whenever there is a reference to this polytheistic religious environment in *Job*, we should examine it carefully in its context to seek to find out what is being said, and why. It could be an allusion to something that was current at the time and no more. But it could be more — much more (for example in Job 3:7, where Job seems to recognize Leviathan's power). As Job was in a life-and-death struggle with a superhuman and devilish adversary, is it surprising that his mind was invaded as well as his body, and that he was plagued with fears and doubts and those spectres as if they had power over life, death and the grave? They too become part of Job's 'perceptual nightmare'. Care must be taken with this line of thought, however, because Job never practised idolatry (see 31:26).

But what shall we say about Jehovah's use of these allusions? (e.g., 41:1). The question of whether there is some reference to death and Satan in Behemoth and Leviathan will have to be considered later.[47] It is sufficient at this point to make clear that no dualism is being countenanced in *Job* by the inclusion of these references to other gods, or to Satan. They are merely man's 'creations'; Satan is God's creature. The one God who is Jehovah is the Creator of all beings and things. He upholds and directs all to his own glory and also the good of his people, who include outsiders like Job as well as Jews. Jehovah is supreme, but not remote; alone, but not aloof, and he 'does all things well'.

1. The Prologue

(Job 1:1 – 2:13)

The first two chapters are usually designated as the Prologue to *Job*. They are almost entirely in prose and that singles them out from a literary point of view. They function as an introduction in two ways. First, the events they describe clearly took place prior to what is recorded in the chapters that follow, and there is no other suitable place for them in the narrative. Secondly, they are also preparatory from a theological point of view, and this is important because this book is about God's dealings with one of his faithful servants.

The opening verse of the Bible declares: 'In the beginning, God created the heavens and the earth.' This indicates that one God created two realms, the supernatural and the terrestrial, and that he rules over both by virtue of being their Creator. It is such a framework for reality that is presented in Job 1:1 – 2:10.

Two 'locations' are referred to: the land of Uz (the earth) and the heavenly court. Between these there is an immense distinction, but they are not totally separate from, and closed to, each other. There is a relation between them, and that is made clear by the ways in which they interact with each other. What happens in Uz is noted in the court, and what is enacted there is what transpires on earth. Each has its own significance — the 'heavenly' and the earthly

— with priority being given to the 'heavenly'. What is
more, the snapshots of both realms that are contained in these chapters are sequentially arranged.
This means that the unfolding of human history is
related to the process of redemptive history.

This background is of the utmost importance for
what is recorded in *Job* and in the biography of every
Christian believer.

'The greatest of all the people of the east' (Job 1:1-5)

The words of our title (1:3) state the point which the author wants to emphasize. They come at the end of a multifaceted description of Job and apply to everything contained in it. Readers and students of the book often tend to connect them to the details about his numerous family and vast possessions rather than to his piety, but, in reality, these words are a summary of all that precedes them.

It is true that 'great' can sometimes carry the meaning of 'rich' or 'powerful', and Job was both. But his greatness did not exclude his piety. Indeed, it was his piety that was reflected in his progeny and prosperity — the numbers of which are symbolic of completeness — and that constituted the prelude to all that follows. His piety contributed to his prestige no less than did his possessions.

1:1. There was a man in the land of Uz whose name was Job, and that man was blameless and upright, one who feared God and turned away from evil.

What the opening verse presents is, first, his place of origin and then his piety. It is anticipatory of the form of address in New Testament epistles, where people are identified in terms of where they happen to live, but also of their relationship to God through the Lord Jesus Christ. Clearly, the author thinks it noteworthy that there was a man in Uz who could be

described in the way that Job was. We shall use
these two categories of place and character to consider the section of text that we have isolated.

Job lived in the land of Uz

Uz was not in the promised land but to the east of it,
across the Jordan, whether to the north or south of
it. Uz was therefore outside the confines of much of
the saving revelation given to Abraham, but not
destitute of what had been made known by God prior
to that, namely what is recorded in Genesis 1-11.

Working on the basis that place names were
derived from the names of people, **'Uz'** is to be connected either with Aram, a son of Shem (Gen.
10:23), or with Nahor (Gen. 22:21), Abraham's brother. The
covenant line did not include Aram but Arpachshad,
his brother (Gen. 10:22,24). Nahor's son, Uz, had a
brother named Buz (Gen. 22:21) and their people
settled later in Edom (Gen. 36:1, Jer. 25:20-23; Lam.
4:21).

Given the state of our knowledge of the times
referred to, it is hazardous to make firm identifi-
cations. Edom is a likely locale given the mention of
the Sabeans. The Chaldeans, however, were in the
Fertile Crescent to the north and east of that region. Whichever option is taken, we can be sure that
Job did not belong to the covenant line from Shem to
Abraham and that he shared in the promised blessing in the same sort of way as did Melchizedek.

Blameless, upright, fearing God and turning from evil

This is a summary statement of Job's piety. It is
made up of two couplets. The first describes him

from an outward aspect; the other describes his inward motivation.

First, and to an observer, he was **'blameless and upright'**. This refers to the outward manifestation of his piety. **'Blameless'** is used to describe what is physically perfect — for example, animals that were acceptable for sacrifice (see Num.19:2). But it is also used of human beings (see Josh. 24:14) and then it refers to sincere and consistent compliance with God's will. It is this that is the point of contention in the subsequent narrative at the level of the 'heavenly' debate between Satan and God which is mirrored, or played out, on the earthly plane between Job and the Friends (see 8:20; 9:2-3; 12:4; 36:4; 37:16).

The second adjective is clearly associated with being 'straight', or 'righteous', in accord with law or divine command (1 Kings 14:8). Job lived in the light which he had been given, as an intelligent, moral being who knew something about sin and mercy and justice, as we shall see. It could have been said of him that 'he walked with God', as it was of Enoch and Noah (see Gen. 5:21-24; 6:9). There was a roundedness and a straightness about his character and conduct. There were no glaring sins in his life of either omission or commission.

His inner life is described in the next couplet, which tells us that he **'feared God'** and **'turned away from evil'**. These complementary aspects sum up the very essence of wisdom (see 28:28). Aware of the power, wisdom and justice of God displayed in creation and providence, but also of his kindness and mercy, Job was conscious of his own moral dignity and accountability as God's creature. Loving the one true and living God whom he knew, he forsook what he knew to be evil in God's sight. These themes are all present in his speeches.

This summary of his piety is endorsed personally by God (1:8) and repeated later by him (2:3; cf. 2:9).

We shall put some flesh on those bones, so to speak, by borrowing statements from chapters 23, 29 and 31 – 33. It is useful to do this in order to gain an appreciation of Job's significance in God's purpose and kingdom in his own time and place. We shall list these in relation to Job in private, in his family and in society.

1. Job in private

In 23:12 Job indicates how much he valued God's words. For him what came out of God's mouth was more important than what went into his own. The fact that man does 'not live by bread alone' was something he well understood.

In 29:3-5 he describes how he enjoyed God's presence. God communed with him and protected him. Darkness was no terror or perplexity to him. The light and life God gave him resulted in his being at his best. He flourished in every way, as was evidenced by the fact that his flocks and olives produced abundantly.

In 31:33 he indicates that he had not hidden from God like Adam,[1] but confessed every sin he was aware of. He had known what it was to have communion with God broken and also to have it restored. Job knew what divine mercy was all about.

2. Job in his family

In 1:4-5 and 1:20-21 we have descriptions of Job as a father. As is obvious, two very different situations are mentioned in these two passages.

1:4-5. His sons used to go and hold a feast in the house of each one on his day, and they would send and invite their three sisters to eat and drink with them. And when the days of the feast had run their course, Job would send and consecrate them, and he would rise early in the morning and offer burnt offerings according to the number of them all. For Job said, 'It may be that my children have sinned, and cursed God in their hearts.' Thus Job did continually.

The first passage refers to the fact that, while Job was no killjoy, he was concerned about the 'killing' effects of sin, and its subtlety. In particular, the focus of his concern is interesting in the light of what follows. He was afraid that his children might have done something similar to what Satan would attempt to get him to do, namely 'curse God'. There was, however, this difference: Job was aware that his children might have done so **'in their hearts'** — that is, in their minds; Satan was intent on making Job do it 'to [God's] face' (1:11; 2:5).

But what exactly is in view here? The Hebrew word that is here translated **'cursed'** normally means 'to bless', but that meaning is obviously out of place because Satan would not try to get Job to bless God openly and directly. It has therefore been suggested that the verb 'bless', rather than 'curse', was written in the original text because in the sentence it immediately preceded the word for 'God'![2]

But there is another way of understanding the use of the verb 'bless'. It also means to 'greet' or, alternatively to 'bid farewell' to someone,[3] in much the same way as our 'Goodbye' is a contraction of 'God be with you'. So I would suggest that 'bless' in this verse here in *Job* should be understood as the equivalent of 'to take one's leave of' — that is, 'to renounce'.

Job was therefore concerned that, in the midst of their birthday celebrations, his children might have set God aside in order that they might enjoy themselves. The very possibility that such thoughtlessness might have occurred was serious enough for him. He watched for their souls like a good father and summoned them to reflection and repentance before God

like a good priest, directing them to the need for
cleansing and pardon via sacrifice. He did this time
and time again. Furthermore, when they died he
reacted in a spirit that indicated intense grief but
also immense appreciation for God's goodness in ever
having granted them to him (1:20-21).

But Job was of course a husband before he was
ever a father, and a glimpse into his relationship with
his wife is provided in the text (2:9-10). His wife
urges him (in effect) to do Satan's bidding. Job's reply
to her is often construed as if he were accusing her of
being 'a foolish woman' — a serious accusation. In
my view, that is not the case. He says that she has
spoken **'as'** a foolish woman would, implying that her
words were not revealing her true self. He follows
that statement by stretching out a helping hand to
bring her to a better mind and to bind her to him
again — note the use of the first person plural (**'Shall
we receive good from God...?'**) — and to help her to
receive calamity at God's hand, just as they had
together received of his bounty. He is here holding
fast to her (Gen. 2:24) and maintaining his marriage
covenant (see 31:1).

3. Job in society

Chapters 29 and 31 are relevant in this connection,
and they depict Job as involved in public affairs but
not in sinful practices.

In 29:7-25 his status as a judge is referred to and
the respect which was accorded to him by all classes
of society. This was as a result of the way in which he
ascertained the true facts of a case brought before
him, was no respecter of persons, defended the
vulnerable and opposed the unscrupulous. Righteousness was his habit because it was his heart.

In 31:1-12 he describes how intent he was on
banishing impurity even from his thoughts and

deceit and covetousness from his ways. (It is as if he had not only read the Decalogue aright, but also the Sermon on the Mount!)

In 31:13-23,29-32 he describes how he has dealt with his servants, with the poor, with his enemies and with strangers. Here is one who 'loved his neighbour as himself'. In addition, he indicates that it was his awareness that they all had one Creator and one Judge that animated his words and deeds. He is aware of the teaching of Genesis 1:26-28 and confirms in advance what Paul says about Gentiles and the law in Romans 2:14-16.

In 31:24-27 he reacts against the idolatry of his day, refusing to trust in 'uncertain riches' (see 1 Tim. 6:6-10), or attribute their provision or continuance to false gods.

This is the picture presented to us of that **'man in the land of Uz whose name was Job'**. His piety is rounded and straight — in the eyes of God, and not just of his contemporaries. This means that those afflictions which are described in the first two chapters of the book are not occasioned by sin and are not disciplinary or chastening in character and purpose. What is said about them later in the book is another matter.

But what does his name mean? The name **'Job'** can be connected with the word that means 'an enemy'. There is a play on this meaning (see 13:24; 33:10) and in those passages the idea is that God treats Job as his enemy. (For God read Satan!) But whose enemy was Job, or whose could he have been? To judge from his character and conduct, he was neither the enemy of God nor of man! But he was the enemy of the one who was the enemy of both, and so the enemy of God and man cannot dismiss him.

Job was included in the 'seed of the woman' which would be opposed by 'the seed of the serpent', and in his case not only the serpent's seed but 'the Satan' himself. Here in Job the saving purpose and promise of God are being wonderfully manifested relatively soon after the promise had been announced, and this manifestation is taking place in the land of Uz!

Behind the scenes
(Job 1:6-12)

So far we have seen an example of a man who had served God faithfully in a fallen world and who was richly blessed by him. His piety provoked two very different reactions in the higher realm of God's creation, and that is what these verses make clear. Two matters must be noted before we consider the interaction between Satan and the LORD: the setting and the Sovereign.

The setting

1:6. Now there was a day when the sons of God came to present themselves before the LORD, and Satan also came among them.

The action in these verses is not to be thought of as taking place 'in heaven', and so there is no need to wonder how Satan could appear there. What is depicted is a royal court, a feature of other ancient Near-Eastern cultures and religions.[4] Shorn of all its polytheistic associations, it is here used to depict a supernatural reality, namely God's sovereign administration and the execution of his purposes (see 1 Kings 22:19; Ps. 89:5-7). The **'sons of God'** (1:6; 2:1; 38:7) who appear there are angelic beings. Elsewhere they are described as 'the holy ones' (5:1; 15:15) or the 'mighty ones' (Ps. 29:1, NKJV, NIV).

'Presenting oneself' is a way of describing the appearance of a servant before a master (see Zech. 6:5), and so they stand and wait to receive commands, or report on tasks performed. It is therefore the duty of all the angelic hosts to attend. And Satan comes too, not as a gatecrasher but out of necessity, because he too is one of them! The same verb is used of him in 2:1.

The Sovereign

Before looking more closely at what is implied by the expression, **'Satan ... among [the sons of God]'**, we should note that the Sovereign before whom they appeared is identified not only as God, but also as **'the LORD'** — not 'the Lord'.[5] The spelling 'LORD' is of the utmost significance because it represents the divine name. Two things should be remembered about it. The first is that uses of the divine name are rare in *Job* and so whenever it occurs, there is a particular reason for its inclusion. The second is that, although the meaning of the name was only disclosed in Moses' time and in connection with the Exodus deliverance (Exod. 3:13-15; 6:2-3), it was not completely unknown before that (see Gen. 4:26). No objection should therefore be made against Job's own uses of it in 12:9, and particularly in 1:21. His use of a different name for God in his reply to his wife in 2:10 is a reflection of the language that she had used in what she had said to him.

But here in 1:6 the author uses the divine name in distinction from the more common word for **'God'** in the earlier part of the verse, and he does so again in 2:1 and frequently from 38:1 to the end of the book. He evidently has a point to make and it is that the divine Sovereign is the LORD.[6] Names of God are significant in the Old Testament, and here is a clear example of that. The Sovereign is not just 'God' but also 'the LORD' — that is, the covenant Redeemer. It is no accident that this name is absent from Genesis 1, where the creative acts of God are recorded, but very common in Genesis 2 and 3, where his rule over all his kingdom and his redemptive purpose are introduced. Such sovereign administration is the point that is being stressed here at the beginning of *Job* and also at the end. It is only because the 'Great Jehovah' manages affairs that there can, and there will, be a resolution of them that is to his glory *and also* to the good of his people. He rules not only over his own handiwork but over Satan's too and, come what may, he will achieve his saving purpose and bring about Satan's downfall and utter disgrace. That is what is unfolded in the rest of the book, and it is that which makes it relevant to the Christian.

The subject and the servant

That Satan should appear in the heavenly court and that Job's name should be mentioned there is significant. Both are related to the Sovereign Redeemer but in very different ways. Satan is an unwilling subject whereas Job is a glad and grateful servant.

1. The subject

'Satan' has become a personal name,[7] but originally the word represented any kind of opponent. It is used for an adversary in a lawsuit or trial (see Ps. 109:6,29) and even for the Angel of the LORD who opposed Balaam in order to defend his people (see Num. 22:22). But in Job 'Satan' is designated as *'the* Satan', and by the use of the definite article someone special is identified, just as is the case with *'the* serpent' in Genesis 3:1. He is the arch-opponent of

Jehovah's reign of grace in the world and is not just a literary symbol for a prosecutor. He is as real as God and Job, and is more opposed to God and to godliness than any human opponent can be. It is therefore no wonder that both terms, 'serpent' and 'Satan', are used in Revelation 12:9 with reference to the devil. But when Jehovah holds court even Satan has to appear, and not only turn up but own up, as we shall see from his remarks when he was interrogated. Having incited rebellion in Eden, he was made subject to Jehovah's saving purpose then and there (Gen. 3:14-15).

Two aspects about him need to be highlighted before we look at the interrogation to which he was subjected.

1. His inferiority

Satan is among the angels because that is his rank in the order of created beings. Man is on the lowest plane of animate and rational existence; one level above is the angelic host, and separated from both by an infinite distance is God. Satan is therefore superhuman but not divine. Like God he is invisible and incorporeal, but unlike him neither omnipresent, omnipotent nor omniscient. His words indicate that he is not everywhere, that he does not understand grace in the human heart and that he does not have the power either to dethrone God or to assault God's people at will.

II. His insubordination

He is not only subject to Jehovah, but he cannot free himself from his subjugation. That increases his malevolence, for not only does he have to serve the one he hates, but he can only do what will advance the gracious purpose of Jehovah. God the Saviour is the Sovereign and he rules the Satan! These are basic truths about Satan and his activity that the New Testament amplifies but nowhere contradicts.

III. His interrogation

1:7. The LORD said to Satan, 'From where have you come?' Satan answered the LORD and said, 'From going to and fro on the earth, and from walking up and down on it.'

Jehovah holds court and begins by putting Satan in the dock by means of the question: **'From where have you come?'** Satan's reply to this may seem to be evasive but it is not. True, he does not say everything, as is made clear by what he adds in reply to the next question that he has to answer. But his first answer is true as far as it goes. He is asked where he has been, and that form of words also implies the question as to what he has been doing (see Gen. 3:9; cf. 2 Kings 5:25, where Elisha questions Gehazi).

Satan's reply contains an admission but not a confession! The verbs he uses (1:7) are both graphic and meaningful. They indicate what a restless spirit he is. **'Going to and fro'** is the expression used to describe Joab's tour of all Israel with a view to numbering the people of God (see 2 Sam. 24:2), and **'walking up and down'** is used elsewhere with regard to conducting a survey of affairs in God's kingdom (see Zech. 1:10). But the latter verb can also denote turbulence in water, whether caused by an oar (Jonah 1:13) or by a swimmer (Isa. 25:11), or in the air produced by the crack of a whip (Nahum 3:2; Prov. 26:3). What Satan is therefore admitting is that he has been engaged in a tour of inspection of the earth with a view to causing a commotion wherever he can. He is always seeking to gain an advantage over the people of God and he forms his schemes for doing so, whether as a lion or as an angel of light (see 2 Cor. 2:11; 11:14; 1 Peter 5:8). But Jehovah knows

all this already because his eyes 'run to and fro
throughout the whole earth' as well (2 Chr. 16:9).

1:8. And the LORD said to Satan, 'Have you considered my
servant Job, that there is none like him on the earth, a
blameless and upright man, who fears God and turns away
from evil?'

By means of his follow-up question (1:8) Jehovah not
only shows his delight in Job, but also brings to light
Satan's malice against him. Designating Job as his
'servant', Jehovah honours him and, by implication,
reminds Satan that Job is no longer his slave. But in
asking, **'Have you considered...?'** Jehovah is charging Satan with having been 'eyeing' Job. This is a
much better rendering than the rather insipid term
'considered'. The Hebrew verb means literally 'to set
[the] mind on [something or someone]'. It is used in
1 Samuel 9:20, where Saul is told not 'to set [his]
mind' on his donkeys — that is, not to 'worry about
them' (NIV) — because they had been found. Satan
had therefore noticed not only Job's existence, but
also his character. Job had not just crossed Satan's
mind but his schemes, and as a result Satan had
designs on him, just as he had later on Simon Peter
(see Luke 22:31).

1:9,11. Then Satan answered the LORD and said, 'Does Job
fear God for no reason? ... But stretch out your hand and
touch all that he has, and he will curse you to your face.'

That this is the drift of Jehovah's second question is
indicated by Satan's reply to it (1:9). He can neither
speak dispassionately about Job nor confine his
remarks to him. He has to speak about God as well.
Piety infuriates him on sight, and the fact that God
protects and prospers his people even more so. But
his reply is not just a vicious outburst. It is also a

distortion. Satan is no atheist and he cannot deny the existence of piety. But he sees everything through his own perverted understanding. **'For no reason'** (1:9) is the dark filter through which he views both human piety and divine praise. For him true religion is a protection racket. It cannot ever be that anyone serves the Lord 'for no reason' — that is, for love's sake. Piety is self-centred, and so is God! God buys praise by selling protection and Job pays for prosperity by his loyalty — and Satan is utterly confident that he can prove that to be so. If all that Job had were to be taken from him, he would not just put Jehovah out of his mind temporarily, but renounce him openly and permanently. Satan therefore makes an indirect request for that to be done and, what is more, he wants God himself to do it.

2. The servant

Jehovah has exulted in Job and honoured him among the angelic hosts with the dignified title of being **'my servant'**. In point of fact he has so described Job to Satan with the inference that Job gives willing and thorough service, and not forced labour. All that has been mentioned about Job from other parts of the book is relevant here.

But a cloud has been cast over Job's character and conduct by Satan's claim that it is not genuine. This dark view of things impugns not only Job's good name, but also the truthfulness and honour of Jehovah. Seeing this larger picture enables a better perspective to be adopted about the permission that Satan is given to test Job. It shows that Jehovah was not only concerned for his own glory, but also for Job's good, and that he has a larger purpose than just refuting Satan's lie. (Elihu makes this clear later in the narrative.) The book is about Job, but it is not only about him. It is also about God as Jehovah —

and in the forthcoming conflict both are going to
stand or fall together. Indeed the honour and glory of
his entire redemptive programme are at stake. Job is
only the principal human 'actor', whereas God as
Jehovah is the primary figure.

I. Permission needed

Though Satan has designs on Job and is also much
stronger than he, yet he cannot **'touch'** Job at will,
and he knows it. Jehovah has indeed put a protective
hedge around him and his household, while his
flocks and herds have been amazingly productive
(1:10). Satan can only gnash his teeth at him. He
knows that he is incapable of acting without divine
permission. He therefore seeks it, but in a way that is
so typical of him. Rejecting Jehovah's evaluation of
Job, Satan requests him to deprive Job of **'all that
he has'** been so abundantly given. He wants the
hand that blessed to be the hand that takes, so that
Job's view of Jehovah will change and that, instead
of blessing the LORD, he will renounce him. In that
way Job's testimony and influence will be destroyed
and Jehovah will be dishonoured.

II. Permission given

1:12. And the LORD said to Satan, 'Behold, all that he has is
in your hand. Only against him do not stretch out your hand.'
So Satan went out from the presence of the LORD.

Jehovah is faithful to his promise, and to his people
and he will neither be a turncoat nor a tempter (see
James 1:13-15). However, he can test while Satan
does the tempting, and that is what happens with
regard to Job, but only within the limit requested
and with a prohibition specifically added. Job *himself*
is not to be 'touched' — that is, physically harmed.
Jehovah opens his protecting hand just a little, as it

were, and permits Satan to deprive Job of all that outwardly marked him as one greatly favoured by God. But Job's life is sacrosanct, so that he might live to give the lie to Satan's claim and so to bring praise to Jehovah.

But for Jehovah to concede to the request even to this degree is awe-inspiring because it is as much an expression of confidence in Job as in the work of divine grace within him. Job is going to be the buffer state, the cockpit of war between Satan and Jehovah — and he is completely ignorant of what is about to happen and why.

Job's 'evil day' (Job 1:13-22)

We move now from 'a day' in Jehovah's court to a day on earth. A storm is about to break on an unsuspecting head! When will it happen? What form will it take and what will its result be? These questions are all answered in Job 1:13-22, which we shall consider in two parts: the action of Satan and the reaction of Job.

The action of Satan (1:13-19)

1:13,18-19. Now there was a day when his sons and daughters were eating and drinking wine in their oldest brother's house... While he was yet speaking, there came another and said, 'Your sons and daughters were eating and drinking wine in their oldest brother's house, and behold, a great wind came across the wilderness and struck the four corners of the house, and it fell upon the young people, and they are dead, and I alone have escaped to tell you.'

Having been given permission to 'touch' all that Job has, Satan leaves Jehovah's presence to go about his nefarious activity. All that now follows discloses his 'craft and power', although he is not mentioned by name in these verses. That omission is worthy of note. It has often been said that Satan disappears from the book after chapter 2. I do not accept that for a moment. The events recorded in this section are his acts no less than the ones attributed personally to him in chapter 2, and this variation opens up the possibility that he continues to be active in what is recorded in the subsequent narrative. Are not all discord and doubt traceable to him? Adopting this view enables a connection to be made between Satan and the speeches that follow and the struggle that they record. Did he not leave the Servant of the Lord 'until an opportune time' after his initial onslaught? (See Luke 4:13).

There are four things to note here which indicate Satan's activity.

1. The time he chose

Whatever a 'day' may represent in the supernatural realm (1:6; 2:1), we understand **'a day'** on earth as having its natural meaning. All that is recorded in these verses befell Job in one twenty-four-hour period. It might be thought that, having such ill will towards Job, Satan would have put the permission to proceed against him into immediate effect. (That is possibly what happened in 2:7, although the form of words there may be a case of compression or summary.) But it seems from 1:13 that he waited for a special day to come around, the birthday celebrations of Job's firstborn son. Satan is not only cruel but also crafty. He chooses his time and his methods. He is out for maximum effect. He chose a day of special family celebration, which was also a day when Job feared that thoughtless sin might have been committed.

2. The losses he inflicted

Satan had been given leave to touch 'all' that Job had' (1:11,12). Here he goes about that progressively, as can be seen by comparing what was taken with the list of Job's possessions given earlier (see 1:2-3).

Proceeding in reverse order, we have first the oxen and (female) donkeys and the servants who were ploughing with them — preparations were being made for the next year's harvest. The sheep (and goats) and shepherds were next, and then the camels and the servants who attended to them. Finally and climactically, we have the deaths of Job's sons and daughters. Nothing was left — well, almost nothing: only his wife and four servants! Why were these spared? It was not that they were off-limits, as Job himself was. Satan could have included them too had he wished to do so. He left them in order to be able to use them against Job.

3. The reports he brought

Four servants (out of a large number) were spared in order that they might bear reports to Job of what had happened. They were therefore 'messenger(s) of Satan to harass' him (cf. 2 Cor. 12:7). Their arrival was orchestrated so that a rapid succession of blows might rain down on Job. After the arrival of the first messenger, three times we have the words: **'While he was yet speaking, there came another and said, "... and I alone have escaped to tell you"'** (1:16,17,18-19). This repetitiveness indicates something of Satan's brutality. He not only uses subtlety, but force. He bludgeons the saints.

4. The means he used

He uses natural disaster as well as human activity, and does so in equal measure, so to speak. Two of the four calamities are attributed to the plundering activities of marauding tribes, the Sabeans and the Chaldeans, while the other two are traced to lightning and the hot desert wind. Such a distribution of causes makes it impossible for Job to avoid bringing God into the picture, because the latter two are 'acts of God' in judgement on the wicked (see 20:26; Jer. 4:11-12). That of course was what Satan intended, and the fact that it was 'an act of God', and not of men, that brought about the death of Job's children is particularly noteworthy. The other losses were intended to soften him up; this one was to shatter him.

The loss of his children was meant to sow doubt in his mind about the character of the God to whom he had prayed. Why would God do such a thing — especially after Job had prayed for them so often (and, doubtless, had been going to do so again) in connection with sin and sacrifice? Clearly Satan not only uses a club, but also a rapier. He not only crushes bones with a succession of blows (like Giant Despair), but he pierces the mind with excruciating thoughts and doubts.

The reaction of Job (1:20-22)

This was Job's 'evil day' (Eph. 6:13). How did he react? Satan was sure of what would happen; he had confidently predicted it. But Jehovah was in no suspense as to what the outcome would be and had therefore allowed the trial. Job, unaware of both, was left to grapple with all that had taken place — alone. He responded as a frail man but as a godly man, and he did so magnificently in both respects.

1:20-21. Then Job arose and tore his robe and shaved his head and fell on the ground and worshipped. And he said, 'Naked I came from my mother's womb, and naked shall I return. The LORD gave, and the LORD has taken away; blessed be the name of the LORD.'

1. As a frail man

This is how people reacted to adversity and bereavement in Job's day and in his society. A **'robe'** was worn over a tunic, and it was this outer garment which Job tore, as Jacob did for Joseph (Gen. 37:34). Doubtless, Job's robe was ornate and costly. Shaving of the head was a common custom too in such circumstances (see Jer. 7:29; Ezra 9:3). While the latter was forbidden in the law, the fact that Job did not inflict gashes on his body, as was done by the heathen, is significant (Lev. 19:27-28). In no way was he either insensitive to all that had befallen him or excessive in the way in which he manifested his grief like the heathen. His godliness did not destroy his humanness.

2. As a godly man

He fell to the ground and worshipped. His prostration was with a view to expressing his own frailty but also exalting God. His words indicate his thoughts. They are full of his own smallness and Jehovah's great goodness, and he does not misrepresent God.

First, *he abases himself before God.* His torn finery and bared head manifest his awareness of the transience of earthly glory and his vulnerability in the presence of death. He recalls his birth in terms of his having nothing and envisages his death in terms of his being deprived of everything. His mother's womb becomes the symbol of the earth to which he returns and from which he was made (Gen. 3:19; Ps.139:15). The sudden and colossal change that has taken place is a reminder to him of his lowly condition. He faces his own mortality, but he does so in the presence of the God who is Jehovah.

Secondly, *he exalts God* by acknowledging that he was no less good in taking from him than he had been in giving to him. But what is so striking and glorious is that Job in this circumstance of bereavement addresses God as 'Jehovah' — the one who spoke of life amid death in the Garden of Eden. Faced with fleeting life and fearful death, he trusts again in a living Redeemer and blesses, instead of cursing, him. He draws near to the immortal Jehovah rather than departing from him.

Hostilities resumed
(Job 2:1-10)

In spite of the obvious similarities between this section and the one just considered, it would be a great mistake to regard it as no more than a repetition of what had already taken place. It records a resumption of hostilities — one that results in a significant extension of the front over which the war was to be fought. It is important to remember that, while there was no respite between the blows that fell successively in Satan's first assault, there was some intermission between them and what is now about to start up all over again.

This passage will be considered in two parts, namely verses 1-6 and 7-10.

The conversation (2:1-6)

Another glimpse is provided into the heavenly court and another conversation (if we may call it that) between Jehovah and Satan with respect to Job is overheard. As the same state of affairs continues, comment will not be made about the aspects which have already been noted. Instead, attention will be focused on the significant differences that are now introduced. These are found in verses 3 and 4 and we shall follow the course of the dialogue.

1. Jehovah to Satan (2:1-3)

2:3. And the LORD said to Satan, 'Have you considered my servant Job, that there is none like him on the earth, a blameless and upright man, who fears God and turns away from evil? He still holds fast his integrity, although you incited me against him to destroy him without reason.'

Jehovah again takes the initiative and the second part of verse 3 is richly significant. The important words in it are **'still'** and **'though'**. The first indicates Jehovah's delight at Job's steadfastness, and by inference Satan's failure; the second is Jehovah's censure of Satan's malignity. These will now be considered in turn.

I. The pleasure of Jehovah

By means of the addition of the word **'still'**, Jehovah exults in Job's continuing sincerity and righteousness, and he does so before the angelic host and 'the Satan'. In spite of the many losses Job has sustained, he has not forsaken his **'integrity'**. He has maintained his 'blamelessness' before God and man. God does not use his people for his own glory and praise in the earth without delighting in them. Although his people are not to boast in themselves, he boasts in them — especially when they glorify him. He is 'not ashamed to be called their God' (Heb. 11:16).

II. The failure of Satan

But **'still'** also means that Satan's attacks have not succeeded and his prediction has not come to pass. Indeed, the exact reverse has taken place. Instead of cursing, Job has blessed. He turned his face towards God, instead of turning his back on him. Jehovah here derides Satan's failure to overcome his servant (cf. Ps. 2:4).

III. The censure of Satan

Job's afflictions are here put down entirely to Satan's malignity. This is reminiscent of Jehovah's charge to the serpent in Eden: 'Because you have done this...' (Gen. 3:14). God is not the author of sin, and even calamity is only to be traced mediately to him (see Isa. 45:7). Satan is therefore held responsible for all the afflictions that Job has suffered, and Jehovah's permission does not amount to any complicity on his part. It is Satan's intent **'to destroy'** Job, not God's, although Satan has tried to make it look as if it is. But it is all to no avail — so far.

2. Satan to Jehovah (2:4-5)

2:4-5. Then Satan answered the LORD and said, 'Skin for skin! All that a man has he will give for his life. But stretch out your hand and touch his bone and his flesh, and he will curse you to your face.'

The Lord has been delighted by Job's perseverance, but Satan has learned nothing from it at all. One might have thought that, after being proved so wrong and defeated so soundly, any adversary would have left the field. But he is 'the' Satan and is not only malicious but also incorrigible. His reply to Jehovah shows that his ignorance is invincible and his hatred of godliness is implacable. He is convinced that with greater leeway he can achieve his purpose. But of course he has to appear again before the Sovereign for permission to extend his activity.

To do this he uses the expression, **'Skin for skin!'** There is no parallel use of this cryptic expression in the Old Testament, and so its meaning has to be sought in the immediate context. Jehovah has just spoken to Satan about Job's consistency, and these words are therefore Satan's immediate outburst by

way of negative reaction. They express a very different view of Job, which Satan backs up by saying that
Job still has **'his life'** (2:4). He still has something
valuable although he has lost so much. There is
therefore a connection between 'skin' and 'life'. Bearing that in mind, there are two ways in which this
saying and the preposition **'for'** can be understood,
and both are so typical of Satan.

I. Others' skin on behalf of one's own skin

Understood in this way, the sense is that Job can
adjust to the loss of his servants, and even that of his
sons and daughters, because he himself is still alive.
His own life is more valuable to him than theirs and
that is why he 'still holds fast his integrity'. This
means that Job is selfish and serves God because he
realizes it still pays him to do so, although to a lesser
extent than before. Satan is therefore 'holding fast' to
his own distorted analysis of Job's piety and also of
Jehovah's praise of him.

II. Skin behind skin

It is noteworthy that the word **'skin'** is introduced
here soon after Job's use of the word 'naked' in 1:21.
Those two words come from the same root. Satan is
therefore parodying Job's confession of faith by
saying that, though 'naked', he still has 'skin' — by
which he means 'life' — **'bone** [frame] **and ... flesh'**
and is so full of health and vigour. Rendered in this
way, the meaning is that the removal of one layer of
skin after another will soon leave Job with absolutely
nothing, and so he will have no reason to maintain
his adherence to God. It is as if Satan were the first
to think that health and wealth equalled piety! In his
view, if health can be removed as well as wealth, then
so will piety!

3. Jehovah to Satan (2:6)

2:6. And the LORD said to Satan, 'Behold, he is in your hand; only spare his life.'

Again Jehovah refuses to act personally against Job, but he does act permissively. The word **'Behold'** is used to draw attention to the fact that it is God who puts Job in Satan's **'hand'** — that is, his power. Greater latitude is given to Satan with regard to Job's body, but still Job's life, his real self, is sacrosanct. That belongs to the great Jehovah. Job must live to give the lie to Satan by giving honour to Jehovah (and to be further blessed by him). What an obligation! What an opportunity! But Job is as unaware of all that as he is of what is about to restart on a much more intense and demanding level.

The consequence (2:7-10)

Armed with divine permission, Satan immediately leaves the court and without delay, it seems, assaults Job with a disease that is painful, extensive and loathsome. Its exact nature has been a subject of investigation and the favoured view is that it was something akin to leprosy or elephantiasis. Descriptions of it can be gleaned from statements that Job makes later in the book — for example, he refers to being unable to sleep (7:4), to having crusted sores (7:5) and nightmares (7:14) and suffering from depression (7:16). Here in Job 2:7-10 we have a picture of agony and ostracism. Job's only relief (2:8) causes him more anguish, and all the while he sits on the rubbish heap. The most honoured citizen has become the most offensive and rejected.

2:9-10. Then his wife said to him, 'Do you still hold fast your integrity? Curse God and die.' But he said to her, 'You speak as one of the foolish women would speak. Shall we receive good from God, and shall we not receive evil?'

It is while he is in this condition that his wife speaks to him. Comments have already been made about this incident, but from the perspective of Job. Now we look at it from the standpoint of his wife and of Satan. There is no doubt that, just as he spared four servants to be unwitting messengers in his employ, so Satan has done the same with regard to Job's wife. This is borne out by what she says to Job. It is in two parts and both are echoes of things that have already been said. The first part, **'Do you still hold fast your integrity?'** (2:9), is an echo of Jehovah's words to Satan about Job, but now they are distorted because they are no longer in the form of a statement but a question. The second is a loud expression of Satan's design.

What she says is therefore an extension of Satan's activity. Previously he had pursued his aim by battering Job, but now he insinuates a question into his mind and follows it up by a proposed action — all put into the mouth of Job's wife!

What does this say about Job's wife? In the history of interpretation she has suffered much by being described as negatively as Job is described positively at the beginning of the book. However, just as it is important to make a distinction between Job's words and his real standing before God, and also between those of his friends and their original intention, so we should not take the worst possible view of Job's wife. After all, the only other negative thing that is explicitly said about her describes an understandable reaction to Job's physical repulsiveness (see 19:17), but it seems from what is said at the end of the book about Job's restoration that she had not left him.

It should also be remembered that the children that had died were not only Job's but hers too! A mother's grief and a wife's sorrow are therefore present in these intemperate and unwise words. In addition, we need to realize that Job held out only a little longer than she did (see chapter 3). Frailty, and not folly, is what is evidenced here. This is borne out by Job's reply, which described her words — not her personally — as resembling those of **'the foolish women'**.[8] He does not charge her with being one of these women, but invites and encourages her to join with him in receiving calamity from the hand of God just as they had together received so many good gifts from him.

Job was still the same gracious and godly man without health as he had been without wealth. He did not speak perversely against God, but controlled 'his lips' (see James 3:6-10). The 'tongue' is here used only to praise God and benefit the one made in his image (Job's wife), and not to renounce the former or denounce the latter.

Three good men and true
(Job 2:11-13)

Job's friends enter the narrative somewhat abruptly at the close of chapter 2⁹ and we must be careful how we consider them. Like Job's wife, they have acquired something of a reputation in the minds of many, as is evidenced by the derogatory expression 'Job's comforter'. Such an estimate of them is not without support in the text, for later Job describes them as 'miserable comforters' (16:1) and later still Jehovah declares that they had 'not spoken of [him] what [was] right' (42:7-8). But we must not read those assessments back into this passage, as if they were true from the very beginning. We must keep pace with the narrative and include all the relevant data about the Friends that we are given in the book. This means giving these verses their full weight, irrespective of whatever adjustments need to be made later. That is what we shall now do.

What we are told about them in these verses indicates that they were kind, wise and good.

2:11. Now when Job's three friends heard of all this evil that had come upon him, they came each from his own place, Eliphaz the Temanite, Bildad the Shuhite, and Zophar the Naamathite. They made an appointment together to come to show him sympathy and comfort him.

They were kind men

They are here called Job's **'three friends'** and that indicates something of what made them special. Job refers to a degree of intimacy having existed between him and them (see 19:19) that he compares with a relationship to the Almighty (6:14). There was therefore some solemn mutual commitment involved between them, as between David and Jonathan. That they were not friends of the 'fair-weather' kind is shown by what they did after they heard of Job's calamity. They arranged to meet and to travel to bring him some comfort by not leaving him alone in his grief. Theirs was a noble, gentle spirit. They were sincere, and that is shown by their reaction when they saw him. There was an immediate outburst of fellow feeling. They knew it was he, even from a distance, but what a change!

They wept and tore their robes because Job's condition rent their hearts and they could not but show how they felt. They threw dust **'towards heaven'** — that is, upwards, so that it descended **'on their heads'** in order to identify with him as closely as they could (see Josh. 7:6). They were stunned and sat in silence for seven days, as Joseph did when mourning for his father (see Gen. 50:10).

They were wise men

This is how Job describes them, although he does so sarcastically (12:2-3), and it is what Eliphaz claims, albeit pompously (15:10). But that is what they were — and so was Job too. Their places of origin may be said to point this out. The information we are given about Eliphaz is the easiest to identify and it supplies an indicator for the other two. The descendants of Teman, the first-named of Esau's grandsons (Gen.

36:11), were in Edom in Ezekiel's day (Ezek. 25:13). Teman was well known for its wisdom (Jer. 49:7; Obad. 8-9). Uncertainty exists about both Shuah and Naamah, where Bildad and Zophar came from respectively. The former name exists in connection with Abraham and Keturah (Gen. 25:2) and the latter with both Cain and Solomon (Gen. 4:22; 1 Kings 14:21).

They were good men

The comfort and wisdom they brought Job was offered to him in God's name. They sought to advise him (5:27), relating what they knew to his condition and circumstances. They spoke of God's justice and goodness, of his power and his kindness. They declared that God punished sin, answered prayer and rewarded piety (see 4:7-9,17-18; 8:3; 11:5-6). All this was true and they were also sincere, a fact that was demonstrated by their obedient response to Jehovah's rebuke and directive (42:9).

But, as was mentioned at the beginning, there are other facts to consider about them that are of a different kind. These too will be given due weight at the proper time and place. Here we shall just draw attention to the question of how these things can *all* be true. How can sense be made of them all? These men came to comfort Job with truth from God, but they were soon mangling Job and misrepresenting God. How could things take such a course? Merely to frame that question in the light of what has just gone before is to answer it.

It is not enough to say that Job's sudden outburst in the following chapter (3:1-26) contributed to their reaction, though doubtless it did. Nor is it enough — and this is more to the point — to say that Job's firm and repeated rejection of what they were confident was the explanation of, and remedy for, his condition

greatly increased their concern about him. Someone
else was at work in them as well as in Job, and by
setting them at odds with each other his identity is
revealed. Satan is the one who sows strife and he is
'the accuser of the brethren'. Like Job's wife, the
Friends unwittingly became a further weapon in
Satan's arsenal against poor Job.

It has been mentioned that Satan left the Lord
Jesus until 'an opportune time' and returned via one
disciple who betrayed him and another who denied
him (John 13:26-27; Matt. 16:22-23) and then when
the rest fled. Joseph Caryl says, 'Satan used Job's
wife to jeer him out of his religion and his friends to
dispute him out of it.' (Whether or not we agree with
Caryl in his view of Job's wife, we should agree with
him about the Friends.) It is the only view that does
justice to the whole text and is supported by the
following considerations:

1. Their coming was 'timed', just as in the
case of Job's servants. He had been left alone
on the rubbish heap with his losses, pains *and
his thoughts*.

2. They mourned with him — or was it over
him, as if he were already a dead man? They
said nothing to him. They were like a mirror in
which he could see himself and his own funeral.

3. The fact that they were friends gave them
(as in the case of Job's wife) a unique entrance
into his anguished thoughts and made their
remarks all the more hurtful.

4. But finally, it was they who consistently
depicted God as punishing Job for his sin. Job's
wife had not done that. This meant that Job
was faced with a choice — an awful choice between his own integrity and God's injustice, and
one he faced repeatedly.

2. The debate between Job and the Friends (I)

(Job 3:1 – 19:29)

Chapters 3 – 31 form a distinct sub-section in *Job*. For one thing, they are in poetry, unlike the previous chapters. But secondly, and more importantly, they contain a series of speeches which are part of the trial of Job's faith as it is progressively unfolded. It is true that they can seem repetitive and desultory and they do contain considerable difficulties. But they should be given serious attention because they have an important place and function in the narrative. They should not be passed over in haste to get to 19:25-27 and then by another jump to move on to the Epilogue. Their importance to the whole book is further seen from the fact that Jehovah sums them up in the conclusion with words whose meaning is crucial but not immediately obvious (see 42:7-9). These chapters cannot therefore be overlooked because they return in the denouement, albeit in a more complex form.

Given all this, it seems appropriate to include a prefatory comment to these chapters so that some matters which are important to them all might be highlighted and considered. There are four of these and we shall examine them in turn.

Their literary character

Our age does not often hear good debate and, while these speeches can cross the line into argument, they are never merely 'full of noise and fury, signifying nothing'. They are full of raw emotion and explosive language, but also twists and turns of argument which have as their single focus why Job is in the condition he is and what he must do in order to be restored. This point needs to be appreciated and remembered.

Attention must therefore be given to the forward movement in these chapters, exhibited in the speech / reply pattern, while trying to preserve the continuity that they all present. There is no interval between one speech and the reply to it, as there was between the two phases of Job's afflictions. In addition, the author seems to indicate that no sooner is a reply given than another speech is made. The cyclical arrangement of the material conveys the idea of a series of attacks being mounted, each contributing to the next and, in Job's case, each needing to be repulsed over and over again. Job has not only been battered personally, physically and psychologically, but now verbally and mentally as well. This is no classroom debate, no phoney war. A fifth columnist is at work here.

The points of view expressed

The role of human perception in the narrative was mentioned in the introduction (see pages 30-32) and this is where it begins to be really significant. All four men, Job and his three friends, describe things as they see them, and not one of them is completely right all the time. They disagree in their views about each other, about God's dealings with Job and also over what needs to happen in order that Job might be restored. Their different convictions are a very important feature in the struggle recorded in these chapters, and care needs to be exercised in interpreting the statements they make.

Two extra details have also to be borne in mind. The first is that 'the Satan', the accusing adversary, continues to be active, although this is not explicitly indicated in the text. The second is that Jehovah is doing a new thing and is in perfect and total control.

Their overall coherence

Debates can turn into arguments, and even into a slanging match if they are not moderated. This one does become personal, but the author of the book preserves the point at issue for us. It is the nexus between God's dealings and Job's sufferings, viewed from the standpoint of Job in his relationship with God. That is brought out in the way this section is structured.

It opens and closes with a speech of Job, and both speeches are in somewhat the same vein. The first is lamentation and the second is protestation. Both are loud. There is something pitiable in the first, but something assertive about the second. Job is no longer agonizingly perplexed by the pressures of his afflictions (cf. the question 'Why?' in chapter 3) but filled with confidence as he conducts his own defence before God, throwing down a gauntlet in his presence. This indicates that there is forward movement in this section, and not just a 'round and round again' motion that goes nowhere. Readers should be able to sense this and find that their interest is piqued by it. We shall look at these closing chapters later, but here we content ourselves with the point that, just as Job's lament gave rise to the Friends' speeches, so his self-defence opens the way for Elihu's intervention.

A turning point

An overview of this entire section reveals that the Friends' speeches begin to peter out towards its conclusion. Eliphaz has less to say in his final address than he had previously, and Zophar has nothing to say at all! How can this be explained? In my view this is due to the self-disclosure of God to Job recorded in 19:25-27 which, not surprisingly, produces a change in Job and marks a turning point in the debate. Job's words indicate that he has reached some solid ground in the midst of all his troubles, the effect of which becomes evident in his subsequent addresses to the Friends, as we shall see later.

'Why?'
(Job 3:1-26)

The seven-day silence between Job and his friends is brought to an end by this unexpected outburst. In it Job is sinning 'with his lips' (cf. 2:10). He has fallen from the high plateau of spirituality that he had occupied. This speech is neither thankful praise nor glad submission. In it we have the agitation of a troubled and gloomy spirit most powerfully expressed — even in translation. In the original it is powerful poetry, full of alliteration and allusion.

We shall consider it under the headings of what Job said and, finally, what he did not say.

What Job said

Questions abound in this chapter. In the original Hebrew the word **'Why?'** is voiced three times (3:11,12,20) and it is implied twice (3:16,23).[1] In using it Job is not asking for information, but expressing a lament (cf. Ps. 44:23-24). But he is going further even than that, because he begins with a curse! A curse is worse than a lament because it is more than just an appeal for pity. It is a determination to destroy, or to have something or someone destroyed. How Satan must have been delighted to hear that word on Job's lips!

These same elements of piteous appeal coupled with vehement cursing are found in Jeremiah

20:7-18, but they are there in the reverse order. With Job, curse predominates and the questions expressed in his lament are introduced as supportive reasons for his desire to desecrate, not consecrate. We shall therefore begin with the curse and then move on to the lament. Job's desire for rest, which is expressed in verse 13 and echoed in verse 26, marks a transition in, and the culmination of, his *cri de coeur* respectively.

1. The curse (3:1- 13)

3:1-3 After this Job opened his mouth and cursed the day of his birth. And Job said:

> Let the day perish on which I was born,
>   and the night that said,
>   'A man is conceived.'

3:7-8
Behold, let that night be barren;
    let no joyful cry enter it.
Let those curse it who curse the day,
    who are ready to rouse up Leviathan.

Two things need to be noted about this poem. First, Job's outcry contains echoes of the account of creation in Genesis 1:1 – 2: 4. God's handiwork on all of the days, except Day 3, is referred to in these verses. We have darkness and light, days and years, sea monsters (Leviathan) and humankind (Job himself) and then rest.[2] But they are set out all in reverse. Job wants light turned to darkness; Moses recorded how darkness gave way to light.

This way of speaking has led to this chapter being described as a 'counter-cosmic incantation' — a literary feature which is derived from a pagan environment. It was a common idea in the ancient Near

East that 'a primordial womb' gave rise and order to everything, whether on the human or superhuman level. Rites of sympathetic magic could secure the continuance of life and order, or the latter could be destroyed by a 'magic' of a deeper and darker kind. Spells were regarded as having power and if Leviathan (3:8), who conquered in the primeval chaos battle, could be roused to act against the day of Job's birth, then an eclipse could be caused which would obliterate it. This feature of the surrounding pagan culture has clearly filtered into Job's mind. But is he adopting it wholesale, or just using it as a metaphor? Whichever is the case, the fact is that this idea is in his mind and in his mouth — and who might have put it there?

In my view Job is not endorsing paganism. Later he denies that he has ever practised pagan rites (31:26-28). But is he here affirming pagan *thoughts*? The highly rhetorical nature of this poem must be borne in mind at this point. Clearly he is expressing such thoughts, but that does not have to mean that he is affirming them. However, he is so aggrieved that he not only has this concept in mind it but he also expresses it in words — and that is bad enough. Just as his wife had thought and spoken foolishly, he is now doing the same. Satan has not only maimed his body; he has muddled his mind.

Secondly, it is not surprising that contrasting his condition and circumstances with God's orderly creative handiwork should lead him to think about rest, its peak and goal. He mentions this subject twice (3:13,26) but the similar terms that he uses in this passage are a pale shadow of the reality that he had enjoyed with God and which resembled the consummation of creation (see 29:3-4). Job is sinking spiritually. He prefers chaos to cosmos and supports his 'thinking' by a threefold lament.

2. The lament

I. 'Why did I have to be born?' (3:3-10)

Job wants action, not an explanation! Reflecting on his origin, he brackets together birth and conception, the former with day and the latter with night. He then proceeds to desire the obliteration of each: the day (3:4-5) and the night (3:6-10). His first longing is that such darkness may engulf 'his day' so that it will pass from God's view and then out of the human calendar. Similarly, with regard to the night, his desire is that it may be deprived of such light as stars provide, and that it may never see the dawn that it expects. He connects the **'eyelids'** of the dawn with the **'doors'** of his mother's abdomen, on the basis that if both had remained closed then his own eyes would never have been opened to see nothing but trouble! (3:9-10). He would have died in the womb (see 10:18).

II. 'Why was I born alive?' (3:11-19)

3:11,13
Why did I not die at birth,
    come out from the womb and expire? ...
For then I would have lain down and been quiet;
    I would have slept; then I would have been at rest.

3:16-17
Or why was I not as a hidden stillborn child,
    as infants who never see the light?
There the wicked cease from troubling,
    and there the weary are at rest.

Moving on from the fact that his birth was not prevented, he asks why he did not die as soon as he was born (3:11) or why he had not been stillborn (3:16). But neither had been the case. He had been born **'a man'** (3:3) and that noun means a healthy vigorous male. He had been received, perhaps by his father (3:12; cf. Gen. 50:23), but certainly by his mother, who nourished him.

He backs up his seriously meant death wish by listing all the 'benefits' which the deceased enjoy and which are being denied to him (3:13-19). It is note-worthy that they are all negative. As someone who had possessed wealth and exercised authority, he thinks of kings, counsellors and princes on the one hand, but also of the wicked, the burdened, prison-ers and slaves on the other. What brings them to-gether is that they all share in a rest that is better than rank, and all that goes with it, and that is the end of all hardship. Social distinctions are all abol-ished. No one harms others; no one suffers at the hands of others. All is quiet — deathly so.

III. 'Why can't I die here and now?' (3:20-26)

3:20
Why is light given to him who is in misery,
    and life to the bitter in soul...?

3:23-24,26
Why is light given to a man whose way is hidden,
    whom God has hedged in?
For my sighing comes instead of my bread,
    and my groanings are poured out like water...
I am not at ease, nor am I quiet,
    I have no rest, but trouble comes.

What Job has been expressing is of course a vain regret, for he is still alive. He therefore wishes that he could just stop living. **'Why is light given?'** he asks in verse 20, and continues with the same thought in verse 23, doing so as one for whom a darkness that is greater than the physical kind has been made attractive. But light continues to be seen, and with it comes life — yet again. No rest is given (3:26). He is so embittered (3:20) that only death will bring him joy (3:22); he regards himself as being confined (3:23), and not protected. His meagre rations of bread and water are coupled with sighs and groans (3:24) — these are strong words. What he had been apprehensive might occur has indeed come to pass (3:25).

What he did not say

In Hebrew the order of words in the opening verse is: 'After this opened Job his mouth and cursed.' We should stop there, catch our breath and ask the question: 'What is going to be cursed, or whom?' 'Blessed' is Job's word, whereas 'curse[d]' is Satan's word. Consecration is Job's language, and not desecration. We should therefore feel some relief that he pronounces evil only on himself, and not on Jehovah.

But what he says is serious enough! He is no longer exercising self-control; he is sinning with his mouth (cf. 2:10) and he is charging God with wrong (cf. 1:22). He refers to God at the beginning and the end of his outburst (3:4,23). Job is not only questioning God's wisdom, but also his goodness.

But still there is no renunciation of God. He implicates God, but he does so by cursing his own birth, his own life and his mother (3:12); that is not the same as cursing God to his face (see 2:5). So Satan has still failed. Nevertheless Job has now fallen, and he is no longer honouring Jehovah. What does the future hold? Will he fall further?

'Remember! Repent!'
(Job 4:1 – 5:27)

Although Job's vehement and mournful soliloquy was not addressed to his friends, it gave rise to the debate that followed. Eliphaz picked up on some of the things that Job said, and so did Bildad and Zophar in their turn. As Eliphaz was the one who spoke first, he was almost certainly the oldest of the three. He spoke in the name of them all (see 5:27). He began in a kindly manner, but that soon wore thin.

'Now it has come to you' (4:1-6)

4:5-6
But now it has come to you, and you are impatient;
  it touches you, and you are dismayed.
Is not your fear of God your confidence,
  and the integrity of your ways your hope?

Having heard what Job has said, and how he has said it, Eliphaz begins with sensitivity. He is conscious that anything he says might provoke another outburst from Job, but finds that he can no longer remain silent because he has become so concerned. With moderation but with clarity (and friends do have licence to speak plainly), he therefore reminds Job of how he had formerly reacted to trouble. He is not here thinking of Job's magnificent responses recorded in chapters 1 and 2, which he had not heard. What he has in mind is what he and his friends knew of Job's previous conduct, as that is summarized in chapters 29-31. Job had instructed and encouraged others in their times of perplexity and weakness (4:3-4), but now that the shoe is on the other foot, Job the comforter has become Job the impatient (4:5), and that militates against Job's piety.

Although Eliphaz refers to Job's **'fear'** (4:6), he does not specify God as its object (as the ESV implies). But it is the **'fear of God'** that he has in mind, as can be seen from the fact that his speech is full of references to God (4:9,17; 5:8-27). He is conscious of speaking in God's name and says that Job has lost his confidence because he no longer fears God as he used to do. By pointing this out he is not encouraging Job to trust in his own piety, but to be hopeful in God, whom he had served with integrity, and to cease to be impatient and dismayed (see 4:5; cf. 3:1-26). Eliphaz is at this point being a true, good friend.

'Remember [now]' (4:7-11)

4:7-11
Remember: who that was innocent ever perished?
    Or where were the upright cut off?
As I have seen, those who plough iniquity
    and sow trouble reap the same.
By the breath of God they perish,
    and by the blast of his anger they are consumed.
The roar of the lion, the voice of the fierce lion,
    the teeth of the young lions are broken.
The strong lion perishes for lack of prey,
    and the cubs of the lioness are scattered.

Eliphaz reminds Job that the **'innocent'** and the **'upright'** (4:7 — a variation on 1:1) do not perish by God's judgement. Drawing from his observation of life

(4:8), he declares that it is the wicked — those who **'plough iniquity'** (sowing evil) and those who prey on others (he uses five words for **'lion'** in verses 10-11) — who perish at the blast of God's hot wind of judgement. Eliphaz is therefore saying to Job that he is not going to have his death wish fulfilled. But there is a kind of *double entendre* in Eliphaz' language, because the illustrations he employs of the desert wind and the **'young'** lions have associations with the calamities that have befallen Job (see chapter 1). Whether Eliphaz intended this allusion is difficult to say, but his language was certainly unfortunate.[3] Was his sensitivity to Job's plight already wearing off? Or was the likelihood that Job was suffering because of some sin on his part already forming in his mind? Given what he has heard from Job's own lips, and his theory that affliction indicates sin, such a conclusion is probable. (He will state it clearly later — see 5:17.)

A further revelation (4:12-17)

4:17
Can mortal man be in the right before God?
    Can a man be pure before his Maker?

Eliphaz now adds supernatural revelation to natural observation by way of confirmation of what he has just said. In moving and graphic terms he recounts a message from God that he was given. His **'deep sleep'** (4:13) is an indication of total passivity on his part, as it was with Adam and Abraham (see Gen. 2:21; 15:12). The announcement made was that no **'mortal man'** can **'be in the right before God'**. It is the application of this statement to Job, rather than its truth *per se*, that is the critical factor. (Job was well aware of its truth and says so later — see 9:2.)

They die without wisdom (4:18-21)

4:18-19,21
Even in his servants he puts no trust,
    and his angels he charges with error;
how much more those who dwell in houses of clay,
    whose foundation is in the dust,
    who are crushed like the moth...
Is not their tent-cord plucked up within them,
    do they not die, and that without wisdom?

What follows in these verses are probably the words
of Eliphaz, and not those of the supernatural visitor.
For Eliphaz, the divine declaration served to prove
that Job had sinned and that his affliction was
commensurate with its gravity in the sight of God.[4] It
means that Job's affliction was in the nature of
punishment from God because his sin had put him
'in the wrong before God'. Job is therefore being
chastened (see 5:17). This is where Eliphaz did not
speak 'what was right about God' (see 42:7). At this
point we do well to recall that truth misapplied is
part of Satan's stock in trade. His use of Scripture is
always twisted, whether by way of supplementation,
contradiction or omission (see Gen. 3:1,5; Luke
4:1-12).
    Eliphaz reinforces the divine declaration by point-
ing out that even the angelic hosts find a gulf between themselves and God, and that they depend on
him rather than his being dependent on them. How
much more is this the case with frail, defenceless
beings! God is mighty and wise, and humans are
weak and unwise, vulnerable and transient.
    Although there is no second-person singular verb
in this section, Eliphaz is speaking to Job, but he
does so obliquely. He is pressing an accusation
against Job. The allusion to a tent collapsing (4:21)
recalls the calamity that was associated with the loss

of Job's children (see 1:19). The charge that he has no wisdom, after the acknowledgement that he has 'instructed' many (4:3), is an indication that Eliphaz' judgement has become affected. Satan is at work!

'Call now ... who will answer you?' (5:1-7)

5:1
Call now; is there anyone who will answer you?
    To which of the holy ones will you turn?

The chapter division at the end of chapter 4 can be overlooked in the interests of sense and continuity.

Eliphaz now becomes unmistakably censorious and denunciatory. His rhetorical invitation to **'call'** out is a reference to Job's outburst in chapter 3 and it is also in keeping with what he has just said about the distance between God and mortals. **'The holy ones'** are God's angelic servants (see 4:18), who, though they are above man, are below God. Not being God's equals, not one of them can act as Job's intermediary with him (see 9:33). This is not because God does not speak — after all, he has spoken to Eliphaz — but because Job's fiery indignation against God, expressed in chapter 3, has put him outside the pale of whatever intervention they can be thought to exert. Job has become a **'fool'**, and Eliphaz proceeds to describe the judgement that fools receive in terms that are pointedly reminiscent of Job's own tragedies! In an echo of the curse on the ground in Genesis 3, Eliphaz connects calamity with human birth (5:6) — that is, with sin.

'As for me I would...' (5:8-27)

5:8-9
As for me, I would seek God,
   and to God would I commit my cause,
who does great things and unsearchable,
   marvellous things without number...

5:27
Behold, this we have searched out; it is true.
   Hear, and know it for your good.

In this passage Eliphaz adopts the role of a mediator.
(We shall see later that Zophar and Bildad do so as
well — in antithesis to Elihu.) Eliphaz believes himself to be qualified to advise Job by what he has seen
of God's acts (see 4:8; 5:3) and heard of God's words
(see 4:16). Having told Job that there is no answer
from God to his outspoken questions (see chapter 3)
and that no angelic intervention is possible, he
makes it clear by his final words that Job's only way
forward is to listen to what he himself has to say to
him: **'Behold, this we have searched out... Hear
and know it...'** Beginning with the emphatic word
'Behold', these words convey the authority that
Eliphaz wants Job to be aware of. What began defer-
entially ends most dogmatically. This is a trap of
Satan.

Eliphaz begins with a personal word, telling Job
what he himself would do in Job's position. (Job will
use this ploy later — see 16:4 — but in a very different spirit.)

Eliphaz has two songs to sing, so to speak. They
correspond to one another but by way of contrast.
They are the way of the 'fool' (see 5:3-7) and the way
of the wise (see 5:17-26). Clearly, Eliphaz wants what
characterizes the life of the wise to be true of Job.
But he is certain that currently it is the opposite that

is true. What Job therefore needs to do in committing his cause to God is to acknowledge that he has been foolish (has sinned) and that is why he has been dealt with as he has. In that event, God will reverse his condition and circumstances — peace and plenty, in family and to old age, will ensue. He advises Job to submit his cause to God, rather than complaining against his ways.

To encourage him to do this, Eliphaz describes how God **'does great things and unsearchable, marvellous things without number'** (5:9). He describes God's abundant beneficence in providence and deliverance, frustrating the wicked and delivering the needy in his just governance of mankind. This is a marvellous description of God's kindness to encourage Job to believe in restoration. Isn't this true, we may wonder? And doesn't it happen at the end of the narrative? The answer to both questions is in the affirmative. But at this point it is important to remember that Job is being told to seek God as someone *who has forsaken the way of wisdom.*

5:17
Behold, blessed is the one whom God reproves;
  therefore despise not the discipline of the Almighty.

What, then, does Eliphaz mean by what is for Job's **'good'**? (5:27). It is that God is 'reproving' Job and training him (see 5:17). This verse is quoted several times in the New Testament. Its general truth is certain, but the question is: how does it apply to Job, if it applies at all? Is divine chastisement the explanation of Job's calamities? It is not! Has Job sinned in complaining? Yes, he has, and that will not be overlooked by God as the narrative unfolds and comes to a climax. (Elihu will begin to deal with it, and then Jehovah will complete the process, as only he can.)

But Eliphaz is dealing with *the cause of Job's afflictions*, and that is not Job's sin.[5] The Prologue has made that clear. Consequently, for Job to admit that he has so sinned in the hope of gaining a wonderful restoration is for him to depart from his integrity — and whose purpose will that serve? Whose case will that prove — Jehovah's, or Satan's? Working on the principle that wickedness will be judged in this life in strict accord with the degree of sin that has been committed, Eliphaz views Job's affliction as proof positive of grievous sin. But Job's spiritual integrity is such that he will not use pretence as a way (back) to prestige and prosperity.

'Oh that I might have my request!'
(Job 6:1 – 7:21)

With this reply of Job the battle is really joined. But it does not only contain a reply to Eliphaz and his colleagues; Job also turns to God and addresses him (see 7:12). This is a pattern that Job often follows in his speeches, but it is not always easy to determine with certainty the point of transition.

This twofold focus should make us aware that, just as there was an unseen dimension to Job's troubles, so there is to the debate about them. We have noted that, in spite of Eliphaz' good intentions, somehow he speaks to Job the words that Satan would have Job hear. Given this, we should remember that each time Job resists the arguments of the Friends, he is resisting Satan, and when he turns to God (not away from him) he is to some degree glorifying God, whatever else has to be said about his remarks.

To the Friends (6:1-30)

Although it is only Eliphaz who has spoken, Job is here addressing them all. He is using plural verbs throughout. Eliphaz has provoked the very outburst that he intended to avoid by his opening remarks.

1. 'Oh that my vexation were weighed!' (6: 1-7)

6:2-3
Oh that my vexation were weighed,
    and all my calamity laid in the balances!
For then it would be heavier than the sand of the sea;
    therefore my words have been rash.

Job here uses the word **'vexation'** which Eliphaz had used in 5:2 in connection with the fool. By doing so he indicates that there has been a rush to judgement about the cause of his plight and the weight of his woe. The fact is that his anguish is heavier than the sand of the sea, and that is what explains the way in which he has spoken. It is not just that his adversity has come from God, but that God has become his adversary! Using military imagery, Job describes how **'the Almighty'** (that designation is significant in this context) is shooting poisoned arrows at him which sap his strength, physically and mentally (6:4). And, according to Eliphaz, Job is expected to be silent, even though animals, whether wild or tame, 'complain' when they have no food (6:5), and to accept meekly an insipid explanation, when even humans try to make what is tasteless palatable (6:7).

2. 'Oh that I might have my request!' (6:8-13)

6:8-10
Oh that I might have my request,
    and that God would fulfil my hope,
that it would please God to crush me,
    that he would let loose his hand and cut me off!
This would be my comfort;
    I would even exult in pain unsparing,
    for I have not denied the words of the Holy One.

Job is referring here to his desire to die — a desire
that Eliphaz, speaking in God's name, has denied
him. Job says that if God were to kill him, by whatever means (the thought of killing himself never
crosses his mind!), then he would endure it gladly.
While it would be a *coup de grâce* because Job knows
that his physical and mental resources are limited, it
would also be a personal triumph because he would
die knowing that he had maintained his spiritual
integrity. Job summarizes his life and conduct in
order to support his refusal to repent, as Eliphaz has
urged him to do. It is remarkable on three counts
(6:10).

1. He refers to **'words'** of God that had been
made known to him (cf. 23:12). These are quite
the opposite of his own 'words' (6:3), which he
acknowledges to have been **'rash'**, a word used
in Proverbs 20:25 in order to designate impetu-
ous speech. God always thinks before he
speaks; he says only what is true and never
needs to recant, but it is not so with Job.
2. He refers to God as **'holy'**, and this adjective is in the singular. It therefore does not relate to words, but to 'something', or rather
'someone', namely the one Job has in view, and
that is God. This term 'holy' is ubiquitous in
Scripture. It points to what is special, unique —
different from everything created, and particularly from everything sinful.
3. Finally, the word 'deny' that Job uses combines both testimony and conduct. He has neither **'denied'** God's word to him — attested in
the universe and inscribed on his moral consti-
tution (Rom. 1:19-20; 2:14-16) and also in the
promise of a deliverer from Satan (see Gen. 3:15
and in Job's use of 'Jehovah' in 12:9) — nor has
he refused to make it known to others.

But he has sinned with his lips (see 1:22; 2:10) because he has accused and complained against God (see 6:4,8).

3. 'My brothers are treacherous' (6:14-30)

6:14-15
He who withholds kindness from a friend
    forsakes the fear of the Almighty.
My brothers are treacherous as a torrent-bed,
    as torrential streams that pass away...

6:24-25
Teach me, and I will be silent;
    make me understand how I have gone astray.
How forceful are upright words!
    But what does reproof from you reprove?

Although Job uses the singular (6:14) he is not just thinking of Eliphaz alone, but of the two other Friends as well (a plural term appears in verse 15 and the verses that follow). All three of them have departed from the cardinal principle of loyal kindness that is of the essence of a covenant of friendship, and also of piety. Later Job will recall his own kindness to the needy and unfortunate (see chapter 29).

Job uses here the same name for God that Eliphaz had used (**'the Almighty'** — see 5:17), but turns it back on him and on them all. In this section he sees the Friends as afraid to get too involved in his condition and compares them to the bed of a torrent which disappoints desert travellers so sorely when they find it dry (6:15). At the very time when it needs to be full it is empty! So it is with his friends, who have no **'upright words'** (see 6:25) to offer him, although he has not asked them for anything. Still, he is willing to be taught and promises to listen (6:24) provided that they enter into his condition and perplexity in a substantial, and not a superficial, manner (6:26). They have to show him how he has sinned, and not just assert it. (Their failure to do this was what Elihu censured them for.) Job is in earnest because his righteous standing (his vindication) is what is at stake. He is sure that he is right and they are wrong, but he is willing to listen to what they have to say.

To God (7:1-21)

Although Job begins in soliloquy he is soon addressing God directly (7:7). The Friends of course overhear all that he says and that fuels their antagonistic responses to him.

1. 'Remember that my life is a breath' (7:1-10)

7:7-8
Remember that my life is a breath;
    my eye will never again see good.
The eye of him who sees me will behold me no more;
    while your eyes are on me, I shall be gone.

In these verses he describes his plight that leads up to the plea quoted above. He begins by alluding to the **'days'** of a mercenary who can look forward to wages after the campaign, or to a slave who can expect the comfort of the shade after toil in the sun (7:1-2). But in marked contrast to them, Job's **'nights'** are no different from his days. They are full of nothing but restless, painful endlessness. His only hope is in the inexorable passage of time and in the end that will surely come (7:3-6).

So he pleads with his Creator to **'remember'** (the verb is in the singular) how frail he is. He reminds God that he cannot last for ever and there is no way back to the **'good'** he knew. Soon he will not be

visible to his friends and others, and perhaps God
will look for him (7:8) but not be able to find him. His
house will be empty and he will be in the grave
(7:9-10). This matter is therefore most urgent! But
what is the explanation of this strange or unexpected
notion of God looking for him? Instead of Job turning
his back on God, he thinks of the possibility that God
may turn his face to him! Isn't this an echo of grace
in his heart?

2. 'Leave me alone, for my days are a breath' (7:11-21)

7:11-12
Therefore I will not restrain my mouth;
   I will speak in the anguish of my spirit;
   I will complain in the bitterness of my soul.
Am I the sea, or a sea monster,
   that you set a guard over me?

7:17
What is man, that you make so much of him,
   and that you set your heart on him...?

7: 20-21
If I sin, what do I do to you, you watcher of mankind?
   Why have you made me your mark?
   Why have I become a burden to you?
Why do you not pardon my transgression
   and take away my iniquity?
For now I shall lie in the earth;
   you will seek me, but I shall not be.

In these verses Job repeats the kind of outburst that
chapter 3 contains. He wants to be left alone to die.
He uses three verbs to express his determination to
explode against the God who will not give him a
moment's relief (7:11). He interrogates God with a
number of questions, all of which are based on the

notion that God is a malign invigilator and violent invader (7:20), concluding with the charge that God is making much too much of his sin (there is no **'if'** in the Hebrew of verse 20). For Job is not a huge sinner (7:20), like the monsters of the deep (7:12), who were depictions of evil in Canaanite mythology and of **'death'** (7:15). God is God and he has power to control (7:12) or to cleanse (7:21). So why the prolonged agony? Why does God insist on making **'much'** of him (7:17) — by way, not of blessing, but of torture and terror, by day and by night? This is out of all proportion to any grief he might have brought to God (7:20). Why doesn't God just pardon him? Soon it will be too late for him to do so.

Job says that God is great and man is small — a sentiment that is echoed by David in the well-known words of Psalm 8:4. But David talks about the way in which God has ennobled man by, literally, 'setting his heart [mind] on him'. Job has a darker view of this regard of God. He sees it as resulting in man's being burdened, being 'eyed' (7:18) and assaulted, used as a target for archery practice (7:20). This is a satanically inspired parody of Psalm 8. What Job says is in fact a description of the Satan and not of God. Satan is the one who has set his mind on Job (see 1:8; 2:3).

Job therefore talks to God about 'leaving' (7:19) but he does not mean that he is going to depart from God. Rather he wants God to leave him — that is, not to keep looking at him and treating him as if he were some massive threat to himself. Little did Job know that he had been (and was) presenting a massive threat to Satan, whereas God was preserving him with a view to blessing him and communicating a blessing to others through him.

'Does God pervert justice?'
(Job 8:1-22)

In considering this speech of Bildad it is important to keep in mind all that has gone before, and particularly the exchange that has taken place between Eliphaz and Job. It is also worth noting that Bildad does not have as much to say as Eliphaz, whereas Job has more to say in reply to him than he had to Eliphaz. What Bildad says to Job can be considered in terms of censure and counsel. He takes Job to task for what he has said and points out the way forward for him.

'Does God pervert justice?' (8:1-7)

8:2-3
How long will you say these things,
    and the words of your mouth be a great wind?
Does God pervert justice?
    Or does the Almighty pervert the right?

Bildad opens without any of the courteousness of Eliphaz. With the words **'How long ...?'** (8:2), he expresses not only impatience, but also indignation at what Job has just said by way of reply to Eliphaz. Job had described the way that his anguished words had been treated as if they were **'wind'** (see 6:26). Now Bildad says that that is exactly what they are! (8:2).

But he does not take issue with Job merely because of the vehemence with which the latter has spoken. Perceiving that Job's remarks have questioned the justice of God's dealings, he censures Job on that account. Indeed, all that he has to say is by way of an assertion of the equity of God, as seen in an exposition of his ways.

The foundation of his remarks is that God never 'perverts justice', which means that God's practice always conforms to his character, the highest standard of all. Bildad asserts this by means of a rhetorical question with a negative cast (8:3) to which, of course, there can be no contrary reply. The answer must be: 'Never!' In doing this Bildad is not just being rhetorical but polemical. He is launching a further broadside at Job, one which is all the more pointed because **'justice'** is something that has not figured prominently in Job's previous thinking. Instead, Job has been wondering what has happened to God's goodness and wisdom because of the losses and sufferings he is enduring whereas, from now on, he has to engage with the reality of God's justice as well. This is more formidable opposition, and such heightening is so typical of Satan. Job is now faced with a choice between his own sense of being just and God's (seeming) injustice towards him. So who is right, and who is wrong?

8:4-6
If your children have sinned against him,
    he has delivered them into the hand of their transgression.
If you will seek God
    and plead with the Almighty for mercy,
if you are pure and upright,
    surely then he will rouse himself for you
    and restore your rightful habitation...

To demonstrate that God is always just, Bildad uses a conditional argument, expressed by the words **'if ... then'**, in verses 4-7. But there is nothing theoretical about it because he relates it first to Job's children (8:4) and then to Job himself (8:5-7). He could not be more personal.

First, he is not expressing uncertainty when he refers to the sins of Job's children because he immediately refers to their deaths. In his world, where inflexible justice always rules, sudden death proves serious sin. Such a comment would have brought to the surface Job's fears about his children (see 1:5) and opened up the wound of Job's bereavement once more (see 1:20). Bildad is not just being insensitive. He is being downright brutal. What is more, he is inferring that Job's prayers for his children were unavailing and that for him to go on serving a God who neither answers prayer nor regards sacrifice is fruitless. The hands may be those of Bildad, but the voice is the voice of Satan. Fraud and force are his stock in trade.

But how does this 'if ... then' argument relate to Job himself? His children are now beyond the reach of his prayers, Bildad suggests, but Job yet has time to seek God. What is more, if he does so, he will be wonderfully restored, but that is dependent on Job's acknowledging that what was true of his children is also in measure true of him. He must seek God's favour and mercy, rather than complain that God is not seeking him (see 7:21). Bildad declares that because God is just he will undoubtedly restore Job if, but only if, Job returns to him. But has Job departed from God? Has he told God so to his face?

'Enquire of ... the fathers' (8:8-22)

8:8,10
For enquire, please, of bygone ages,
and consider what the fathers have searched out...
Will they not teach you and tell you
and utter words out of their understanding?

Eliphaz had invoked the authority of a supernatural revelation for his advice but Bildad refers to venerable tradition for support for what he says. Although he uses the third person in doing so (8:8-10) and in the process acknowledges his own relative youth, he not only argues that antiquity should be listened to, but claims that he is conveying its message.

8:13,20
Such are the paths of all who forget God;
the hope of the godless shall perish...
Behold, God will not reject a blameless man,
nor take the hand of evildoers...

What he then says (8:11-22) is an outworking of his basic principle of divine equity that is all-encompassing. He refers to those who depart from God (8:13) and those who serve him truly (8:20-22), and he shows how both will be dealt with justly.

He identifies those who **'forget God'** as being **'godless'** — that is, profane. They deliberately put God out of their mind and their **'paths'**, and cherish hopes that are insubstantial.[6] They are described by two metaphors drawn from nature. The first is the papyrus plant which, though it stands tall, dries up suddenly when it is deprived of water (8:11-12) and the second is the **'spider's web'** which collapses when any weight is placed upon it (8:14-15). That 'frailty' seems at first sight to be out of keeping with what follows in verses 16-19, where there is a picture

of productivity even in rocky soil that is in contrast to
the reed and the web, and there is even hope for
future growth for such a plant if it were to be uprooted. This is hardly consistent with the sudden and
final devastation threatened against the wicked.

The question that has to be faced is: 'Do verses
16-19 refer to "the wicked" or "the righteous"?' In my
view the double use of the word **'behold'** in verses 19
and 20 is important. It points up a contrast —
between the wicked in verses 16-19 and the righteous in verses 20-22.

In verses 16-18 we have the same picture as in the
previous verses, of growth leading to collapse —
whether papyrus plant, spider's web or a lush plant
among the stones. Verse 19 highlights a **'joy'**
(growth) that is short-lived, but also points to the fact
that such a process will be repeated. Others will rise
up in the place vacated. The verse expresses both
sarcasm and sadness. Reading these verses in this
way means that it is the godless who are being described by Bildad in this section beginning at verse
11. What is more, it means that it is Job that he has
in view as he speaks.

But by way of conclusion, he affirms that God
knows the difference between the righteous and the
godless and, being just, he will neither reject the one
nor receive the other (8:20-22). He can therefore hold
out to Job the sure and certain hope of a joyful and
victorious future — but only if Job ceases to be
unjust, 'if' he will admit sin (which must be the case
because he is suffering) and ask God for mercy. This
of course resembles the offer of recovery made by
Eliphaz which he based on the fact that Job was
being chastened for sin. But for Job to implore for
mercy means denying his integrity, which would
prove Satan's lie and disprove God's estimate of him
— and that he will not do.

'How can a man be right before God?' (9:1 – 10:22)

In addition to replying to Bildad (and his friends) Job addresses God. As in the case of his earlier speech, there is some uncertainty as to where the transition is best placed. There is a second-person singular verb in 9:28 that refers to God, but there are third-person singular verbs prior to that verse which also refer to him. Job is therefore talking to the Friends about God before he actually addresses him. Bearing this in mind, we shall adopt the ESV division of the text.

'I know that it is so: but how can a man be in the right before God?' (9:1-24)

9:2-3
Truly I know that it is so:
　　But how can a man be in the right before God?
If one wished to contend with him,
　　one could not answer him once in a thousand times.

It is impossible to determine whether or not Job is being sarcastic when he says, **'Truly I know that it is so.'** All we have are his words, and not his tone of voice.[7] However, we shall take him as doing no more than expressing agreement with Bildad here because, initially, his objection is lodged against Bildad's exposition of God's justice in relation to him, and not against the principle itself. Indeed, Job expresses wonderment at God's greatness in much the same words as Eliphaz had used (9:10; cf. 5:9). We need not therefore set Job and his friends at odds with regard to every statement made.

However, the point that Job wants to make is expressed in his next words: **'But how can a man be in the right before God?'** Job believes in God's justice, but points out that his present suffering condition is not covered by Bildad's explanation of it. Realizing that Bildad has been thinking about him in his afflicted state, Job asks how a righteous man *who is afflicted* may gain vindication from God. That is a matter that neither Bildad nor Eliphaz has addressed because there is no place in their world view for a good man suffering who has not sinned. All they think of is a good man suffering because he has sinned.[8] They therefore have only one way back to fellowship with God to offer Job, and that is the way of a penitent.

Being convinced that he has not lived a secretly profane life, Job wants to establish his righteousness before God. He therefore wants to enter a court of law, and not a confessional. **'Contend'** in verse 3 is a legal term. But here he encounters his great difficulty, because it is God that he wants to interrogate. How can that be done at all, let alone successfully? He expands on this in the verses that follow and in so doing he comes close to denying the principle of God's justice as well as its operation.

Job believes he has a case, but will he be given a hearing? He knows that he cannot prevail in a lawsuit with God because even if there were to be a hearing, God could either refuse to answer, or he would not be able to answer God. God is **'wise ... and mighty in strength'**, far too skilful and powerful for a human being to gain the upper hand over him. Even so, Job has no other recourse than to contemplate the unattainable because he desires to find God again.

But it is not only Bildad (and Eliphaz) who can talk about God's greatness. Job can do so as well (9:5-10). Here he describes God's great works of creation and providence. Earth and skies, sea and stars are all at his behest and command. But he not only directs their movements with regularity; at times he also disrupts them in his anger — yet still retains control. His ways are unfathomable and innumerable.

Job is certain that it is such a God that has stalked him and savaged him (9:11). God is invisible and invincible, and in comparison with him even the fearsome personifications of evil in Canaanite mythology like Rahab (see 26:12) and Leviathan (see 3:8; 41:1-34) are powerless. Devastated by his anger, Job is helpless. Who can overcome God and stop him doing what he wants to do? Who can arraign him and call him to account for what he has done? Job wants to present his case to God, but he knows that he will be dumbstruck when he appears before him (9:14) and that he will only be able to plead for mercy. But he will not do that prematurely. He believes that he is in the right (9:15) and wants God to entertain his case (9:16). But in his darkened state of mind he cannot believe that God would do that, even if he were to grant Job a hearing.

9:15
Though I am in the right, I cannot answer him;
    I must appeal for mercy to my accuser.

9:20-21
Though I am in the right, my own mouth would condemn me;
    though I am blameless, he would prove me perverse.
I am blameless; I regard not myself;
    I loathe my life.

Job's world that had God at both its centre and circumference (see the opening chapter) has totally changed, except for one thing — something that is so vital for him that he refers to it several times. Twice he says, **'Though I am in the right'** (9:15,20) and three times, **'I am blameless'** (9:20,21,22). This is his fixed point — his spiritual integrity. It is what the Friends (and the Satan, but not God) are attacking, and it is what Job is defending and wanting to have vindicated by God. In verse 19 Job combines imagery from a wrestling bout with the legal process that he desires (see chapters 38 – 40).

This fivefold assertion amounts to a resounding plea of 'Not guilty' in defiance of the fact that he is so obviously suffering and his friends' argument that he is doing so under the hand of God. But, refusing to acknowledge guilt and being refused a hearing by God, what alternative does he have left? It is to renounce himself and to denounce God. That is what he does — both. He hates himself (9:21) and wishes himself dead. He has done that before, and at length, in chapter 3. He now does it again. And what does he say about God? Does he curse God and wish him dead too? No! He does not. He 'merely' says that God is not just!

9:22,24
It is all one; therefore I say,
    He destroys both the blameless and the wicked...
The earth is given into the hand of the wicked;
    he covers the faces of its judges —
    if it is not he, who then is it?

In verse 22, Job says, **'It is all one'**, and goes on to explain what he means by saying that God makes no difference between **'the blameless and the wicked'**. He is here refuting Bildad's simplistic and universal dictum. But he goes beyond that and says that God is heartless, for he mocks when the blameless are ground down by the wicked. In this downward spiral of thought, he even appears to say that God has 'given' the (whole?) earth to the wicked to rule over! He is so convinced by the force of his own logic that he says with a rhetorical flourish (or is it a moment of speaking more wisely than he knew?), **'If it is not he, who then is it?'** He still attributes everything to God and does not know that there is someone else involved.

So it seems to Job that God has no moral discrimination, and he says so! This serious distortion of the character of God, and not only of his ways, is something for which he will later be called to account (see 32:2). In maintaining his own integrity he has denied the integrity of God.

'There is no arbiter between us…' (9:25-35)

9:32-33
For he is not a man, as I am, that I might answer him,
    that we should come to trial together.
There is no arbiter between us,
    who might lay his hand on us both.

This part of Job's reply contains both lament and determination. He senses that his life is fleeting. He compares it to a swift runner, a papyrus boat and a swooping eagle (9:25-26). In addition, his spirit is failing. He cannot put on a forced smile and pretend that all is well (9:27). His incessant suffering is a harbinger of condemnation to him. Why then should he **'labour'** — that is, soldier on? (9:28-29). He knows he cannot win an argument because God is wiser than he is; he cannot win a fight because God is stronger (9:19); he cannot dictate because God is sovereign, and now he says that he cannot cleanse himself because God will reject him. What is more, the difference between him and God is so great that there is no one who can intervene and bring them both together. So what can he do? He is in a paralysis of hopelessness. He asks God to **'take his rod away'** and to become less terrifying, so that Job might not be afraid in speaking to him (9:34-35). He appeals to God to become more human, as it were, making it possible for Job to conduct his own defence, secure his vindication before God and bring about their reconciliation. (This is an anticipation of 16:19; 19:25; 33:6 and of the close of the book.)

'Remember that you have made me like clay ... granted me life and steadfast love' (10:1-22)

10:2-3
I will say to God, Do not condemn me;
    let me know why you contend against me.
Does it seem good to you to oppress,
    to despise the work of your hands
    and favour the designs of the wicked?

10:9,12
Remember that you have made me like clay;
    and will you return me to the dust?...
You have granted me life and steadfast love,
    and your care has preserved my spirit.

As Job proceeds to give vent to his anguish and the reasons for it, the chapter division can be overlooked at this point. He pours out his grief without waiting for his request even to be entertained. At the root of his bitterness is the inconsistency between the God he had previously known and the phantom deity that has now been created in his own mind. He wants to acquaint God with this conundrum and to get an explanation for it. He therefore voices the kind of questions that he would put to God if he were to have the opportunity of a day in court.

He asks why God has issued a writ against him and left the charge sheet blank (10:2). This seems so astounding to him in the light of God's being a beneficent Creator and bountiful provider, and not only on the basis of his knowledge and experience of due legal process. He therefore reasons with God in those terms.

God's silence seems to Job to be in contradiction of the fact that God is good. **'Does it seem good to you?'** harks back to Genesis 1 and 2, where God pronounced everything that he had made to be 'good'. In Job's mind, benevolence and malevolence cannot harmonize. What is more, God elevates, and does not **'oppress'** like wicked men do. He is good and he gives. In addition, he made man with the capacity of sensation, but his dealings with Job seem to depict him as being destitute of anything akin to those susceptibilities. The comparison in verses 4 and 5 serves to point up the fact that God does not need to hurry about his business because he does not have very long to complete it. Man does have to, and that is why mistakes are made in human courts. But God does not! He is eternal. And now such a God is destroying the good work on which he bestowed so much labour and such love! Job cannot believe that this is possible! He knows that it cannot be because he has been the object and manifestation of God's glory — a marvellous affirmation of intelligent and indomitable faith.

But this confidence rapidly subsides, and in verses 14-17 Job speaks in a very different way. He reverts to his previously expressed view that it is of no moment to God whether he is in the right or not. God will treat him as if he were guilty. Such a fluctuation is not difficult to understand, given his condition and all its fresh pangs of torment (10:17).

10:20-21
Are not my days few?
  Then cease, and leave me alone, that I may find a little
      cheer
before I go — and I shall not return —
  to the land of darkness and deep shadow.

The close of this chapter in verses 18-22 is an echo of
Job's lament in chapter 3. In view of his sufferings,
he wishes that he had not been given one day of
conscious existence and that no one had ever seen
him. But, as he has only a few days remaining, he
now wants the little comfort of being left alone before
he goes to the grave. Nevertheless the parting of the
ways between him and God that he once more envisages is to be brought about by God's leaving him,
and not by his leaving God.

    Job is crushed by what he now knows of God and
yet he is talking to God. In maintaining his spiritual
integrity (see 1:1), Job is not making his little self the
centre of the world, but is trying to locate himself in
God's big world — a world that has become 'bigger'
than he had previously thought. Even so, he will
neither give up on all that he had previously been,
nor on what God has previously been to him.

'Less than you deserve!'
(Job 11:1-20)

The first round of speeches comes to an end with this address of Zophar and Job's reply. It is worth observing at the outset that Zophar has about as much to say as had each of his friends, but that Job has considerably more to say by way of reply to him than he had to either of them. By means of this growing disproportion, the author hints that Job was no more overcome by his adversaries than he was by his adversities and that already he was beginning to gain the ascendancy in the debate with them (and with Satan).

Zophar uses the same stick-and-carrot approach to Job as Bildad, but he does so with greater intensity. He beats Job mercilessly (11:1-12) and then dangles before him, in the most attractive terms, the promise of God's restoring mercy and power (11:13-20).

'God exacts less than your guilt deserves' (11:1-12)

11:4-6
For you say, 'My doctrine is pure,
    and I am clean in God's eyes.'
But oh, that God would speak
    and open his lips to you,
and that he would tell you the secrets of wisdom!
    For he is manifold in understanding.
Know then that God exacts of you less than your guilt
        deserves.

Zophar is convinced that Job is condemning himself
out of his own mouth. To be **'full of talk'** (11:2) and
scoffing was the mark of the fool (see Prov. 29:20). It
was therefore only right that Job should be told this
— and told so plainly! (11:3). But Zophar is not just
blunt. He is savage and also unfair. He has not
listened carefully to what Job has said because he
charges Job with claiming that his **'doctrine is pure'**
and that he is **'clean in God's eyes'** (11:4). Two
different adjectives are used here and both mean
'pure'. When he speaks about **'doctrine'**, what Zophar has in mind is what Job has been saying over
against the teaching of the wise, as presented by
Bildad (see 8:8). But all that Job has claimed in this
regard is that what Eliphaz and Bildad have said has
not dealt with his precise circumstances (see 6:2).
Secondly, and with reference to himself, the claim
that Job has made before God is not that he is
sinless, but that he is 'blameless' (see 9:20-21). He
denies that he has in any way merited the afflictions
that have come upon him.

It will be remembered that Eliphaz had appealed
to a revelation and Bildad had invoked tradition as
sources of, and supports for, their teaching (see
4:12-21; 8:8-10). Job, however, had set aside both as
inadequate to his case and had appealed directly to
God. Zophar has heard all this and so he resolves
that if Job has appealed to God, to God he shall go,
and Zophar will, as it were, take him there! On the
one hand he declares that God has infinite knowledge and understanding, and on the other that he
knows what God would say to Job if he were to
address him! (On the face of it this is at least as
impertinent as Job's alleged claim to 'purity'.)

Zophar is certain that God is not only punishing
Job, but that he is doing so less than Job truly deserves (11:6). He declares that God is overlooking part
of Job's enormous sin. It is indeed surprising that he

is able to quantify Job's (alleged) guilt in relation to God's just punishment and yet he does not measure his own 'knowledge' over against God's greater understanding! Job is facing more than human opposition here. The 'father of lies' is perpetrating a wicked distortion of the truth.

11:7-9

Can you find out the deep things of God?
  Can you find out the limit of the Almighty?
It is higher than heaven — what can you do?
  Deeper than Sheol — what can you know?
Its measure is longer than the earth
  and broader than the sea.

Zophar declares that God's wisdom exceeds anything that Job can imagine or discover. God knows what is above, what is beneath and what is all around. Zophar refers to 'the heights of heaven' (11:8, literal translation) in order to exceed the level to which human knowledge can reach. Similarly, he refers to Sheol, the realm of the dead that the living cannot plumb, and to the extent of the earth and sea, which is beyond measurement. Zophar is seeking to encompass all created reality. While **'higher'**, **'deeper'** and **'broader'** are terms that exceed the dimensions of lesser things, they have their limits because God is beyond them all; he is infinite (11:7). Is this terminology perhaps echoed by Paul in Ephesians 3:18?

Therefore, when God issues a writ and summons someone into court (11:10), it is on the basis of his perfect knowledge. This is what he has done with Job, who is **'worthless'**. Job has demanded that God explain both himself and his actions (see 9:12). Zophar says that God always has good moral reasons for what he does (11:11). He knows more than Job can ever know and, more to the point, he knows Job better than he knows himself — indeed, better than

Job will ever know himself, because he is as un-
teachable as the colt of a wild donkey (11:12). Bildad
had only broached with Job his need for wisdom (see
8:8), whereas Zophar declares him to be invincibly
ignorant — and arrogant to boot. Job has nothing to
complain about; he deserves all he has got; in fact he
is being treated leniently.

'If ... then ... and' (11:13-21)

11:14-16,19
If iniquity is in your hand, put it far away,
   and let not injustice dwell in your tents.
Surely then you will lift up your face without blemish;
   you will be secure and will not fear...
You will lie down, and none will make you afraid;
   many will court your favour.

Having adopted such a perspective about Job, the
wonderful promises Zophar makes in this section
might seem hollow or insincere. But that is not the
case. Zophar is urging Job to see sense and turn to
God. These promises are not empty in themselves —
although they amount to a temptation for Job (as we
shall see later).[9] A call to repentance and a promise of
blessing are the stock in trade not only of the Friends
(see what Eliphaz has said in 5:17-26 and Bildad in
8:21-22), but also of the Old Testament prophets, for
example in Isaiah 1:16-20. But they spoke like this
because there was sin to be repented of and divine
judgement to be averted, and that is not so in Job's
case. For Zophar to speak in this way is therefore a
misuse of truth and it is also an indication of the
activity of Satan.

The promises that Zophar holds out are all echoes
of Job's past, as well as a portent of the future. He
speaks of a 'tent' at peace, a **'face without blemish'**

and a mind and heart without **'fear'** (11:14,15); misery will be a thing of the past (11:16), light and peace will abound, and usefulness to others will return (11:17-19). This is an anticipation of the Epilogue because safety, comfort and prosperity did return for Job. But when, and why? Was it after Job humbled himself? Yes, but not for the reason that Zophar and his friends have been urging upon him. Ironically, but righteously, it is after they have (at Jehovah's direction) asked Job to pray for them — and while he was still in his afflicted state, out-wardly. Job thus prays for his foes, but not for him-self, and God, the LORD, hears and answers. The sincerity of godliness is displayed and rewarded.

But Zophar concludes as he began, with a solemn prediction of what awaits the wicked. Job is therefore left with one route of hope. He must set himself to seek God and put away his iniquity and injustice. But this is a snare, because if Job does this in order to recover his prosperity, he demonstrates insincer-ity; if he refuses to do so, he demonstrates his per-versity. Integrity is forfeited either way, and if it is, then Satan wins.

'I am a laughing stock'
(Job 12:1 – 13:28)

The considerable length of Job's reply to Zophar has
already been noted and commented on. We shall
therefore divide it into two parts. Leaving chapter 14
for treatment on its own because of the importance of
its theme, I will focus our attention here on the first
section of the speech.

Just as in his earlier responses, Job moves in this
speech from addressing the Friends to talking to
God, but at what point he does so is difficult to
determine. Obviously he has God in view in 13:20,
but there are signs in several of the immediately
preceding verses that he is speaking in the hearing of
his Friends rather than addressing them directly.
Taking note of this, I will divide my comments after
13:17 because the **'you'** in that verse is in the plural.
It clearly refers to the Friends.

'I am a laughing stock to my friends' (12:1-6)

12:4
I am a laughing stock to my friends;
    I, who called to God and he answered me,
    a just and blameless man, am a laughing stock.

Job addresses all the Friends as he begins his speech
(12:2-6) and then he singles out Zophar (verses 7,8
have a singular pronoun). Stung no doubt by being

called a donkey, he sarcastically refers to his friends as **'the people'**, those with whom wisdom begins and ends (12:2). Vigorously defending himself, he asserts that he is not without **'understanding'**, as Zophar had said (see 11:12), and claims that what the Friends presented is no more than common knowledge (12:3). His quarrel with them, therefore, is not about God's power (about which Eliphaz had spoken, see 5:8-9), nor about his justice (which was Bildad's theme, see 8:3); nor was it about his wisdom (which Zophar trumpeted, see 11:6). His argument with them is that they had used these truths to 'frame him'. They had turned all these divine attributes into accusations and had just not dealt with *the facts* of his case.

He therefore proceeds to set out those facts before them as plainly as he can. In order to do this, he uses the term **'laughing stock'** twice. First he connects it with his friends, and also by implication with God (12:4), implying that neither they nor God should have treated him so. Human friendship should have prevented their mocking him; divine friendship should have prevented God from attacking him. But the one who **'called to God'** and was **'answered'** by him, the **'just and blameless man'** (see 1:1), is *now* held up to open ridicule and disgrace. 'Explain that!' he says to them in effect. He then proceeds to further his challenge in two ways — and in both he is speaking more wisely than he knew.

First, he says that for someone who is at ease to treat a sufferer contemptuously is to increase the latter's anguish greatly. To add scorn to pain makes that pain so much harder to bear (12:5). That was something Job never did — not even to someone who was his enemy (see 31:29). It is therefore not how friends should behave — but it is something that is Satan's stock in trade. It is he who 'kicks a person when he is down'.

Secondly, Job refers to the fact that ungodly,[10] marauding bands often live securely themselves (12:6), and that is something that the Friends seem not to have observed, or reflected on, in connection with their representation of God to Job. Indeed, Job himself has not yet realized the full significance of this fact and its potential as a rebuttal of the thesis of his Friends (the distortion of Satan), but he will do so later (see chapter 21).

'Ask the beasts, and they will teach you' (12:7-12)

12:7,9-10
But ask the beasts, and they will teach you;
    the birds of the heavens, and they will tell you...
Who among all these does not know
    that the hand of the LORD has done this?
In his hand is the life of every living thing
    and the breath of all mankind.

Job continues in a sarcastic vein. He has already charged the Friends with dressing up common knowledge as if it were the preserve of only a few. Here he says four times that the animals **'teach'** such truth (12:7-8). Climactically (and rhetorically) he says that all the creatures know that the hand of Jehovah has made them! (Cf. Gen. 1; Rom. 1:20).

God's wisdom and power are therefore known by all that he has made, and not only by the pompous Zophar. Job majors on these themes because Zophar had spoken about them (see 11:7-12). This sub-section is therefore not just a discussion of a truth in the form of a hymn of praise; it is a continuation of the debate. By what he says Job is showing God to be his friend, whereas Zophar has been making God out to be Job's foe!

In a way that is typical of wisdom, Job uses an analogy to present the point that he is driving at. Observing that an ear and a tongue are given to a human being for the purpose of evaluating words and foods, he deduces that corresponding critical faculties are also provided (by God) so that what passes for wisdom may be evaluated by others (12:11). The wisdom of the aged is therefore not to be regarded as the last word (nor of course is it to be sniffed at). What Job has been, and is still, doing in replying to his Friends is reflecting on what they have said to him, agreeing with the accuracy of their general principles, but challenging the correctness of the interpretation that they based upon them in relation to his case. He is therefore exalting 'the right of private judgement' over against community consensus as represented by the Friends and the view of the aged (see 13:1-4).

Treading such a path can, of course, be hazardous but when an individual evaluates his circumstances in the light of what God has revealed about himself the danger is greatly reduced. That is what Job is doing by way of these magnificent statements about God's power and wisdom. He is not making himself the centre of God's world, but just trying to find a corner for himself in a world that has become bigger and more mysterious as a result of the tragedy that has befallen him. In doing so he points out that such a world is also larger than the platitudes which the Friends are uttering! Job is a believing pioneer.

His opening statements about God's wisdom are built around the question, **'Who ... does not know?'** (12:9), and this supports Job's allegation that his friends are not the pundits they think they are. Zophar's remarks had tended in the direction of God's being inaccessible, but here Job asserts that God has not entirely concealed himself; he has shown his hand in what he has done. There are

many echoes of Genesis 1 here. The animal world
and the human world — birds, beasts, reptiles and
humans — all come from God. Their lives (literally,
their breath) are upheld by him and their habitats
are determined by him (12:7-10). **'Life'** is therefore
common to all, but only human beings possess
'spirit'. So Zophar's claim that God knows wicked
men (see 11:11) is a commonplace, rather than a
wonderful discovery! To this Job adds a sarcastic
comment about the Friends' belief that those who
have lived longest must know the most (12:12).

'With him are wisdom and might' (12:13-25)

12:13-16 (NASB)
With him are wisdom and might;
   To him belong counsel and understanding.
Behold, he tears down, and it cannot be rebuilt;
   He imprisons a man and there can be no release.
Behold, he restrains the waters, and they dry up;
   And he sends them out, and they inundate the earth.
With him are strength and sound wisdom,
   The misled and the misleader belong to him.

Although there is no word in the Hebrew text of these
verses that corresponds to 'God', the use of the terms
'wisdom and might' and **'counsel and understanding'** (12:13,16) and the activities described in this
passage are hardly applicable to anyone else. This
section therefore stands in contrast to the sarcastic
comment about the aged (12:12) and also to the
Friends, who are regurgitating their teaching. This
section is more than a positive statement; it has a
polemical edge — throughout.

   The main focus of Job's remarks is on what God
does in his wisdom and power. Twice the word **'Behold'** occurs in order to underline the stupendous

features of the divine sovereignty (12:14,15). Job describes the manifold nature of God's activity with regard to nature and mankind. God is regarded as the source of everything, and nothing can be conceived of that either lies beyond the scope of his reign, or that can effectively resist its exercise. Three things should be noted about this description.

First, Job majors on *the human realm*. In what he says he only makes one statement about natural things (12:15; verse 22 is a metaphor). The remainder concentrates on the world of human affairs, whether religious or political, judges or priests.

Secondly, this is a declaration of *God's power* rather than his wisdom. Job is asserting that power is what is uppermost in God's activity. None can rebuild what he pulls down, or open what he closes (12:14). Job here picks up what Zophar had said (see 11:10). He agrees with it as a fact, but not with the explanation Zophar had given of it. Zophar had declared how God arrests offenders and imprisons them, believing this to be what has happened to Job. By a strange irony that is also exactly what Job believes has happened to him — but not for the reason that Zophar had advanced, which was that God always acts on the basis of human morality, or its opposite in the case of Job. Job therefore rejects Zophar's explanation as being too simplistic by far.

Thirdly, Job's chosen examples are full of *the imagery of loss and reversal*. Those that are wise, mighty, noble or strong are all deprived of what makes them great. (Did Paul have this in mind when he wrote 1 Corinthians 1:18-25?) This depiction matches Job's experience of course, but he is not just looking at the world through the window of his own affliction; he wants the Friends to focus their attention on the bigger picture too.

By implication, Job is refuting Zophar's thesis that adversity always points to iniquity and he is seeking to confront the Friends with the mystery of God's administration. While he is right in this, there is also something that he needs to learn about God's power, namely that it is also exercised with his goodness, and thus for a beneficent purpose. Elihu will teach him that.

But Job has been seized and bound and is being denied due process of law. So he sees a world in which the wise and the strong, the deceiver and the deceived, the ruler and the ruled are all vulnerable to an intervention of God. Counsellors, priests and princes are exhibited to derision and contempt (12:17,19,21). Nations rise and fall (12:23). It is a world in which things are often turned upside down and inside out — and by God, seemingly without any human agency. He is the one who does all these things, and he cannot be resisted.

'I would speak to the Almighty. Oh that you would keep silent!' (13:1-17)

13:3,5
But I would speak to the Almighty,
    and I desire to argue my case with God...
Oh that you would keep silent,
    and it would be your wisdom!

Job here gives notice to the Friends that he would rather talk to a God who does not answer than listen to what they have to say. In taking this attitude he is unknowingly turning from Satan's masquerade to Jehovah's mysteriousness — and triumphing once again. But it hardly seems like a triumph to him.

He begins by rejecting the Friends' thesis (13:1-12) which he describes as whitewash and ashes (13:4,12). This is something that he has consistently done, but here he does it for another reason, one that is exceedingly bold. He accuses them of trying to defend God, of standing up for his honour — but doing so with lies. He even goes further and warns them that God would not take kindly to being defended with untruth! (Cf. 42:7). They are seeking to exonerate God, but their defence is flawed, and because God is just he will not tolerate misrepresentation.

13:15-16
Though he slay me, I will hope in him;
    yet I will argue my ways to his face.
This will be my salvation,
    that the godless shall not come before him.

Commanding them to be silent, he turns to argue with God, risking all (13:13). There is a long-standing manuscript variation in verse 15 which would change the sense from **'I will hope in him'** (ESV) to 'I will not hope' — that is, 'I have no hope'. While it may seem as if that reading is not as good, it does highlight how remarkable it is that Job is determined to defend his ways **'to [God's] face'** and not just **'before him'**. This combination of an expected death at God's hands with a determination to conduct his own defence before God's very eyes, in the hope of salvation, is most remarkable. It is a *tour de force* of faith — in the dark. It is not blind self-confidence, however. It rests on the fact that, however unjustly God may be treating him, in the last analysis God will be just and will not accept the godless (13:16) — and, whatever others may think, Job knows that he is not among them.

'Call, and I will answer' (13:18-28)

13:20-22
Only grant me two things,
    then I will not hide myself from your face:

withdraw your hand far from me,
   and let not dread of you terrify me.
Then call, and I will answer;
   or let me speak, and you reply to me.

He therefore professes himself ready and willing, not
only to risk all in an approach to God (13:13-14), but
also to rest his case and die (13:19) if God were to
take it up. But this is something that is easier said
than done, because while he has breath he cannot
but appeal to God (13:20-28). So he tries to make a
bargain with God. If God were to lessen the terrors
that surround him and inform him of his sins, then
Job would not hide from God (as Adam did in the
garden?), but he would turn up for the hearing. But
why, oh why, does the Almighty (13:3) punish him for
the sins of so long ago (his youth), hide from him,
treat him as an enemy and confine him?
(13:24,26,27). He is just a moth-eaten garment, a
frail, decaying leaf (13:28).
   We know the answer to these questions. Job did
not!

'If a man dies, shall he live again?' (Job 14:1-22)

The theme of this chapter is very obviously that of life and death. Job and his friends have reflected on this already from their differing vantage points. But here a new perspective is opened up. Job explores the possibility of life after death. That is something surprising.

Of course, Job's statements in this chapter are a continuation of his reply to Zophar (and his colleagues), but they are directed more to God than to them. Although no word for 'God' is used in this chapter, he questions God (14:3), issues commands to him (14:6) and also communes with him meditatively (14:7-15, especially verse 13). Job is therefore talking to God, the God he once knew, but he is doing so in the hearing of his friends.

Life and death are the themes of this chapter — as Job saw them at the time. He will have more to say on this matter later. Here he first describes the character of life before death (14:1-6). He then wonders about the possibility of a life after death (14:7-17) before describing death as bringing life to an end.

Life before death (14:1-6)

14:1
Man who is born of a woman
   is few of days and full of trouble.

Job here meditates on the fact of human frailty and mortality in relation to God's transcendence and inscrutability. The last verse of the previous chapter fits in with this emphasis because it speaks generally of the fact of human corruptibility. It has no specified subject, merely the third-person singular pronoun.

The word **'man'** is used in several places in this chapter. It represents four different Hebrew words. The common word for a 'male person' appears in verse 12. In verses 10 and 14 we have a term which describes man in his greatness. By contrast we have man in his frailty described in verse 19. The dominant term, however, is the one with which the chapter opens, the word *'adham'*. This refers both to the first male and to the whole human race, to mankind. The fact of divine creation is therefore in the background. But so is the fact of sin, as is indicated by the expression **'born of a woman'** and the description of the brevity and difficulty of life (see Gen. 3:16-19).

14:4
Who can bring a clean thing out of an unclean?
    There is not one.

Given this setting, it is not at all surprising that Job connects impurity with infirmity (14:4). Several have thought it so, but in my view this is the result of a failure to take seriously the teaching of Genesis 3 and the fact of original sin that is mysteriously connected with it.[11] Job seems to have no problem with such a connection, and neither does Eliphaz (see 15:14). Job's rhetorical question is therefore calculated to deny the possibility that anyone who is unclean (and that means everyone) can make himself clean (see Jer. 13:23). In Job's mouth this is an attempt at self-defence, meaning that he cannot be held responsible for not being able to cleanse himself. It is not a denial that God could do such a thing.

For Job, to be frail and prone to trouble is part of what it means for someone to be human and sinful. Life is full of trouble, as is shown by the fact that flowers that bloom soon wither and shadows vanish (14:2). As man's (i.e. Job's) life is so brief, why is God so intent on judging him? (14:3). Why does God keep looking at him, instead of **'[looking] away from him'**? (14:6). The duration of his life is not only short but also fixed. Its days and months are numbered (14:5). There is a possible allusion here to the fact recorded in Genesis 6:3, to the abbreviating of man's life in comparison with the era before the Flood.[12] But as man's life is frail and brief, why can Job not be allowed the little relief that every hired hand is given by his master? Why does he have to bear the divine stare and not only the divine stroke — and both uninterruptedly? Life before death is *nothing but* great trouble.

Life after death? (14:7-17)

14:7
For there is hope for a tree,
   if it be cut down, that it will sprout again,
   and that its shoots will not cease.

14:14-15
If a man dies, shall he live again?
   All the days of my service I would wait,
   till my renewal should come.
You would call, and I would answer you;
   you would long for the work of your hands.

Job has likened his life to the existence of a flower and the duration of a shadow (14:2). The first of these is less than what it means to be human; the other has no existence at all. Perhaps shocked by a realization of how superficial such a comparison was, he now reflects on the great difference between a man (himself) and a tree — but after both have died.

The thought in this section is based on the vast difference between plant life and human life. It is all of a piece with the record in Genesis 1. Man, in this case Job, is **'the work of [God's] hands'** in such a unique way that fellowship is possible between him and God (14:15; cf. 10:8-12). That is not true of any other created thing, even if it has life.

Reflecting on what happens to a tree, Job realizes that it may revive and grow after it has been cut down. Retaining some vitality, its stump may sprout again, even after an interval has passed. If only it may scent water, it will produce shoots and flourish again. A new tree can take its place. It has a form of life that is self-propagating (see Gen. 1:11-13).

So, why should something like that not happen to man, whom God made *for himself*? That is the question that Job begins to explore: **'If a man** [that is a mighty man, even a warrior] **dies, shall he live again?'** It seems that he lies down and never gets up and is gone — and to where? His breath is extinguished like water which evaporates from a lake or a river. Unlike the tree, there is no return to life for him (14:12).

It is this discrepancy between a tree and a man that propels Job from speculation to supplication as he contemplates Sheol[13] (see 7:9-10). Sheol, the abode of all the dead, is inevitable, but is it interminable? Might there not be an interval there too, after the pattern of the tree stump, which seemed to be lifeless, sprouting again? Might not a God who created and animated reanimate?

What if God were to hide Job from his own anger during the time when it was being vented, and then, when it was past, remember him so as to renew their previous relationship? Might it not be the case that the God who had given him a human frame (see 10:10-11) would give him then a 'change' or a **'renewal'**? (14:14). That word is used of a change of clothing, or release from military service. All God would need to do would be to say the word to **'call'** (14:15) — that is, to speak as he did at the dawn of time. Such a mighty word (and not any inherent power of self-propagation), expressing God's desire for renewed communion, would meet with an immediate response by a *dead* Job! (14:15).

There is an element of uncertainty and of ambiguity in verses 16 and 17. The former relates to the opening words of verse 16, which could be a continuation of Job's optimistic, but not groundless, longing. If that is so they are to be rendered **'For then ...'**, as in the ESV. If not, they are in contrast to his hope and they should be rendered, 'But now ...'. The ambiguity relates to the metaphors of 'numbering steps' and 'sealing in a bag' (14:16,17). The first of these could describe either God's care (see 31:4) or his scrutiny (see 10:14). The second could represent either the way in which something precious was guarded (see Prov. 7:20) or the way in which a record was kept for accounting purposes (Hosea 13:12). Which of these two sets of alternatives should be adopted?

For two reasons I favour the first options in both cases and see these statements of Job as a continuation of his positive frame of mind. First, the strophe division comes after verse 17, and not after verse 15, as modern translations make clear, and that points to a continuity of theme. Secondly, the expression which concludes verse 17 is parallel to the clause that concludes verse 16, which says that God will *not* keep watch over Job's sin; in other words, God will not present an account for payment. This means that in these verses Job is describing a further element of his 'renewal' that amounts to his being protected and pardoned by God. (All this is important background for a consideration of Job 19:25-27.)

Death extinguishing life (14:18-22)

14:21-22
His sons come to honour, and he does not know it;
    they are brought low, and he perceives it not.
He feels only the pain of his own body,
    and he mourns only for himself.

Job now reverts to thinking about life as being defenceless before death, and what he says amounts to a picture of unrelieved gloom. He is describing the eclipse of the hope he had and uses the picture of a landslide (an inanimate thing) in order to do so (14:19). That is the kind of thing that God does. He does not answer man's longings; he destroys them! That is the kind of 'change' and 'recovery' that God effects. It is one for the worse; it is expulsion, not recall (14:20). Such a fluctuation of outlook is not to be wondered at, given Job's distressed condition, psychological as well as physical, and also the limited amount of information on the subject of life beyond the grave that was available to him.

But two things should be noted. The first is that what Job says in these verses goes beyond his lament in chapter 3. There he envisaged death as bringing all hardship to an end; here he just speaks of total oblivion. The deceased is unaware of the past and all that subsequently transpires on earth, even the pleasurable aspects (14:21). Job does not find anything about the prospect that gives him the least scintilla of pleasure. On the other hand, oblivion is not annihilation — there is pain and continuation of identity (14:22).

Secondly, the extinction of all hope with which this chapter ends is not the end of the story. Job will have more to say about life beyond death and life with God.

'You are doing away with the fear of God! (Job 15:1-35)

The second cycle of speeches begins with this address of Eliphaz and it continues until chapter 21, where we have Job's reply to Zophar. So far the Friends have proposed a lie in the name of truth as an explanation of Job's suffering, which he has rejected as being inapplicable to him. In what he says Job has maintained his integrity before God, but he has also (and frequently) taken issue with God on the basis of his actions being inexplicable and even unjustifiable. In the early part of this section there is an increase in the heat of this dispute and a consequent deepening of Job's gloom and anguish leading to a transforming moment of light, life and love.

A comparison of this speech of Eliphaz with his first address demonstrates how strained the relationship with Job has become. His viewpoint is one and the same as in that earlier speech, but this one contains no introductory courtesies and no counsel for restoration. In addition, its decibel level is higher. This reaction on the part of Eliphaz shows that he has paid little attention to what Job has just said in chapter 14!

The chapter divides itself very naturally into two parts: in verses 1-16 we have a denunciation of Job and his views, and then, in the remaining verses, a description of the fate of the wicked.

'You are doing away with the fear of God' (15:1-16)

15:4
But you are doing away with the fear of God
  and hindering meditation before God.

15:7-8
Are you the first man who was born?
  Or were you brought forth before the hills?
Have you listened in the council of God?
  And do you limit wisdom to yourself?

15:11
Are the comforts of God too small for you,
  or the word that deals gently with you?

Eliphaz begins by declaring that Job's words are not only devoid of substance but are also the height of impertinence. They are useless and profitless verbiage (15:2-3), as vain as they are vehement. But, more seriously, they express the wickedness of Job's mind and they amount to a rejection of God (15:4-5). Job is therefore self-condemned and he will also most certainly be judged by God (see 15:17-35).

Eliphaz then mounts an assault on Job that is as vigorous as he alleges Job's words to have been against God (15:7-16). With a series of rhetorical questions, he seeks to batter down the doors of Job's resistance. He asks him whether he was the first man to be born (15:7), and although the word 'Adam' is used the reference cannot be to the husband of Eve because he was not **'born'** but 'made' and he was the crown of God's creative handiwork. Here is a **'man'** whose existence predated the 'hills' and who listened to wisdom being uttered **'in the council of God'** (15:8).[14] Eliphaz continues with withering scorn to belittle Job's claim to wisdom by referring to his relative youth (15:9,10).

What he is aiming to do is to reply in kind to Job's words uttered at the beginning of his reply to Zophar (see 12:2-3; see also 13:1-2). Eliphaz is in effect saying that Job does not even know what he and others know from their mentors, and yet he is claiming to know more than they do! But all the while Job is rejecting with derision (15:12-13) the many comforts of God extended to him through the 'gentle word' that someone has spoken. Eliphaz is of course referring to himself at this point, and this is shown by the fact that he repeats the **'word'** that he had heard and made known to Job (15:14-15; cf. 4:12-18). But it is noteworthy that he does not now repeat what he said then which referred to human frailty (see 4:19). Instead he speaks of human sinfulness, using adjectives that combine inward turpitude and outward offensiveness (15:16).

God will do away with the wicked (15:17-35)

15:17-20
I will show you; hear me,
   and what I have seen I will declare
(what wise men have told,
   without hiding it from their fathers,
to whom alone the land was given,
   and no stranger passed among them).
The wicked man writhes in pain all his days,
   through all the years that are laid up for the ruthless.

This passage is only about **'the wicked man'** (15:20). It exceeds everything that has been said before by the Friends on this matter (see Eliphaz in 5:12-14; Bildad in 8:8-18; and Zophar in 11:11). It is a sustained, detailed and unrelieved denunciation.

The opening of it is impressive, as Eliphaz intends it to be (15:17-19). In it he refers, in that order, to himself (and his friends), to the wise, to the fathers and to strangers (or rather to the absence of the latter). In differing ways each group contributes to the significance of what Eliphaz is going to say to Job about the wicked. Eliphaz declares that the fate of the wicked was found out by the wise at a time when no stranger was in the land to introduce alien elements into their thinking. The wise then declared it fully to the fathers, who transmitted it to their descendants. That is how it came to Eliphaz (and his friends) and he is now declaring it to Job, confirming it by his own observation of life.

Job is therefore being confronted by the weight of venerable, unanimous tradition, which declares that judgement awaits the wicked (15:20-24), on account of the wickedness that he has perpetrated (15:25-26), a judgement into which he slips unconsciously — and irrecoverably (15:27-35).[15]

15:29-32,34
He will not be rich, and his wealth will not endure,
    nor will his possessions spread over the earth;
he will not depart from darkness;
    the flame will dry up his shoots,
    and by the breath of his mouth he will depart.
Let him not trust in emptiness, deceiving himself,
    for emptiness will be his payment.
It will be paid in full before his time,
    and his branch will not be green...
For the company of the godless is barren,
    and fire consumes the tents of bribery.

Eliphaz describes the judgement of God from the standpoint of those who will bear it and he uses terms that bear obvious similarities to Job's sufferings. The 'wicked man' (Job) is not only wracked with pain but also with fear; or perhaps the pain is a metaphor for fear, because it is described as birth pangs that are the prelude to something. In this case what is brought forth is merely the consequence of his ways, namely loss of prosperity and the darkness of death (15:21-22). He is famished and full of foreboding because he has raised his hand, stiffened his neck and with an embossed shield run against the Almighty (15:23-26). This is how Eliphaz and his friends understand Job's previous refusals to admit that he has sinned against God and that he is being punished by him.

But **'fat'** — a symbol of power and prosperity — will come to an end (15:27-29). Death will extinguish breath and its darkness and dryness will have a desolating and desiccating effect (15:30). In direct response to Job's words about 'hope for a tree' (see 14:7), Eliphaz here uses the same analogy — but with the opposite meaning. Beginning with shoots being consumed, and going on to vines and olive trees bearing no fruit, he describes the hope that Job has entertained as 'empty' (15:30-31). He then speaks about the land of the **'godless'** becoming **'barren'**, and **'fire'** destroying the tents of those who become rich through corrupt and underhanded ways. This is intended to call to Job's mind what happened to his land through the 'fire of God' (see 1:14-16). What is more, Eliphaz says, **'It will be paid in full before his time'** (15:32). What he has in mind is how it was for Job — these calamities came upon him all in 'one day' and unexpectedly.

'My witness is in heaven'
(Job 16:1-22)

This speech of Job (16:1 – 17:16) is difficult to classify. It seems to be in the nature of a soliloquy rather than either a response to the Friends or an address to God. However, there are places in it where Job does speak directly to each (16:2-5; 17:3-4,10). It is therefore clear that, although Job is speaking about himself (he does so in almost every verse in one way or another), he knows that he is being heard by the Friends and by God — and what is more, he does not care!

We shall use the chapter divisions in the English Bible to consider this material.

'If I were in your place' (16:1-5)

16:2-5
I have heard many such things;
    miserable comforters are you all.
Shall windy words have an end?
    Or what provokes you that you answer?
I also could speak as you do,
    if you were in my place;
I could join words together against you
    and shake my head at you.
I could strengthen you with my mouth,
    and the solace of my lips would assuage your pain.

Job makes a remarkable transition in these verses. It is from biting sarcasm to a genuine empathy. He begins by deriding his friends and their remarks, and claims that they are all harping on the same theme. Picking up on Eliphaz' use of the term for 'trouble' in 15:35, Job associates with it his claim that he has been bringing comfort (see 15:11). The result is an expression that approaches the ultimate oxymoron — **'miserable comforters'**, which Job applies to them all. The word 'wind' has been used pejoratively by each side in the debate to describe the speech that has just been made. Job is doing so here (16:3) by way of responding to Eliphaz in particular (see 15:2; but also Zophar in 11:2-3; Bildad in 8:2).

Suddenly, however, Job discloses a piety that is not characterized by self-interest (as Satan had claimed) but one that is genuinely altruistic. He envisages what he would do if circumstances were reversed (16:4-5). He declares that, although he could speak to them as they had been speaking to him, he would not do so. Something had gone badly awry. The Friends had come to lessen Job's troubles (see 2:11-13) but were doing the very opposite. While all the blame cannot be laid at their door for what ensued, because Job was the one who gave vent to remarks that astounded them, they cannot be totally absolved either, because they made his burden immensely heavier. Such a turnabout of affairs discloses the activity of Satan.

But Job declares that, if he were in their position, he would speak as they had intended to speak. He would bring real and effective comfort. Underneath all the agony and anger the same gracious person exists. Satan has not been able to uproot that love for God and one's neighbour that is the sum of true piety.

God hands me over to ruffians (16:6-17)

16:7,9,11
Surely now God[16] has worn me out;
   he has made desolate all my company...
He has torn me in his wrath and hated me;
   he has gnashed his teeth at me;
   my adversary sharpens his eyes against me...
God gives me up to the ungodly
   and casts me into the hands of the wicked.

This is another lament and complaint. In it Job refers to his condition as being so serious that neither speech nor silence can alleviate it (16:6). Lean and lonely, his shrivelled skin proclaims how dispirited he is and how deprived of company, both divine and human. As a wild beast seizes on its prey, he is assaulted by God; like a beggar on a rubbish heap, he is derided by men (16:10) as they pass him by (cf. Lam. 1:12; Matt. 27:36-39).

Referring to how God hates him, Job uses a word that differs only in one letter from the noun 'Satan' to describe him as **'my adversary'** (16:9), and what immediately follows is a perfect portrait of Satan's attitude and actions (16:12-14). But Job pins the image on the wrong face! He thinks that it is God who has seized and shattered him, shot arrows at him and disembowelled him. Job has covered his scabbed skin with rough sackcloth; his face is flushed with tears; he is ready to lie down and die, but he will not acknowledge that his piety has been pretence (16:15-17). He has not wronged or hurt others and he has served God sincerely. His **'prayer'** (his worship of God) has been sincere and he will maintain his spiritual integrity even as his strength departs.

'My witness is in heaven' (16:18-22)

Although the same themes of lament and complaint
are present in these verses, they are being treated in
a sub-section of their own because of the remarkable
appeal and assertion that they contain (16:19,21).

16:18,22
O earth, cover not my blood,
   and let my cry find no resting-place...
For when a few years have come
   I shall go the way from which I shall not return.

In this passage Job is once more contemplating
death (see 7:7,21; 10:21-22; 14:1-2), but he is doing
so with a sense of greater imminence than ever
before. He refers to **'a few years'** (16:22). Literally, he
speaks of 'a number of years', but that is an idiom for
'few', as opposed to what cannot be numbered (cf.
5:9). It is therefore a way of indicating brevity.

Job had asked God for a charge sheet (see
13:20-23) and he has not received one. He therefore
thinks that all hope for vindication before death has
been extinguished and that there will be no way in
which he can return from the grave to pursue the
matter again (18:22). He therefore turns to the earth
where he will be buried and makes an appeal that his
unjust death (his murder at the hands of God, we
might say) will not be forgotten and go unavenged.
The widespread belief in the ancient Near East was
that a murdered person would have no rest until his
death was avenged (see Gen. 4:10; Isa. 26:21) or his
body was buried (Ezek. 24:7-8). By calling on the
earth not to cover his blood he is in effect issuing his
own writ against God!

16:19
Even now, behold my witness is in heaven,
   and he who testifies for me is on high.

Job uses a term here that indicates a contrast to
what he has just said, and what follows is indeed
staggering. Job expresses assurance! But there is
more here than a change of mood or spirit. He is
filled with confidence that he does have someone who
will be a defence **'witness'** for him after all. Yet even
that does not reach the height of what he says here.
The most surprising and distinctive feature of this
statement is that he now knows he has a witness **'in
heaven'**. Who might that be, and how does Job reach
such a staggering conclusion?

To understand Job's advocate as being his own
'cry' in verse 18 is inaccurate because in verse 21 he
refers to the one who is arguing his case using a
masculine form, whereas the Hebrew word for 'cry' is
a feminine noun. There is no real alternative to the
view that the one Job regarded as the counsel for his
defence was no other than **'God'**, the nearest antece-
dent noun that can function as a subject for the verb
'argue'.

But how does Job make such a 'leap of faith'? The
answer (if one is available to us) must be found in the
previous verse, where Job personifies the dumb earth
and gives it a voice that God must surely hear and
answer because it is a cry for justice. (This is an echo
of the account of Cain and Abel.) This leads him to
realize that God is no more unjust than he is deaf,
and so he too will be heard. This is then translated
into the existence of an advocate in heaven who will
speak for Job in God's court. There is someone in
God's realm who will 'lay his hand' on Job and God
and bring them together in a legal setting (see 9:33).

16:20-21
My friends scorn me;
   my eye pours out tears to God,
that he would argue the case of a man with God,
   as a son of man does with his neighbour.

There are real difficulties in the first part of verse 20, but they do not undermine what has been said. They concern both words in it, namely **'friends'** and **'scorn'**. The verb which is translated **'scorn'** can also mean to 'interpret or' 'intercede'. The NIV has therefore opted for 'My intercessor is my friend' and we accept that here.

But how can the plural words 'friends' and 'scorners' be turned into the singular 'friend' and 'intercessor'? This is not as great a problem as might appear, because the difference between the words in Hebrew is only a matter of vowels, and not of consonants. The Hebrew text was originally written only in consonantal form and the vowels were supplied later. The possibility therefore exists that different vowels might provide a reading that is more in keeping with the context. That is what explains this variation. The consonantal text should always be treated with the utmost respect and any vowel changes that are suggested should be tested by the context.

With regard to the second half of the verse, the verb that is used means 'to drip'. Related to the eye, it refers to tears. But why should Job weep at such a wonderful prospect of someone presenting his case in heaven? What follows provides the answer to that question. The NIV is preferable to the ESV at this point. It reads:

My intercessor is my friend
   as my eyes pour out tears to God;
on behalf of a man he pleads with God
   as a man pleads for his friend.

Job therefore weeps imploring tears, desiring that what he has glimpsed may become reality and that his witness may speak to God as one man does with another. That actually happened!

'My spirit is broken'
(Job 17:1-16)

A hasty reading of this short chapter might lead one to think that it contains nothing that Job has not said before. Such a conclusion would be understandable, but it should be resisted. No portion of Holy Scripture should be dismissed in this way before it has been carefully examined. In this connection it is salutary to recall that there are differences, as well as similarities, between the first two chapters of the book and that those differences are of significant importance. So this chapter ought to be examined, and not passed over, because there might be something here that has not been mentioned before. Even if there is not, the way in which the details are laid out will shed new light on old truths. We shall therefore follow the verses in their order.

17:1-2
My spirit is broken; my days are extinct;
   the graveyard is ready for me.
Surely there are mockers about me,
   and my eye dwells on their provocation.

Job begins by making clear that he feels his life force is spent, the grave is imminent and he is surrounded by those who mock him (17:1-2). He is not only persecuted by God, but also provoked by man. He is alone and death is his only companion.

17:3-4
Lay down a pledge for me with yourself;
   who is there who will put up security for me?
Since you have closed their hearts to understanding,
   therefore you will not let them triumph.

But then Job makes a surprising request and declaration (17:3-5). This is a section that must not be overlooked. It expresses daring faith and remarkable insight. He asks God to give him a pledge that he will not forget him (17:3; cf. Deut. 24:10-13). Earlier Job had said to his friends that he has not asked them for a pledge, even though it was the kind of thing that might be expected by one friend of another (see 6:14-23). This is an allusion to someone paying an oppressor to release a friend, or standing bail for him to guarantee that he will not flee the country but will turn up in court on the date when the case is due to be heard. But having no one else to do this for him, Job asks *the Judge* to be his surety! The psalmist does the same in Psalm 119:121-122.

This request is of the same sort as Job's surprising testimony that God will somehow plead with God on Job's behalf (see 16:19-21). To many commentators this tautology is inexplicable, but to those who know anything about the daring power of 'faith without sight' and the reality of the unseen realm there is nothing about this that is difficult to understand. All that is required is more revelation, more light, and that is supplied in 19:25-27 and the remainder of *Job* and, of course, in the New Testament. Even so, mystery, great mystery, remains for the Christian, and not only for Job.

Continuing in this daring frame of mind, Job declares that the Friends' misreading of his condition is part of God's will (17:4) and that if God allows their argument to stand, then not only will Job not be vindicated, but God will not be exalted. This appeal to God's glory is an extra reason that Job uses in an attempt to constrain God to intervene on his behalf. Using a proverb of some sort, he castigates the Friends as behaving like traitors and vultures who at a time of calamity violate the law of sacred friendship for the sake of gain (17:5). He who has been made childless warns them that the same fate could befall them.

In a way that is not untypical of a sufferer, Job's mood fluctuates once more (17:6,7). He recalls how others mock and execrate him and how he is weary and weak because of it all. He descends again into a whirlpool of blackness, but once more he finds a measure of hope and solid ground under his feet (17:8-10). There are, however, some difficulties in these verses.

17:8-9
The upright are appalled at this,
    and the innocent stirs himself up against the godless.
Yet the righteous holds to his way,
    and he who has clean hands grows stronger and
        stronger.

In the second line of verse 8 Job refers to two sorts of people and he contrasts them. They are the **'innocent'**, on the one hand, and the **'godless'**, or 'profane', on the other. Both words are singular adjectives that function as nouns, and so the two individuals that are in view here are probably representative of a larger number of persons in each case.

But what about the **'upright'** in the earlier part of the verse? This is a plural adjective. Who are these? They are spectators, or observers, of the innocent person who is afflicted. It is therefore likely that they are Job's 'upright' friends who are **'appalled'** because they see someone who is desolate and devastated by what to them appears to be divine judgement. Job is therefore describing himself as the person who is 'innocent' of the charges brought against him and also as the **'righteous'** person who resolves that, whether he is seen as righteous or not, he is going to persevere to the end (17:9), confident that extra strength will be given to him to do so. This is indomitable faith. He is maintaining his integrity.

17:10
But you, come on again, all of you,
　　and I shall not find a wise man among you.

In verse 10 Job is either calling on the Friends to come to a better mind — that is, to repent (the phrase translated **'come on again'** could be rendered 'turn', which is the word for 'repent') — or he is inviting them to try again to overcome him. The latter seems more likely in view of the fact that he closes by saying that not one of them will show that he is really wise.

17:11
My days are past; my plans are broken off,
　　the desires of my heart.

Verse 11 returns to the note that Job struck at the beginning concerning the brevity of life. But this time he also describes it as fragile. His plans are **'broken'** as well as his spirit. Death is his home and despondency is his next of kin (17:12-16). Darkness, dust and defeat seem to engulf his faith. But it has only been eclipsed and not extinguished. It will rise and emerge again.

Black darkness
(Job 18:1 – 19:24)

In this section we have Bildad's speech and most of Job's reply. Breaking off at 19:24 will provide a context for considering Job's well-known and much-loved words that come immediately afterwards.

The light of the wicked is put out (18:1-21)

18:2,4
How long will you hunt for words?
   Consider, and then we will speak...
You who tear yourself in your anger,
   shall the earth be forsaken for you,
   or the rock be removed out of its place?

In his first speech Bildad did offer Job a ray of hope, but it was on the basis that he would seek mercy from God as one who had sinned (see 8:5-6). In this second address there is not a glimmer of hope extended. In twenty-one verses all but three are a description of the wicked and his fate. This raises the question as to whether Bildad had given up all hope that Job might repent, with the result that he was intending to announce both verdict and sentence — while Job was still alive.

He begins with the same impatient words with which he first addressed Job: **'How long ...?'** (18:2; cf. 8:2). He certainly does not interact with anything that Job has said, but he does react to Job's claim that he had 'clean hands' (see 17:9). He had heard that much at least! But he chooses to regard it as a thinly veiled accusation that he and his colleagues are 'unclean'. In addition Job's appeal to the earth and his words about having a witness on high (16:18-19) leave him completely unmoved.

It might appear from our English translations that Bildad is addressing Job in his opening remarks. But that is so only in verses 3 and 4. In verse 2 the second-person verbs are plural. As the Hebrew text stands, Bildad is therefore describing Eliphaz and Zophar as **'[hunting] for words'** (18:2). This use of the plural is so strange that several emendations have been suggested, but not one is free of some objection or other. However, there is an interesting possibility to consider that does not require any change in the text, and this is that Bildad is some-what dissatisfied with what his two friends have said. (Satan sows discord everywhere!) Neither of them has been as categorical as Bildad believes the case now requires, which is that an unambiguous declaration of the doctrine of strict retribution is called for.

What is clear is that Bildad is exasperated with Job. He regards Job's refusal to kowtow to him and his colleagues as an indication of his sense of superi-ority and disdain for them (18:3). He gives Job a name (of sorts) which it is difficult to express in English as pithily as in Hebrew. He calls Job a 'tearer of himself in [his] anger' (18:4). By this Bildad in-tends to defend God as well as to denounce Job. He is saying to Job that it was not God who was 'tearing' Job, as he had claimed (see 16:9), but that it was he who was ravaging himself by his own anger. Job is therefore the wild beast, and not God! So often Job must have resembled someone who was distracted, if not demented. Bildad thinks that Job is on a con-stant, mad search for words and is refusing to think

and by making an appeal to the 'earth' (16:18) it was
as if Job was expecting the order of natural things to
be overturned in his favour (18:4).

18:5-6
Indeed, the light of the wicked is put out,
    and the flame of his fire does not shine.
The light is dark in his tent,
    and his lamp above him is put out.

18:21
Surely such are the dwellings of the unrighteous,
    such is the place of him who knows not God.

But Bildad thinks that Job is also challenging the
moral fabric of life on earth — and that is far more
serious. He therefore expatiates on the justice of the
moral order (18:5-21). He thinks in terms of strict
retribution. But his world view is not only characterized by this principle; it is totally limited by it —
entirely and everywhere. He begins and concludes his
peroration with synonymous terms whose meaning is
'Surely'. There can be no variation and no exception
to what he says. The wicked will be treated in this life
just as he describes, and wherever such events occur,
there the wicked will be found.

Even if Bildad is still thinking, perhaps even
hoping, that Job may turn to God, his shock tactics
are counterproductive. Although he is speaking in
impersonal terms, it is obvious that he has Job in
mind. Light and darkness are the operative terms in
what Bildad has to say. Light is associated with
God's favour and therefore with strength (18:7,12),
with health (18:13), with home comforts (18:14), with
wealth (18:16) and with a name — that is, with
public regard and personal descendants (18:17). Job
has lost all of these.

Darkness is associated with all sorts of snares that await him (18:8-10) because of his wicked schemes, and with all sorts of terrors that besiege him as a result (18:11). He is chased (18:11), tripped up (18:12), torn away (18:14) and thrust out (18:18). He presents a horrifying spectacle to all who see or hear of him, in the west or the east (18:20). Bildad concludes with a definitive declaration about the fate of the wicked.

All this is hardly likely to mollify Job's agitation or to edify his understanding. It is more calculated to terrify him because it is a description that parallels his own experience in so many ways. Properly interpreted, all that Bildad says about the unrighteous, those who do not know God, is true. Filtered through the teaching of the New Testament about the Last Judgement, his declaration can be used in preaching. Its emphasis on suddenness, certainty, finality and justice is all in keeping with what the Lord Jesus had to say about the destiny and the destination of the wicked. The only thing that was untrue about it was that Bildad applied it to Job, who was *not* **'unrighteous'** and who *did* **'[know] God'**.

So in accusing and condemning Job, Bildad is actually, if unwittingly, serving Satan's purpose. Job has just spoken of his having an advocate and has asked God not to forget him. Bildad challenges that and denies it, and he does so in the name of all the Friends.

'He has set darkness on my paths' (19:1-24)

It is important to keep pace with Job's answer to Bildad in this chapter and not leap to a consideration of verses 25-27. This is because the background provided in verses 1-24 contributes significantly to the meaning and value of his ringing affirmation of faith. We shall use Job's appeal in verse 21 as an integrating theme for these earlier verses and consider them as 'a cry for pity'.

19:21
Have mercy on me, have mercy on me, O you my friends,
    for the hand of God has touched me!

This is a seriously meant plea (he repeats it) in spite of all that Job has had to say about his hard-hearted friends. He is not being sarcastic. Unexpected it might be, but we have to remember that Job is a man in anguish, and people who are desperate do clutch at straws. After all, the Friends had come in order to pity him and, indeed, had done so for a while; this is something that he had reminded them of before (6:14).

When anyone appeals for pity he or she is reduced to the direst of circumstances. After all, it is possible to be in agony but to be resolute. But to ask for pity is to be close to breaking point; in addition, pity is usually asked for from one's enemies, not from one's friends.

1. Unpitied by his friends (19:1-5)

19:2-4
How long will you torment me
    and break me in pieces with words?
These ten times you have cast reproach upon me;
    are you not ashamed to wrong me?
And even if it be true that I have erred,
    my error remains with myself.

In verse 2 he declares that his friends' words, coupled with their looks and gestures, have had a tearing, crushing effect on him. His specification of **'ten times'** (19:3) is of course not to be understood literally, but figuratively. They have engaged in assault and battery of a verbal kind.

Verse 4 is not difficult if it is understood in a narrow sense. In it Job is asserting that his sin only affects himself — if he has committed any. His friends have been seeking to impose their views on him. They have completely discounted him in the interest of their theory. He has not done anything to them.

2. Unpitied by God (19:6-12)

19:7-8
Behold, I cry out 'Violence!' but I am not answered;
    I call for help, but there is no justice.
He has walled up my way, so that I cannot pass,
    and he has set darkness upon my paths.

Job's charge is that God has been unjust. He sees himself as attacked by a surrounding army, or stalked by a preying animal. He has been dethroned (19:9), uprooted (19:10) and besieged (19:11-12).

3. Unpitied by others (19:13-22)

19:13
He has put my brothers far from me,
    and those who knew me are wholly estranged from me.

19:20
My bones stick to my skin and to my flesh,
    and I have escaped by the skin of my teeth.

There is no human sympathy forthcoming from any direction. Reviewing folk from whom he might expect to receive it, he lists his **'brothers'** and other friends (19:13-14), his household guests and servants (19:15-16), his siblings, his wife (19:17), little children (19:18) and his closest friends or colleagues

(19:19). The reference to **'children'** in verse 17 is literally 'sons of my womb'. Understanding this as a reference to his blood brothers (**'the children of my own mother,'** ESV), and not to his own children, means that there is no contradiction between this verse and the record of the deaths of Job's children in chapter 1; it also means that the term **'brothers'** in verse 13 refers to clan members rather than just his immediate family.

Job is nothing but skin and bone and is barely alive. Not only is there no justice for him but there is no kindness either. The Friends (and others) are joining forces with God against him (19:20-22). Job is here at his lowest and Satan is at his strongest.

4. 'Oh that my words were written!' (19:23-24)

19:23-24
Oh that my words were written!
  Oh that they were inscribed in a book!
Oh that with an iron pen and lead
  they were engraved in the rock for ever!

These two verses are of the utmost importance. Job is here declaring his determination to have things put on record. What exactly he is envisaging in verse 23 is uncertain. It might be that he is thinking of a scroll made of strips of papyrus reed flattened and joined together. If this is the case, then he moves on in verse 24 to something more permanent, namely a **'rock'** with incised letters filled with molten lead or something equivalent. But, whatever the precise details, Job is interested in permanence, or that which is ineradicable.

But what does he want recorded? What does he mean by **'my words'**? This is a far more important question. Is it what he goes on to say in the following verses? In several translations (e.g. ESV) the word 'for' that stands at the opening of verse 25 encourages such a view, and there is no doubt that the declaration that follows would be worthy of permanent record. Indeed, it has been given it in a better format than rock that is liable to crumble, or engraving that can be defaced or become weathered!

The word **'for'** is too weak as a rendering of the Hebrew. The NASB has 'as for me', and that is better because it points to a contrast between verses 24 and 25 (cf. Ps. 2:6). What would be even better would be 'but I', or 'but as for me', because that would point up a strong contrast. This would mean that what Job wanted to have recorded was his plea of 'Not guilty'. In other words, there is a shift between verses 24 and 25 that is of exactly the same kind as that between verses 18 and 19 in chapter 16. It is the protestation of his integrity that he wants written as a kind of epitaph — and that leads to an encouraging intervention by God. The darkest hour is before the dawn.

A beam of light
(Job 19:25-29)

Verses 25-27 of this passage contain Job's best-known words. They have endeared themselves to many in the form in which they appear in the King James (or Authorized) Version and Handel's *Messiah*. But there are some difficulties with that translation that just cannot be avoided, as is evident from a comparison with recent translations.

19:25-27

KJV	ESV
For I know *that* my redeemer liveth, and *that* he shall stand at the latter *day* upon the earth:	For I know that my Redeemer lives, and at the last he will stand upon the earth.
And *though* after my skin *worms* destroy this *body,* yet in my flesh shall I see God:	And after my skin has been thus destroyed, yet in my flesh I shall see God,
Whom I shall see for myself, and mine eyes shall behold, and not another; *though* my reins be consumed within me.	whom I shall see for myself, and my eyes shall behold, and not another. My heart faints within me!

The words that appear in italic type in the KJV have no counterpart in the Hebrew text and were inserted by the 1611 translators in the interests of conveying some meaning. These do not appear at all in recent translations, and some of those extra words, namely **'day'**, **'worms'** and **'body'**, carry significant weight in the popular use or understanding of this text. In addition we shall see that there are alternative renderings for the words **'for myself'** and **'not another'** and that the meaning of the verb that is translated **'destroyed'** is difficult to fix with precision. Clearly, there are tasks of some magnitude to consider at a most basic level with regard to this text.[17]

We are going to look at these verses in relation to the rest of the book of Job as a first step in considering them. We shall therefore examine the opening expression, **'I know'**, and then focus on the assertions that **'my Redeemer lives and ... he will stand'** and **'I shall see God.'**

'I know' (19:25)

As this verb is in the first person singular, what follows is an individual affirmation. Job is no longer giving vent to a wish amid the surrounding gloom; he lays claim to a knowledge that is characterized by tremendous, joyful certainty. This knowledge is the same as the assurance of faith; it is a believing of something that has been revealed to him. 'In a moment, in the twinkling of an eye' (after verse 24, so to speak, and like 16:18-19) God had somehow revealed himself to Job, and his **'I know'** introduces an account of what was revealed and his response to it. His 'I know', or 'I have come to know', is equivalent to 'I believe'. It is a testimony that has both content and effect, and that is how we shall consider them.

We shall begin by examining the content.

'My redeemer lives and he will stand' (19:25)

What Job knows is that he has a **'Redeemer'** who lives and who **'will stand'**. The object of believing knowledge is therefore a person and his activity. That is what is summed up in the term 'redeemer'. Questions have been raised about the suitability of this term as a translation of the Hebrew.[18] But it can be allowed to stand provided that it is first thought of in Old Testament terms — that is, before any light from the New Testament is allowed to shine on it. The Hebrew word is used in a number of places in the Old Testament for a person's nearest blood relative who had an obligation to perform certain tasks in differing circumstances. Strictly speaking, it refers to someone's next of kin — which is precisely what Job has just said he does not have (19:13-17).

The circumstances in which the kinsman was to act varied from recovering a relative's lost property or liberty (Lev. 25:25-27,47-49) to avenging his unjust death (Num. 35:9-34) or marrying his brother's childless widow (Deut. 25:5; Ruth 3; 4). Job has in effect lost all of these and needs a next of kin to restore and to release, to avenge and to perpetuate his name. Such recovery was often effected by the payment of a ransom, and that makes the term 'redeemer' entirely appropriate as a translation.

Clearly, the kinsman exercised a significant role in the cohesion of a community and nation, and it was not only in Israel that such a duty was recognized. It was family-based, going back to what was included in the mutual care of husband and wife before ever it was enshrined nationally. It was (and is) part of what it means to be created in the image of God. But it then became bathed in new light when Jehovah became Israel's next of kin by delivering them from bondage in Egypt (see Exod. 6:6).

Job describes his 'Kinsman' by stating that he **'lives'** and he **'will stand'**, and those epithets point in the direction of his being divine. It is possible that each of these verbs might be understood as equivalent to 'existing', on the one hand, and 'being erect', on the other, but that would be incredibly superficial and of little comfort to Job. What Job is saying is that he knows that his Kinsman has life and that he will perform his duty.

With regard to his having 'life', we should remember that Job has just been speaking of inanimate rock and of himself as a dying man. 'Life' therefore stands in contrast to both of those; Job's kinsman is not only alive at the time of speaking, but he will not die. The Hebrew word for 'living' that is used here is used elsewhere of God (Num. 14:21,28; Deut. 32:40; 1 Kings 17:1). Job's 'Redeemer' is therefore the living God who will never die (Deut. 5:26; Job 16:19).

What is in view in the reference to his 'standing up' is equivalent to someone 'taking the stand' in order to act as a witness. Job is envisaging proceedings in a court of law. Earlier he has said that his physical condition rises up as witness against him (see 16:8) and later he will refer to God doing the same, but as a judge (31:14). The verb 'rise up' is also used of false witnesses testifying against the godly (see Ps. 27:12) and of God himself whenever he intervenes to defend and deliver his people in times of need in answer to their prayers (Ps. 7:6; 68:1). It is also used in connection with God's appearing to judge all mankind (Isa. 2:19-21; Zeph. 3:8). Job is expecting that his Kinsman-Redeemer will intervene on his behalf and render a final verdict against which there can be no appeal. These words are therefore all of a piece with the Christian's expectation of being owned and vindicated at the Last Day through his Kinsman-Redeemer, the Lord Jesus Christ.

The timing of his intervention

But when and where does Job think that this Kinsman/Vindicator will intervene? The answers to these questions are bound up with the latter part of verse 25 and the first part of verse 26. In the ESV they read: **'... and at the last he will stand upon the earth. And after my skin has been thus destroyed...'**

There are two uses of the word **'after'** in these verses. The first is rendered in the ESV by the word **'last'**. Both relate to the timing of this intervention. The first use (19:25) is an adjective which lacks a noun and which is difficult to translate. It has therefore been suggested that it should be understood in the same way as Isaiah uses it when he speaks of God as 'the First and *the Last*'. This suggestion has not commended itself generally and it can be set aside without losing all reference in the text to the presence of God, given what has already been said about the word 'lives'.

As these verses are full of legal language and a courtroom scene is envisaged, **'last'** can be a reference to the witness whose testimony is decisive in the case. It is worth noting that, though 'the last word' in the dispute between Job and God comes from Job's mouth (see 42:1-6), it is Jehovah who has the last word as to Job's standing and character. What is more, he makes such a declaration four times (see 42:7-8). This part of Job's testimony could therefore refer to the end of the book, and not to the end of time.

The second use of the term (19:26) raises a question that is of material importance in relation to the timing of the Kinsman's intervention. It relates to what happens to Job's **'skin'**. Sadly, the meaning of the word that is translated **'destroyed'** is difficult to fix with precision because wherever it occurs in the Old Testament it is used metaphorically. As a verb it is used in only one other place (Isa. 10:34) and there it describes the clearing away of thickets in a forest; as a noun it refers to the 'beating' of olives from the tree (Isa. 17:6; 24:13). As it is skin (not body) that is being referred to in verse 26, the English word that seems to be most endorsed as a translation is 'strip' or 'flay'. Either would make good sense but neither settles the all-important question as to whether Job is thinking of 'torn flesh' or of the 'bare bones' of 'this' body as emaciated or as decomposed. As a provisional judgement I would suggest the former, even though it means saying that Job *did not intend* to express his belief in an encounter with God after death or in a resurrected body. Such a loss is to a large extent compensated for by seeing Job's testimony here as being an effective (though unconscious) refutation of Satan's belief that stripping Job of his skin would strip him of his piety (see comment on 2:4-5).

The locale of this intervention

The next question relates to the locale of this intervention because in verse 25 we have the expression **'upon the earth'**. The Hebrew noun means 'dry earth' or 'dust' and Job's use of it in 28:2; 30:6 and 41:33 could be rendered either way. But it is also used in connection with an interred corpse (see 20:11; 21:26) and also for the abode of the dead (see 17:16). The *possibility* that Job has in mind an intervention on his behalf after his death ought not therefore to be dismissed, but whether it can be asserted confidently on the basis of the words in the text is another matter. We shall return to this below.

'I shall see God' (19:26)

Three times Job makes this assertion in verses 26 and 27, and he does so in slightly different ways. Again there are translation questions in connection with each of these.

First, and most doctrinally significant, is the preposition **'in'**, which introduces **'my flesh'**; this would be better rendered *'from* my flesh'. The ESV includes an alternative rendering as a footnote, and this is *'without* my flesh'. The difference between these two readings is obvious and, seeing that it is so great, someone might well wonder whether one and the same Hebrew expression can have both meanings. But the fact of the matter is that both renderings are accurate. The question that is inevitably raised is whether Job is referring to a sight of God 'from within' his flesh or 'from without' his flesh — that is, when he is in a disembodied condition.

If the latter view is adopted the question that then has to be faced is what is meant by **'eyes'** in verse 27. If he was disembodied Job would have no eyes. The reference to his 'eyes' would therefore have to be construed metaphorically, but this would appear unlikely, given the threefold emphasis on sight in this statement. I therefore take the view that Job is referring to the eyes of his present body and so render the expression '[from] in my flesh'.

But when would this be? Does adopting that interpretation mean that Job was declaring that he would see God after he had died and had been given a new body? We have already seen that verse 25 and the first part of verse 26 do not *have to* be understood in this way in order to be treated *fairly*. To regard them as expressing Job's confidence that he would have a personal encounter with his Kinsman-Redeemer while he was in an emaciated condition — *in extremis*, so to speak — which would result in his being vindicated before death is a sufficient exposition of these words in their immediate context. It is also a wonderful testimony of faith against incalculable odds. The following three reasons support this view:

First, in verse 27 he envisages seeing his Kinsman-Redeemer **'for myself'** and **'not another'**. **'For myself'** can be translated as 'on my side' — that is, for him and not against him — and **'not another'** as 'not a stranger'. This means that reconciliation will be effected and fellowship will be restored through the intervention of his Redeemer. God will be for Job and no longer far from him.

Secondly, this is what Elihu holds out to him in 33:24-28.

Thirdly, this is what actually came about when Job said, 'Now my eye sees you' (42:5). Jehovah did vindicate him before he died and he did see God. All that he lost — no, twice as much — was restored to him. He enjoyed life on earth with God again.

Taking this view entails regarding Job 19:25-27 as presenting no advance on what Job had said in chapters 14 and 16 with reference to death. In chapter 14 he considers the possibility of life after death with some longing, but in the most tentative way. In chapter 16 there is no reference even to such a possibility, even though he refers to a witness on high in the face of its imminence. Similarly, there is no clear and firm *textual* evidence in chapter 19 that Job asserted life beyond death. And, most significantly, there is no mention of it afterwards when Job is speaking of death (see chapter 21) — and that is surely to be expected if this passage is speaking of a future resurrection.

But this interpretation will be unacceptable to many, and so I want to state clearly that I do not mean that the 'popular' understanding of 19:25-27 should be entirely given up. We have only been exploring the question as to what Job meant by his words, and doing so contextually — that is, from within the book that bears his name and the era of revelation recorded in it. Not much had been revealed by God of life beyond the tomb up to and during the patriarchal era, beyond Enoch's total and mystifying disappearance. It is therefore not surprising that Job 19:25-27 does not exhibit anything like clarity on the matter. The surprising thing is that it contains as much as it does.

But there is a larger context to be borne in mind, the larger canonical context. Viewed through that lens, Job 19:25-27 *is* messianic in character. It anticipates the beatific vision in glory — and the resurrection of the body. It does have Christological and soteriological dimensions.

But on what basis can such an assertion be made? Is it only because of the fact that *Job* is as much part of divinely inspired Scripture as is Revelation? No. That is certainly true, but there is more to it. There is an expression used in *Job* which is exceedingly important in giving instruction as to how the Lord's appearing, and all that follows it, is to be understood. It is: 'The LORD restored the fortunes of Job' (42:10). Rendered literally, the Hebrew means 'The LORD turned the captivity of Job.' This expression is first used in Deuteronomy 30:3 in connection with Israel's deliverance and restoration from God's covenant displeasure — that is, from exile — and it is also used of Israel's deliverance from bondage in Egypt (see Ps. 126:1). The appearance of the Lord as Kinsman-Redeemer brings Job's captivity to Satan to an end, restores him physically and blesses his latter days much more than the ones before he was afflicted. Our consideration of the Epilogue (42:10-17) will seek to demonstrate that it is an anticipation of heaven expressed in Old Testament terms.

As in many other matters, Christians should understand more of what is presented in the Old Testament than Old Testament figures did. This applies to the words of Job that we have been considering. Magnificent though Job 19:25-27 is, it is less than 'the appearing of our Saviour Christ Jesus, who abolished death and brought life and immortality *to light* through the gospel' (2 Tim. 1:9-10, emphasis added).

The effect of Job's testimony

This knowledge produces an upheaval of two kinds — emotional and mental.

1. Emotional

Job says, **'My heart faints within me!'** (19:27). This describes the emotional effect of what he now knows. The term he uses is literally 'kidneys' — thought to be the most sensitive organ in the human anatomy, and which earlier he had described as having been slashed open by God (see 16:13). Now he says something like, 'My kidneys have ended up in my chest', which is clearly a metaphor. (We have a similar expression in English, namely to 'have one's heart in one's mouth', which we use to describe apprehension. But Job is not apprehensive; he is overjoyed.) Faith is not fact without feeling; it is certainly not feeling alone, but it is equally certain that it is fact that is felt.

2. Mental

This upheaval occurs in the realm of the understanding. Being enlightened, Job is now able to warn the Friends of the judgement of God (19:28-29). He sees that the Friends are persecuting him, believing that the explanation of all his suffering lies within himself. But his new-found certainty enables him to see the unsure ground on which they are standing. He warns them of the **'sword'**, which is a metaphor not only for death, but also for the wrath of God (see 15:22; 27:14) and 'the judgement'.[19]

There are so many wonderful statements in Scripture prefaced by the words, 'I know', but this one (limited as it is) deserves to be ranked among the greatest of them.

3.
The debate between Job and the Friends (II)
(Job 20:1 – 26:14)

Although there is no division in the text itself following the magnificent testimony of Job, it would indeed be surprising if there were no effects of the light that has come into his mind. We shall therefore pause at this point to set out what I believe these to be. There are two things to note and appreciate concerning chapters 20-31.

First, and with regard to the Friends, Job is able to adopt an aggressive approach towards their explanation of his suffering. Secondly, he becomes much more moderate in the words he addresses to God about his suffering. These two features ought to be noted and appreciated.

With regard to the Friends

The Friends have been threatening Job with judgement on account of the sin that they believe he must have committed and that he will not repent of. What Job has been saying by way of reply to them is that their diagnosis of his condition is incorrect and consequently he will not avail himself of the medicine they prescribe. Job has protested against the justice of his treatment, at God's hands as well as theirs, but he has set himself to soldier on in faith. In the course of doing this he has mentioned that their thesis that sin is always followed by judgement in this life is not as watertight as they have made out (see 12:6) and he has also warned them of their danger in misrepresenting God (see 13:7-11).

As a direct result, I believe, of his new-found assurance, he strikes this note of warning more boldly (see 19:28-29), over against Bildad's inflexible and universal dictum, and he proceeds to subject his Friends' thesis to a thorough scrutiny and to refute it. Prior to 19:25-27 it was as if he only half realized the significance of what he had said in 12:6. But, enlightened with his liberating knowledge that God is his Kinsman-Redeemer, he is able to appreciate the significance of his claim that 'The tents of robbers are at peace and those who provoke God are secure,' and to make much more telling use of it (see chapters 21 and 24). Job now has two extra strings to his bow in dealing with his Friends, and of course with Satan, albeit unwittingly.

With regard to God

Job has complained about God's dealings with him and described God as a malicious and merciless foe. But he has also accused God of being fundamentally immoral, asserting that God is completely indifferent as to whether a person is righteous or wicked, treating both in the same way according to his whim. Job has said that God 'destroys both the blameless and the wicked', that he 'mocks at the calamity of the innocent' and that he gives 'the earth ... into the hand of the wicked' (see 9:22-24), but no longer does he utter such wild and sinful allegations. It is true that he still says that he is being dealt with cruelly and unjustly by God, and it is that which Elihu will begin to deal with, and Jehovah will perfect the process. But the wildness has gone out of his spirit.

The conclusion we can draw from these facts is that Job is winning the argument with the Friends, and so with Satan. This is indicated by the fact that the speeches of the Friends become shorter and Job's become longer in chapters 20-31. Indeed, the third cycle is not completed, for Zophar does not speak and Bildad has nothing at all to say apropos of the subject of the debate. They all give up on him (see 32:1), which means that he has seen off their challenge. From chapter 26 onwards it is all Job — but only until Elihu begins to speak.

'I hear an insult'
(Job 20:1-29)

We have detected some changes in Job as a result of his new-found assurance, but there seems to be none in Zophar, or at least none that is for the better, and that goes for both Eliphaz and Bildad too, as we shall see later. But this does not mean that Zophar has taken no note of Job's words. His whole address is a reply to what Job has said and it falls into two stages. First, he takes particular exception to Job's warning, and then he completely distorts Job's exultation.

'I hear censure that insults me' (Job 20:1-3)

20:3
I hear censure that insults me,
    and out of my understanding a spirit answers me.

Zophar does not address Job directly in these opening verses. He treats him dismissively by just saying, **'I hear'**. Overlooking Job's presence, Zophar takes great exception to what has been said. Roused because he thinks he has been insulted, and filled with confidence in his own understanding, he makes a reply that he claims is based on a higher view of things. Zophar is about to pontificate.

The joy of the godless (20:4-29)

20:4-5
Do you not know this from of old,
  since man was placed on earth,
that the exulting of the wicked is short,
  and the joy of the godless but for a moment?

He confronts Job with an assertion that **'The exulting of the wicked is short, and the joy of the godless is but for a moment.'** Why should Zophar speak of **'exultation'** and **'joy'**? The answer must be that he is commenting on Job's testimony, and on the spirit in which it was uttered rather than on what was said. Zophar is so convinced that Job is wicked that even the sight and sound of his joyful restored fellowship with God will not cause him to revise his opinion. Hopelessly prejudiced, he says that such rejoicing is brief and it cannot be anything else. He is not only contradicting what Job had said; he is also dismissing it. Just as Satan had denied the sincerity of Job's piety when speaking to God, Zophar now does the same all over again addressing Job himself.

He also throws down a challenge. It is based on the tradition of venerable antiquity, but it conceals a trap, and the way he poses it continues his derision. By the words, **'Do you not know...?'** he intends to draw Job's thinking into an either/or mode, pitting him over against the wise men of the past, even going back to the dawn of human history. The implication is that Job is an ignorant upstart, and that is proved by the remarkable discovery that he has just spoken about!

Job is therefore in a cleft stick. Either he has to agree with Zophar's statement, or else dismiss respected wisdom. If he agrees, he undermines his own testimony; if he disagrees, he puts himself in the category of the wicked and godless. This is so typical

of Satan. We have only to think of the many traps
that were set for the Lord by the teachers of his day
(see Matt. 19:3; 22:15-46).

20:6,9-10
Though his height mount up to the heavens,
    and his head reach to the clouds...
The eye that saw him will see him no more,
    nor will his place any more behold him.
His children will seek the favour of the poor,
    and his hands will give back his wealth.

But Zophar does not wait for an answer. Having
sown these alternatives in Job's mind, he proceeds
immediately to capitalize on his perceived advantage.
He does so by focusing on the fate of the wicked on
account of his sin (20:12) and on the intervention of
God's **'burning anger'** (20:23) and 'wrath' (20:28). He
uses the twin poles of exaltation and abasement to
depict the wicked (and he means Job, of course),
pointing out that, however high someone ascends,
the lower will his fall inevitably be.

With regard to exaltation, he has relatively little to
say about it (20:6). It is, however, difficult to think of
anything that would exceed what he says, for it is
only God who is above the heavens and the clouds.
Zophar could be repeating the image used by Bildad
in which a mighty man or ruler is depicted as a tall
tree (see 8:16-18; 18:16). Job too had used this
metaphor with regard to all that manifests a man's
dignity (see 14:7-9) and as a basis for speculating
about life beyond the grave. If that is what Zophar is
doing, he is once again turning Job's words back on
himself.

But Zophar speaks of exaltation only in the interests of underlining a colossal abasement, and all that
follows — all twenty-three verses of it — deals with
that theme in a sustained, brutal and even coarse

way. For the triumphant godless person, like Lamech (see Gen. 4:23-24), all joy is extinguished; there will be nothing left to bring him any delight (20:20).

Verses 7-11 refer to Job personally but include one reference to his children. Zophar says that Job will disappear from human view and leave nothing to his children, who will be impoverished (20:9-10). His vigour will not protect him from such calamity (20:11). Zophar is definitely quoting words from Job himself at this point (see 7:8,10). Job had used these words as a lament; Zophar uses them as a judicial sentence. He describes Job as a secret sinner whose entire being will become diseased and poisoned as a result of the sin that he will not renounce (20:12-16), and as an open sinner whose toil will yield no prosperity because he had trodden on the poor and seized property that did not belong to him (20:17-19). The combination of these trumped-up charges denies not only Job's inward sincerity but also his outward integrity.

The final part of Zophar's speech describes Job as being not at ease (20:20) in spite of the plenty and prosperity he had enjoyed (20:21-22), and states that he will only be filled to the full by God's all-consuming anger (20:23), even as he flees from it (20:24-25). Job had appealed to the earth on his own behalf and had received assurance from heaven (see 16:18-19; 19:24-27), but Zophar declares that neither will vindicate him. Inevitable devastation and destruction are his lot — but Zophar, for all his pomposity, is just repeating what Bildad had said before him (see 18:21).

'Why do the wicked live and reach old age?' (Job 21:1-34)

Job's speech resembles Zophar's in structure, but it differs markedly from it in content. Beginning with a reply (21:1-6), Job then develops a theme (21:7-34), which leads up to a conclusion. But this theme breaks new ground in the debate, and so the conclusion it presents is no platitude. Job takes issue directly with the basic plank of the Friends' argument, which is that the wicked are always punished in this life.

'Lay your hand over your mouth' (21:1-6)

21:4-5
As for me, is my complaint against man?
    Why should I not be impatient?
Look at me and be appalled,
    and lay your hand over your mouth.

His opening words to the Friends remind them that they have not given him the comfort that they thought they had (or had intended to give). Although he has no real hope of any real change in their attitude towards him, he nevertheless asks them to suspend their mocking, at least for a while, in order to give attention to what he is going to say. Job uses the full first-person pronoun several times in these first six verses in order to stress that Zophar is not the only one who can claim that he has something important to say. Using rhetorical questions in verse 4, Job makes clear that it is God that he is complaining about, and not man, and so the Friends should not take offence on a personal level. What is more, he has good grounds for complaining against God, given his terrifying physical condition, which he can hardly bear to contemplate himself. His request that they should look at him (21:5) raises the possibility that they had been 'hiding their faces from him' (cf. Isa. 53:3).

'Why do the wicked live and grow mighty in power? (21:7-16)

21:7
Why do the wicked live,
    reach old age, and grow mighty in power?

Job is here challenging the thesis of the Friends. By all the laws the wicked should be judged, and yet that does not happen! Job describes what happens to them, their children and their descendants (21:8), their property and livestock (21:10) and the festivities that they are able to enjoy (21:11-12). Their lives are full of ease and their deaths are not difficult (21:13). Yet they openly and audibly reject God and his ways (21:14), denying that there is any benefit to be gained from serving God!

21:16 (NASB)
Behold, their prosperity is not in their hand;
    The counsel of the wicked is far from me.

Verse 16 expresses Job's conclusion about such wickedness and his repudiation of it. He says that the prosperity of the wicked is not the result of their

own 'hand' — that is, what they can acquire or retain. The implication is that it is God who provides it
and allows them to keep it. But even though Job has
been deprived of what the wicked still enjoy, he will
not endorse their impious thinking, speech or conduct. In this he is maintaining his integrity.

'How often is it that the lamp of the wicked is put out?' (21:17-26)

21:17,19-20
How often is it that the lamp of the wicked is put out?
    That their calamity comes upon them?
    That God distributes pains in his anger? ...
You say, 'God stores up their iniquity for their children.'
    Let him pay it out to them, that they may know it.
Let their own eyes see their destruction,
    and let them drink of the wrath of the Almighty.

Job pursues his point further in this section by
pointing out what does *not* happen to the wicked.
Bildad had asserted that the 'light of the wicked is
put out' (see 18:5) and Zophar had declared that the
prosperity of the wicked would be short-lived (see
20:5). But Job challenges their universal dictum with
the words: **'How often?'** It is far more often the case
that God does not pour out his wrath upon them,
which they so plainly deserve.

At this point he anticipates a reply that the
Friends would make, or perhaps had already made
(see **'You say'** in verses 19,28), namely that God
stores up his wrath for their children. But, using the
Friends' cardinal principle that God always deals
justly with the unjust, Job claims that to speak of
their children being judged in their place is to evade
the issue. It is those who have done the deed who
should reap its consequences because in the grave

the wicked will not know what happens on earth
(21:19-21). If the Friends' evasion were to be correct,
then the wicked would never bear their due punishment. How can that be 'just' justice?

Job is aware, however, that God's ways are beyond
human knowing. Looking at people's lives and circumstances with merely an outward eye and from an
earthly perspective will reveal many inequalities
(21:23-25). But, whatever a life has been, it is ended
in death — however that death may come (see 21:26).
Given such mysteries, Job asks whether it is not wise
to acknowledge that God knows most and he does
what he deems right and best (21:22), instead of
trying to pry into his thoughts, or, what is worse,
thinking that one knows the 'whys and wherefores' of
his ways.

'I know your schemes to wrong me' (21:27-34)

21:27,29-30
Behold, I know your thoughts,
    and your schemes to wrong me...
Have you not asked those who travel the roads,
    and do you not accept their testimony,
that the evil man is spared in the day of calamity,
    that he is rescued in the day of wrath?

Job does not lose the force of his argument when he
comes to his conclusion.

The central point in this conclusion is put in the
form of a question in verse 29. They have claimed to
have been observers of life and learners from the
wise, but Job is now confident enough to challenge
their claim and to ask whether they had in fact
sought information from others as they had claimed.
It is his view that they are trying to frame him by
means of a partial, or slanted, interpretation of the

adversities that have befallen him (21:27). The truth
is rather that the wicked may not be judged *in this
life*. Here he may be buried with honours by many
who will follow in his wake, just as he was preceded
by others like him (see 21:32-33). That being so, how
empty and comfortless are the falsehoods uttered by
the Friends! (21:34).

Job is triumphing in faith and the facts are on his
side.

'There is no end to your iniquities' (Job 22:1-30)

In this opening speech of the third cycle Eliphaz continues to sound the same notes as he and the Friends had done before. He speaks of the judgement and mercy of God, seeing the former clearly manifested in Job's present condition, while the latter will only become evident if he repents.

'Is not your evil abundant?' (22:1-20)

22:3-5
Is it any pleasure to the Almighty if you are in the right,
    or is it gain to him if you make your ways blameless?
Is it for your fear of him that he reproves you
    and enters into judgement with you?
Is not your evil abundant?
    There is no end to your iniquities.

Convinced that the only possible explanation of Job's condition and circumstances is that he has sinned, Eliphaz opens with a series of rhetorical questions that attack Job's confidence. He asserts that Job is only serving his own interests by maintaining his spiritual integrity and that he is not advancing God's glory in any way (22:2-3). What is more, his claimed integrity cannot be genuine because God is reproving him (22:4-5). Eliphaz browbeats Job and baits him sarcastically.

Job's piety is therefore no good to either God or
man! That is what Eliphaz states explicitly (22:2-5)
and then expands on (22:6-20). He begins with the
many injustices that he claims Job has committed
against his own kin, against the weary and the
hungry, and against the widow and the orphan, the
most defenceless and needy in society. Job was **'the
man with power'** (22:8) but no principle. **'Therefore'**
darkness and flood, the portents of Sheol, justly
overwhelm him (22:10,11). These charges are of
course a total fabrication (see chapters 29 and 31)
but Eliphaz announces them as if he had personally
witnessed all these things taking place. This is in
such marked contrast to the theme and tone of his
first speech. It has Satan's trademark all over it. He
and his colleagues have accepted Satan's depiction of
Job, but Job will not accept their depiction of God
(which is in fact Satan's).

22:13-14
But you say, 'What does God know?
    Can he judge through the deep darkness?
Thick clouds veil him, so that he does not see,
    and he walks on the vault of heaven.'

But Eliphaz goes even further than denouncing Job
for his alleged shameful treatment of his fellow
human beings. He charges him with denying that
God knows and judges (22:13-14). Using the 'distance' between God and man, and the fact that God
lives above the clouds and darkness that sweep the
skies, he represents Job as having derided the possibility that God could see what transpires on earth so
as to make a judgement about it. But this is a misin-
terpretation of what Job has just said about the
wicked not always being punished in this life. Job
was not denying that God **'does ... know'** and will
ultimately **'judge'**, but was stating that, for reasons

best known to him, God does not act as instant-aneously and universally as the Friends claim. Their thesis does not therefore cover Job's particular case, because if the wicked are not always judged pound for pound in this life, then there is at the very least the possibility that Job's sufferings may not be due to his being a hypocrite. Their theory of retribution does not apply everywhere and to everyone at all times. But the link between suffering and sin is so firmly entrenched in the mind of Eliphaz that he connects Job with notorious sinners in the past (22:15-17) in what could well be a reference to the state of people before the Flood.

So far it might seem as though Eliphaz has not heard anything Job has said. But that is not the case. In verse 18 he endorses Job's point that God does prosper the wicked, but he has already declared that this is only for a time (22:16). He then echoes Job's words that 'The counsel of the wicked is far from me' (see 21:16), but only in order to distance himself both from the wicked and from Job. Eliphaz is again saying that Job is in the same category as the wicked in spite of his protestations to the contrary. But Eliphaz is being self-righteous as he proceeds to describe the reaction of **'the righteous'** to the judgement of the wicked, including himself in the former group while putting Job in the latter! (22:19-20).

'Agree with God, and be at peace; thereby good will come to you' (22:21-30)

22:21-25
Agree with God, and be at peace;
    thereby good will come to you.
Receive instruction from his mouth,
    and lay up his words in your heart.
If you return to the Almighty you will be built up,

if you remove injustice far from your tents,
if you lay gold in the dust,
    and gold of Ophir among the stones of the torrent bed,
then the Almighty will be your gold
    and your precious silver.

Although Eliphaz has become unscrupulous as well
as insensitive, he still holds out in the most wonderful terms the possibility of restoration for Job. There
is an echo of his opening remarks (see 22:3) in verse
23 by virtue of his repetition of the same name for
God. He says that, although Job's professed righteousness does not advance God's glory, a new submission to God will bring benefit to Job, and Eliphaz
then proceeds to describe the form that such submission and benefit will take. The submission is
described in terms of receiving God's disciplinary
word (22:22) and the setting aside of all that contradicts it, perhaps greed in the light of the reference to
gold and silver that follows. Such humility is costly,
and so Eliphaz depicts it by means of gold being
disdained and laid in dust and water — and the
finest gold of Ophir at that! The benefit is that the
Almighty will be to Job all that gold and silver can
procure, and more besides. (The name Eliphaz
means, 'My God is pure gold.')

Job will be **'built up'** (22:23) — that is, restored —
in every way. First, his fellowship with God will be
renewed. Prayer will be heard and answered; vows
will be paid (22:27). This implies that Job will no
longer be an outcast on the ash heap. Secondly, his
position in society will be restored. He will issue legal
verdicts and they will be approved and brought to
fruition (22:28). Thirdly, his spiritual usefulness will
be renewed as he instructs and encourages others in
their affliction (22:29-30), whether or not they are
suffering as he had.

While these words of Eliphaz should be connected initially with his reply to Job (and Job's subsequent recovery), they should not be limited to that context. We saw earlier that some words of Eliphaz are quoted in the New Testament and that they are given a larger function there. That is not the case with anything that Bildad and Zophar say, though that does not mean that their words are in no way edifying. But it indicates that Eliphaz was much better than they, and yet he needed to be prayed for too. These words in 22:21-30 should be preached through a New Testament filter, and they can be. They are full of the amazing kindness of the Lord to a penitent sinner.

'Who will prove me a liar?'
(Job 23:1 – 24:25)

Job ignores the wonderful prospect that Eliphaz holds out to him because it rests on the condition that he must repent of his many great sins and submit to God. Job replies to Eliphaz in two ways. First, demonstrating his piety, he seeks God as a plaintiff, or suppliant, but not as a penitent (23:1-17). Secondly, he explores the apparent strangeness of God's ways (24:1-25). He is perplexed, first by God's ways with the righteous — namely himself — and then by God's ways with the wicked.

'Oh that I knew where I might find him!' (23:1-17)

23:2-7
Today also my complaint is bitter;
    my hand is heavy on account of my groaning.
Oh, that I knew where I might find him,
    that I might come even to his seat!
I would lay my case before him
    and fill my mouth with arguments.
I would know what he would answer me,
    and understand what he would say to me.
Would he contend with me in the greatness of his power?
    No, he would pay attention to me.
There an upright man could argue with him,
    and I would be acquitted for ever by my judge.

In Job's speeches after chapter 19 we do not find him addressing God directly as he did before. Instead of accusing God, he talks about him, but he does so with complaints. In 23:2, for example, he does not refer to God at all, but what he says must include God's dealings with him. He is describing how his trouble feels to him. It is bitter and it is burdensome — so much so that he takes up a lament. He no longer has the light and strength that were his at the end of chapter 19, but this does not mean that his testimony there amounts to nothing. It is just that his sorrow and grief have eclipsed his joys and triumphs.

His desire is to find God again, but not just to find him somewhere, but specifically at his **'seat'** — that is to say, at his throne (23:3). This is because he has a case that must be settled, one way or the other. Job will present it and he will listen to what God has to say by way of reply. It is important to note that Job does not stand in dread of such an encounter any more, nor does he ask for someone to make God 'bearable'. That is now settled for Job, as he knows he has an Advocate, and so he specifically excludes the possibility that God would terrify him or be unjust to him (23:6-7). On the contrary, Job expects attention to be paid to him, and to be vindicated.

23:8,10
Behold, I go forwards, but he is not there,
    and backwards, but I do not perceive him…
But he knows the way that I take;
    when he has tried me, I shall come out as gold.

But where might such a hearing take place? Here Job knows that he has immense problems because God is as invisible to him as his ways are inscrutable (23:8-9). God is simply inaccessible to him, but he is not without all hope because he knows that God knows where he is and what he is doing (23:10). He also knows that God is refining him, a process that by definition cannot go on for ever (23:10). Job is therefore determined to persevere in obedience to God's commands, which he delights in and which sustain him (23:11-12). God can therefore find Job with great ease whenever he wants to, but Job has no hope of forcing God to change his purpose.

Finally, in verses 15-17, Job feels overawed but not cowed. He will not give up his case or hope although his frailty disables him. He will continue to trust.

Who will prove me a liar? (24:1-25)

24:1
Why are not times of judgement kept by the Almighty,
    and why do those who know him never see his days?

Eliphaz had sidestepped Job's argument that the wicked are not always judged (see chapter 21). Realizing that this issue is fatal to the Friends' case against him, Job now restates it, and he does so at some length and with considerable vigour. He begins by asking why the righteous do not see days of divine judgement following inexorably on from days of human wickedness (24:1). He expands this point in two stages. First, he describes the wicked and their treatment of the poor (see 24:2-8,9-12) and in the remainder of the chapter points out that the wicked are not singled out for judgement.

'Yet God charges no one with wrong' (24:2-12)

24:12
From out of the city the dying groan,
    and the soul of the wounded cries for help;
      yet God charges no one with wrong.

In this little section we have an account of 'man's inhumanity to man', twice over! First, Job describes those who act in a lawless and tyrannical manner (24:1-4). They ignore boundary markers and appropriate others' land (cf. Deut. 19:14; 27:17). They seize livestock, and even the last defence of the weakest against disaster, and they deprive the needy of the protection of the law courts. He then describes the effects of such inhumanity (24:5-8). The poor live in the desert and subsist on animal fodder (24:5-6). Deprived of outer clothing, they are exposed to cold, wind and rain (24:7-8; cf. Deut. 24:10-15).

Verses 9-12 present a second catalogue of such unfeeling cruelty. The fatherless infant is seized (presumably for slavery) and the poor man is made to serve as a forced labourer by taking away his outer garment as a pledge — that is, promising to return it to him at the end of the day's work in the fields or at the wine or oil press. The victims are reduced to the most heartfelt groans for help — but God does not intervene immediately on their behalf and against the wicked!

'They are ... gathered up like all others' (24:13- 25)

24:22,24-25
Yet God prolongs the life of the mighty by his power;
   they rise up when they despair of life....
They are exalted a little while, and then are gone;
   they are brought low and gathered up like all others,
   they are cut off like the ears of the corn.
If it is not so, who will prove me a liar
   and show that there is nothing in what I say?

Job here lists further sins that the wicked perpetrate, all of which are carried out under cover of darkness. There is the murderer (24:14), who is also a thief. Then there is the adulterer (24:15), who, not content with the cover of darkness, disguises his face. The light is hated and feared. 'You shall not commit murder', 'You shall not commit adultery,' 'You shall not steal' and 'You shall not covet' (see Exod. 20:13-15,17) are all treated with disdain.

Verses 18-24 do present several difficulties. Chief among them is the fact that they seem to contain two differing accounts of the fate of the wicked. In verses 18-20 a swift judgement is described, whereas in verses 21-24 their life is prolonged, and even prospered — and that by God. The simplest solution of this question is to read the first of these accounts as a summary of the view of the Friends, which Job proceeds to debunk most effectively. The ESV therefore inserts the words 'You say', as it does in 21:19 (but not in 21:28, where the words are found in the original text).

Reading the text in this way is in keeping with the drift of the whole chapter because Job is here subjecting the Friends' argument to thorough scrutiny. It also involves making no amendment to the text, for there are no marks of direct speech in Hebrew, and a conversation is proceeding in which the Friends would have known what Job was doing. The problem is ours rather than theirs!

In no uncertain terms Job here throws down the gauntlet to his friends. He invites them to contradict what he has said by showing that his claim and the facts he has cited in support of it are not true.

The greatness of God
(Job 25:1 – 26:14)

A careful reading of both these chapters together will show that the greatness of God is at the heart of what they contain. This is so in spite of the fact that they record speeches by two different speakers, Bildad and Job. We shall consider them in turn.

'Behold man is a maggot' (25:1-6)

25:2,5-6
Dominion and fear are with God;
   he makes peace in his high heaven...
Behold, even the moon is not bright,
   and the stars are not pure in his eyes;
how much less man, who is a maggot,
   and the son of man, who is a worm!

This is Bildad's last speech and in it he has nothing new to say! It has all been said before. Two things, however, can be said for it. The first is that it is short (mercifully so from Job's point of view!) and, secondly, it terminates the Friends' participation in the debate in a definitive way. It is therefore not pointless in the narrative because it indicates that the Friends' argument has failed and Job has won the debate — and so Satan has been vanquished and God glorified.

The general claims that Bildad makes for God are true. God does rule above, and numberless hosts of heavenly creatures do hold him in reverence and obey his will, and as a result peace reigns among them (25:2-3). But Bildad had one eye on Job in making these remarks because the opposite state of affairs has been going on here on earth! Job has created an unholy hubbub by contesting God's will as expressed by his servants (that is the Friends)! The result is that Job is not only sinful; he is also impudent. He is a frail man, 'born of a woman' (see 14:1). If the moon and the stars that shine so brightly in the eastern sky are not pure in comparison with God's light, much less is man, who is a **'maggot'** (25:5-6). How dare **'a worm'** (that is, Job) challenge God?

To judge from what Bildad says, one would think that he had not heard Job declare that the wicked are *not* immediately judged by God. He ignores that telling fact, and does so completely. He refuses to face up to Job's claim that he is not wicked even though he is suffering so horribly, and to explore how that might relate to the divine majesty and the fact of universal sinfulness. Bildad is the classical theorist; he deals in generalities. He refuses to face facts or listen to objections. And he is pompous to boot, because all he has to say is to repeat what Eliphaz had already said earlier (see 4:17; 15:14) and what Job had also acknowledged (9:2; 14:4). He did not even have Zophar's sense to say nothing when he had nothing really to say.

Bildad, then, has said his piece and, even though its implication for Job is not true, instruction or benefit may be derived from it by later generations. Peace does reign where sin is absent and where God's righteous will is carried out by way of obedience (25:1-3). It is Satan who creates hubbub by misrepresenting man to God, as in the Prologue, and God to man and man to man, as in the chapters that follow. He does this in the world and in the church. But such nefarious activity will be brought to an end (see chapter 42) and heaven will be a world of peace and righteousness between God and human beings through Jesus Christ.

'Behold the outskirts of his ways' (26:1-14)

Job here silences Bildad (and by implication his friends as well) by answering him in his own coin and by speaking about God in terms that exceed those that Bildad has used. He beats Bildad in theology as well as anthropology.

'Whose breath has come out from you?' (26:1-4)

26:4
With whose help have you uttered words,
    and whose breath has come out from you?

What a thing to say! It is as if Job has at last been able to smell the foul breath of the old dragon on the lips of Bildad (and the same would go for Eliphaz and Zophar), and so to realize that they are not speaking for God. But of course that is not the case. Job is probably referring to the fact that Bildad is merely repeating what Eliphaz had said. Job is therefore being heavily sarcastic. Even so, a touch of irony may be detected in his remark. He mocks all the attempts that have been made by means of **'wisdom'** and **'sound knowledge'** to help him — someone who **'has no power'** and **'no wisdom'**! (26:2-3). The wisdom that the Friends have brought to Job is no wisdom at all in Job's estimate.

'How small a whisper do we hear of him!' (26:5-14)

Job now proceeds to speak about God, but his view of God is greater than that of his friends in two important respects: first, with regard to the scope of God's activity; and, secondly, with reference to the character of his self-revelation. All the statements that follow must be considered in the setting of this noble and true view of God because they do contain several references to Canaanite mythology.

I. The scope of God's sovereignty

26:5-6
The dead tremble
    under the waters and their inhabitants.
Sheol is naked before God,
    and Abaddon has no covering.

Bildad had spoken about the powerful reign of God over the heavenly beings in God's immediate presence and court (cf. 1:6-12; 2:1-6; 5:1). Job does not disagree with this but he includes more, much more, in his summary of who are God's subjects. Job speaks of God's presence and activity in the realm of the dead (see 26:5-6) and in the whole of created reality (see 26:7-13).

The question that arises here is whether Job is using language from Canaanite mythology for effect, or whether he is actually endorsing its view of the origin and structure of the world. This has been discussed in the introduction (see pages 33-36) and we need not go over the ground again. What we shall do is to examine the text.

What must be noted and given full weight is that there is a reference to God in every stanza from verse 8 to verse 13. It is therefore clear that, even if Job were in any sense referring to the views of his day, he is clearly asserting that it is God, and *not* the Canaanite deities, who is responsible for things as they are. Job is a monotheist who believes that God is Creator and Ruler of all that he has made. He is talking about God throughout. The question that arises for us is related more to how we understand his words than to what they actually meant for Job.

With regard to the 'underworld', the important terms to note are the words **'dead'**, **'tremble'**, **'Sheol'** and **'Abaddon'**. The word for **'the dead'** is the term *'rephaim'* (see, for example, Gen. 14:5; 15:20) which was used in Ugaritic not only to describe divine beings but also humans who, in some respect or other, were 'larger than life'. This means that verse 5 does not have to refer to divine beings at all. To think of it as applying to mortals who are greater than ordinary, run-of-the-mill humans would satisfy the requirements both of the text and the larger point that is being made, which is that such great ones are not beyond the powerful reach of God, even when they are no longer in the realm of the terrestrial. Indeed, they are said to **'tremble'** before God's holiness and power. **'Abaddon'** is a poetic synonym for Sheol (see 28:22; 31:12; Ps 88:11; Prov. 15:11; 27:20).

The wonderful variety in this world is then described and brought within the scope of God's rule. Skies, earth, clouds, moon, waters, light, darkness, mountains, sea and heavens are all within his creative work and providential activity. God's power in creating the very structure of the universe (26:7-10) and his providential activity in ruling the forces of nature are asserted. The value of this emphasis is that by means of it Job is supporting the point that he has made, which is that God is not removed from the (grim) reality and the variety of life on earth although he is transcendent.

II. The character of God's self-revelation

26:14
Behold, these are but the outskirts of his ways,
    and how small a whisper do we hear of him!
    But the thunder of his power who can understand?

Bildad had spoken as one who knew that the 'distance' between God and man was greater than that between the moon and a maggot (see 25:5-6) and that God, who is 'light', was always right, while man 'born of woman' could never be. Subject closed! But Job did not need to be taught that. These things were linchpins of his theology too, but, by the same token, he knew that God was greater than his theology — and of course than that of Bildad, Eliphaz and Zophar. He knew that there was a self-limitation in God's self-revelation in creation and providence. Observable phenomena and their processes were merely **'the outskirts'**, or 'edges', **'of [God's] ways'** (26:14), like a small whisper in comparison with **'the thunder of his power'**.

By this statement Job seems to indicate that God will reveal more of himself, beyond what he currently knows. What would that be like? Job was to find out — and so would the Friends. A 'new thing' was being done, and more light was needed in order to provide some explanation for it. God did have an answer for Job's predicament!

4.
Job continues his discourse
(Job 27:1 – 28:28)

In order to consider chapter 27, which is a continuation of Job's reply to Bildad, we must give attention
to two matters. First, there are some connections
between it and the four chapters that follow up to
chapter 31 that we need to note; and, secondly, there
are some difficulties in it that are best dealt with in
advance.

The connections

Speeches abound in the earlier part of Job, but not
one of them has been introduced with the words,
'again took up his discourse' (27:1; see also 29:1).
Instead what we have is 'answered and said' (see
chapters 4-26). Chapters 27 and 29 are different in
this respect and, while that change may seem to be
minimal, it is noteworthy for two reasons:

1. It indicates that the statement-response
pattern that is of the essence of debate has now
come to an end. The debate between Job and
the Friends has been concluded, and Job is the
victor. The brevity of Bildad's speech in chapter
25 points in this direction and the silence of

Zophar shows this to be the case. Job holds centre stage. He is the last man speaking.

2. It also indicates that Job still has more that he wants to say. He wants to make a full statement, rather than just reply to one or more previous speakers. He therefore seizes on Zophar's non-intervention to begin to do so. The repetition of 27:1 in 29:1 makes clear that he does so in two phases. Including chapter 28 for the moment, this layout means that there are two speeches in the section from chapters 27-31, and not five, as might be suggested by the number of the chapters.

The difficulties

Job describes the fate of the wicked in 27:7-23. But whether it was actually he who did so is a matter that has long been debated. Many have concluded that the sentiments contained in these verses prove that he could not have been the speaker. They are regarded as more suitable to one or other of the Friends. Other parts of this section of *Job* have been included in this discussion as well — for example, the brevity of Bildad's last speech and the silence of Zophar. It has been argued that this whole section of *Job* needs to be reconstructed, and several revisions of the text have been proposed. Some have argued that these verses should be appended to Bildad's speech; others that they should be regarded as the 'missing' speech of Zophar. (In the multitude of theories wisdom is often conspicuous by its absence!)

There are two general remarks that I want to make by way of reply to this proposed relocation of material that in my opinion is quite unnecessary:

1. There is no version of *Job* extant, in Hebrew or any other language, that locates 27:7-23 in any other place. The task is therefore to try to do justice to the text as we have it, and not to speculate.

2. It is much easier to explain the relative brevity of Bildad and the silence of Zophar *at this juncture of the narrative* than it would be to explain what would be a seriously truncated reply of Job if only 27:1-6 were to be his. (Those who argue for a restructuring of the text do not see chapter 28 as being part of Job's speech, as we shall see later.)

I would therefore argue for the retention of these verses in their present place and also for recognition of them as words of Job. But doing this presents the challenge as to how these words should be understood in relation both to him and to what he has been saying. By way of initial response to that task, which will be pursued further by means of the exposition, I would offer the following considerations:

1. In 27:11 the word **'you'** is in the plural. Job is here speaking to his Friends. It would need to be in the singular if either Bildad or Zophar were addressing Job. There is no textual support anywhere for changing this plural pronoun into a singular one.

2. What Job goes on to say about God and the wicked — namely, that the wicked will be punished — is something that he has never denied. To regard his earlier statement that God 'destroys both the blameless and the wicked' as a contradiction of what he now says is to fail to see that 9:22 is a cry of anguish, and not a thoughtful conclusion and conviction.

3. What he is going to **'teach'** the Friends is something about the **'hand'** of God which they have witnessed but not appreciated (27:11-12). While 'hand' can be a synonym for God's 'power', it also describes his presence and dealings — that is, the way in which he administers affairs. It is to be connected with his providence, which is pervaded by mystery, as Job had intimated at the end of chapter 26 and as he will show in what he says about the wisdom of God in chapter 28.

We shall now consider this speech in its obvious parts.

'I hold fast my righteousness and will not let it go'
(Job 27:1-23)

'My lips will not speak falsehood' (27:1-6)

27:2,4-6
As God lives, who has taken away my right,
    and the Almighty, who has made my soul bitter ...
my lips will not speak falsehood,
    and my tongue will not utter deceit.
Far be it from me to say that you are right;
    till I die I will not put away my integrity from me.
I hold fast my righteousness and will not let it go;
    my heart does not reproach me for any of my days.

The words quoted above declare that Job is committed to telling the truth as it is (or as he sees it)[1] about God, the Friends and himself. This means that Job is never going to say that he is in the wrong, although this means not only declaring that the Friends are not right (27:5), but also that that God is not in the right either (27:2). His friends have put him in the wrong and God has taken away his right — that is, has denied him a fair trial (27:2) — and that is what he intends to say until he dies (27:5).

This little section is full of legal language and an attempt has been made to point this out in what has just been said by means of the expression 'in the right'. Job has been seeking justice in a world that he perceives to be in the hand of the wicked. This being so, it is worth noting that he does not deny that God exists, or suggest that he has ceased to be powerful. Instead he has affirmed that God lives (see 19:25) and that he is still omnipotent (27:2). But this only accentuates his problem because it entails the fact, the staggering but undeniable fact, that such a God has become, or is being, unjust too. (What a comfort it is to us to know that Satan is such a deceiver that he will even make it seem that God is like him — and all because he has totally failed in his attempt to make himself God!)

But there is one more matter to note, and it concerns the fact that Job takes an oath in these verses. He does so because he is determined to maintain his own dignity and integrity. His dignity is not self-importance. It is bound up with his awareness of having been created and of his being sustained, albeit in his severely diminished circumstances (27:2-3). The life that he has is therefore life from God — and we may add that he only has it because God is preserving it! Conscious therefore that his breath is as sacred as God's own existence, he determines to use his precious last gasp in order to maintain his integrity. He will only say what is right, and that means affirming that he has peace of conscience. He knows that he has not been wicked, in spite of what others claim and what his sufferings may seem to prove. He will not give in or go quietly. This indomitable spirit is a fruit of the life with God that he had formerly enjoyed.

'Let my enemy be as the wicked' (27:7- 23)

27:7
Let my enemy be as the wicked,
>   and let him who rises up against me be as the
>   unrighteous.

In the opening part of this section (27:7-10) there are two important textual features to comment on. The first is that in these verses Job uses the singular when speaking of his **'enemy'**, or the one who **'rises up against'** him, whereas verses 11 and 12 are in the plural. The use of the singular raises a question. Who is Job thinking of as his **'enemy'**? But perhaps this is an inappropriate question, because the literary form of these words (and that is the second feature to note) resembles another kind of oath, namely a curse. There are similarities here with the imprecatory psalms. If we allow form to determine meaning, then the identity of the 'enemy' is immaterial. Job is describing *all* enmity, rather than *an* enemy.

Job describes this 'enemy' as someone who **'rises up against'** him (27:7) — that is, a witness for the prosecution in a court of law (cf. 19:25) — but also as someone who is **'godless'**, or 'profane' (27:8). This fits the Friends, who have accused him and who have never once called on God for help themselves. They are combined into one because of their common enmity. It is therefore they whom Job is thinking of. But, equally, Job is speaking more wisely than he knows and, just as the Friends have spoken for Satan, so now Job's words may be directed against him as well as against them. This is in keeping with the curses in the imprecatory psalms, which express a desire for God's (not the psalmist's) judgement on all the wicked and the 'evil one' (cf. Matt. 6:13). It is part of what is meant by the petitions:

Hallowed be your name.
Your kingdom come;
your will be done, on earth as it is in heaven.

Such a desire will not go unheard or unanswered!

27:11
I will teach you concerning the hand of God;
    what is with the Almighty I will not conceal.

But Job does not only denounce; he also instructs. His statement to the Friends (27:11-12) resembles Eliphaz' counsel to him (see 22:22). It is also a most important preface to his description of the impending fate of the **'wicked man'** (27:13-23) and to the poem on wisdom and its place in the narrative. All that follows is a description of what he calls **'the hand of God'** (27:11), which refers not only to God's power in acting, but also to his wisdom in doing so.

In what he says about the wicked (note that Job includes the word **'oppressors'** as well in verse 13), Job turns his Friends' statements that they have uttered against him back on them. He is saying that the circumstances that they have observed in his life, which they have pointed out to him as proof positive of his wickedness, may yet happen to them because they surely will to all the wicked. That is the **'portion'** of the wicked (27:13); it is part of sin's wages (Rom. 6.23).

The calamities that are listed (27:14-23) make up a composite picture. They are typical of Job's times and ours — war (**'the sword'**); want (not having enough bread) and woe (**'the pestilence'**) — but are not to be understood as each occurring in sequence to a manifestly wicked person. Such calamities do remove the wicked from the earth, and the bereaved mothers and widows strangely do not weep (27:15). His treasures will be plundered and be possessed by better men; his house, which would hardly resemble a shed (27:18), is swept away like a spider's web. Everything is suddenly removed, and so is he by whirlwind and flood. He flees while others (perhaps the reference is to God) clap their hands in anger (see Num. 24:10) and hiss in horror (Jer. 49:17). That is the portion God allots to those who oppress the righteous.

Where can wisdom be found?
(Job 28:1-28)

This chapter is generally lauded as a wonderful piece of poetry, and so it is, in language, structure and theme. But many regard it as having no point of contact with the debate and none with reference to its resolution, and they treat it accordingly. Indeed, they often deny that it has any connection with Job himself and put it into the mouth of one or other of the Friends, or consider it to be a comment made by the narrator.

It has already been indicated that a different view of this chapter is taken in this commentary and the time has now come to support that position and work it out. Two general facts are worth mentioning at the outset. First, this chapter is not found in any other place in any of the extant versions of *Job* and it is not omitted from any of them either. Its position in the text of *Job* is therefore secure. Secondly, it is worth remembering that Job and the Friends are all wise men and in what they have said to each other they have all spoken in the name of wisdom. The appearance of a poem on wisdom is therefore not alien to the theme and character of the book. In the light of these considerations we may well question whether the prevailing consensus about this poem should be given as much credence as it is in many quarters.

Moving on now to the suggestion that this poem is to be traced to the author of the book, we need to take into account two facts. The first is that there is no preface attached to it, indicating a different speaker from the passages which precede or follow it. That is the pattern which the author follows from as far back as chapter 3 and which he perpetuates until chapter 42. Speech follows speech with only one interruption which the author points out, and that is the second fact which should be noted. At the beginning of chapter 32 there is an interjection by the author, but it is in prose, not poetry. Given this, it would be strange if the narrator included a poem of his own in one of Job's speeches in order to provide some disengagement between Job and the Friends and also some relief for the reader. I regard such thinking as unnecessary, given the significance of Job's testimony in chapter 19:25-27, which contributes towards the mood change perceived in this speech.

Finally, as we have noted earlier, Job has indicated to his friends that he is about to instruct them in the 'hand of God' (see 27:11). He begins to do that in the latter part of chapter 27 and it continues in chapter 28. The **'hand of God'** is a metaphor for God's power or authority, and especially so when it is bracketed with the adjective 'right' (for example, in Ps. 110:1,5). But this expression designates more than authority. Just as hands are for doing things, so the Lord's (right) hand describes his activity on earth as well as his authority (as in Ps. 118:15-16). His acts are not only strong; they are also wise. That is what Job intends to talk about to his friends, and he does so in this wonderful poem about the wise working of God.

But is this poem about God? To many it seems as though it is about the wonders that human beings accomplish. But that is a serious misreading of the poem, the point of which lies in what humans fail to discover, in spite of all their explorations and achievements, namely true wisdom. What Job is saying is that man is totally dependent on God for wisdom, and that truth is relevant both to Job's predicament and to the explanations of it that he and the Friends have advanced.

We shall now consider the content of this poem. Its structure is fairly obvious. It is divided into three parts by the question posed in verse 12 and repeated in verse 20: 'Where does wisdom come from?' An introductory section describes its 'place' (28:1-11); the next section describes its price (28:12-20) and finally the path to it is declared.

The place of wisdom (28:1-11)

28:1,3-4,10
Surely there is a mine for silver,
    and a place for gold that they refine…
Man puts an end to darkness
    and searches out to the farthest limit
    the ore in gloom and deep darkness.
He opens shafts in a valley away from where anyone lives,
    they are forgotten by travellers;
    they hang in the air, far away from mankind; they swing to
        and fro…
He cuts out channels in the rocks,
    and his eye sees every precious thing.

The point of these word pictures is to show by contrast that man cannot find the place where wisdom dwells. The lengths to which human beings will go in order to find what is precious and useful are presented by referring to the enterprise of mining. Just as human effort expended on the earth produces bread (28:5), so minerals and metals are available below ground to those who search for them.[2] But great effort is required in order to obtain these and a great risk is incurred in doing so. In localities where these minerals are not near the surface of the ground, shafts are sunk into the solid earth (28:4), channels are cut in subterranean rock (28:10) and streams in the water table are dammed up (28:11). Darkness is overcome and danger is encountered in uninhabited and uninhabitable places (28:4). Alone, miners swing to and fro and dig for such minerals, while above ground there are those who have the skill to refine what is precious and smelt what is useful (28:1). Such discoveries indicate man's superiority to the falcon and the lion, those creatures of air and land, renowned for keenness of sight and fierceness respectively (28:7-8). Man goes where the one has not seen and the other has not trod — but he does not find wisdom.

The price of wisdom (28:12-22)

28:12-14
But where shall wisdom be found?
    And where is the place of understanding?
Man does not know its worth,
    and it is not found in the land of the living.
The deep says, 'It is not in me',
    and the sea says, 'It is not with me.'

28:20
From where, then, does wisdom come?
    And where is the place of understanding?

So there is something that the most intrepid of explorers and the most skilful of engineers cannot lay their hands on. Human beings desire it, but they do not know how precious it is. Its worth exceeds their computation, just as the way to it is beyond their understanding (28:13). Job then reviews places where mining operations were carried on and the precious stones that were discovered. There is Ophir, with its fine gold; the sea, with its coral and pearls; and Ethiopia, with its topaz (28:16-19). It is hidden from man and beast. Its place is neither on earth nor in the sea (28:14), nor is it in the realm of the dead (28:22). Its price exceeds the value of each of the precious stones and of all of them put together. Human beings could not buy it even if it could be found. There is a universal desire for it, coupled with an awareness that it exists — but where is it?

The path to wisdom (28:23-28)

28:23-24,28
God understands the way to it,
    and he knows its place.
For he looks to the ends of the earth
    and sees everything under the heavens...
And he said to man,
 'Behold, the fear of the Lord, that is wisdom,
    and to turn away from evil is understanding.'

Wisdom is therefore beyond human reach and knowledge, in spite of the traces of it evident in the resources of land, sea and air and in the creatures, notably in man himself. It eludes all man's efforts and skills to find it. It is **'wisdom'** or **'understanding'** (28:12), a couplet that is the hallmark of wisdom literature (see Prov. 1:2).

But God knows **'the way to its place'**. This is because he lives with it, or rather it lives with him. He knows it because he sees it; he does not have to search for it. He himself is its 'place' (see Prov. 8:12-21). He knows it because he **'looks to the ends of the earth and sees everything under the heavens'**, and also because of what he does, or has done, in the universe that he has made. He weighs the wind and measures the waters; he decrees the rain and directs the lightning (28:24-26), both samples of his power and wisdom. He is the wise Lord (28:28) — that is, the Ruler of all, assigning everything that he has made its place and function in his world. Wisdom is therefore what he sees and what he does.

But wisdom is also what the Lord says (28:28), and that is the only way in which man can find it. Man gains wisdom by hearing what the God who sees and rules everything is pleased to tell him in order that he might know and do it. Reverence (**'the fear of the Lord'**) and obedience (**'to turn away from evil'**) is man's highest wisdom.

This closing statement is the climax of this wonderful poem. It is no trite conclusion. But it is not the climax of the story in the book. The Friends need to recognize their distorted presentation of the Lord's power and wisdom — and so does Job, in spite of what he says! Here he speaks of the Lord who is great; at the end of the book he meets with the LORD who is also gracious. The wisdom of God is found in the Lord Jesus Christ and in him crucified!

5. Job's final defence

(Job 29:1 – 31:40)

This section comprises three chapters but only one speech. It is Job's last and it is a real *tour de force*. It paves the way for the speeches of Elihu and then those of the Lord, just as Job's curse-lament in chapter 3 initiated the speeches of the Friends and the debate that followed. It has been suggested that it was as a result of Job's magnificent testimony in chapter 19 and the argument that he was able to develop that the Friends have less and less to say. But after his remarks in chapter 31 it is Job who has nothing more to say!

This final speech is made up of three parts which, happily, coincide with the chapter divisions in the English text. Job begins with a review of what his life was like before any calamity befell him and he continues with a lament that it has become so different, notes that have been sounded by him before, although not at such length. They are struck up again, as the prelude to its third part, and that is what makes this speech unique.

What is so special about chapter 31? It is that, having failed in his requests to obtain a hearing of his case from God, he forces the issue by submitting a protestation of innocence. He does the equivalent of appearing before the bar and asking for legal redress — or conviction. As a former judge, he was well aware that this was how those who had been falsely accused would proceed in law (see Luke 18:2-3), and so he now becomes the plaintiff and demands that the judge should adjudicate his claim to innocence. But it is at God's bar that he is appearing and not that of his peers! This is a most dangerous thing to do. It is equally breathtaking whether it is viewed as arrogant or confident. But is it wholly either? That question will be answered in the rest of the narrative. The closing comment of the inspired author, 'The words of Job are ended', is most significant.

Reference was made to some parts of this speech when we considered the opening verses of the first chapter of *Job*. That was necessary in order to gain some appreciation of the significance of Job's character and influence, which is summed up in the familiar words, 'blameless and upright, one who feared God and turned away from evil', which gave rise to God's delight in him and Satan's desire to destroy him. Now we must consider those manifestations of Job's integrity in their proper context, which is that of a legal suit. Job is making a deposition; he has (as he had just said) feared the Lord and turned from evil, and so he demands that he should be vindicated as an upright man. It is vital for all that follows that this new context should be noted and appreciated because it is one thing to demand a hearing from the judge, but it is another thing to put the judge in the dock, which is what Job does in effect here.

Review and lament
(Job 29:1 – 30:31)

'Oh that I were…!' (29:1-29)

29:2,4
Oh, that I were as in the months of old,
 as in the days when God watched over me …
as I was in my prime,
 when the friendship of God was upon my tent…!

Job here speaks of his **'prime'** — literally his 'days of autumn' (29:4). He is therefore using the analogy of harvest-time in order to describe the joy and plenty of days and months gone by. Those good old days still exist clearly in his memory although 'days of affliction' (see 30:27) have now come. Although he longs for their return, he seems able to recall those earlier days without recrimination and to acknowledge 'the LORD [who] gave' them to him. He refers to the light of God's favour (see Ps. 80:3) and friendship (contrast 19:19), which was seen in his home life as well as his role in the community (29:5-7). At home there was the delight of children and an abundance of the finest of fare and of riches. **'Butter'** (29:6; cf. 20:17) and **'oil'** point to the productivity of his animals and his land. He includes these 'home thoughts' again when later he speaks of his **'nest'** (29:18), a term that is used for a shelter in the ark and even in the temple of God (Ps. 84:3), as well as its more ordinary sense. God had cared for Job as he did for animals and for his pilgrim people on their way to Zion.

29:14
I put on righteousness, and it clothed me;
  my righteousness was like a robe and a turban.

What is really significant in this review is that Job gives much less attention to his domestic peace and bliss than to his energetic activity in society. Five verses are devoted to describing his life at home, as opposed to twenty about his social service! This is a prelude to his protestation in chapter 31, but clearly his piety had not been self-centred, as Satan had claimed! He speaks of the way in which he was respected by young and old alike (29:7-11) as he went to the gate in order to hear and determine disputes between the members of his community. He was respected in the public square (see 2 Chr. 32:6; Neh. 8:1) because of the **'righteousness'** and **'justice'** of his verdicts, which his ceremonial dress truly symbolized (29:14). Those whom he represented in law praised and blessed him. He investigated the cause of the stranger and defended the orphan and the widow, the poor and the weak against unrighteous predators whose power he opposed and broke (29:12-17). In his official duty he was not partial, and certainly not corruptible.

29:18-19
Then I thought, I shall die in my nest,
  and I shall multiply my days as the sand,
my roots spread out to the waters,
  with the dew all night on my branches.

So he thought that such an idyllic existence would continue through long life and that he would be constantly renewed as a tree is by unseen dew

(29:18; cf. 14:7-9; Ps.1:3) so that his influence would be like refreshing rain to others (29:23). His smile (29:24) brought a light into their lives. He was their chief, and his counsel gave both direction and comfort to a willing and submissive people. How impudent Satan was to touch him, and how cruel to send him such miserable comforters! Here is a searching example for ministers and elders — and also a salutary warning.

'But now ...' (30:1-31)

Having recalled God's goodness in the past, Job now takes up a lament, but not just to bewail his lot. He has an aim in doing this, and that is to demonstrate the greatness of the change that has come upon him so that God will appreciate its enormity! (30:19-23). He sets about this in two ways. First, he uses a word that stresses the fact of change, and he does so three times. The ESV renders it as **'but now'** (30:1) or **'and now'** (30:9,16), and either rendering is accurate. Secondly, he uses that word to introduce each section of his lament, which contains a number of word pictures from his present circumstances. He therefore builds up a picture for effect and we shall follow its divisions.

1. 'But now they laugh at me' (30:1- 8)

30:1
But now they laugh at me,
    men who are younger than I,
whose fathers I would have disdained
    to set with the dogs of my flock.

Those who are referred to here should not be identified with the young men who withdrew on seeing Job

make his way to the gate of the city (see 29:8). The
men in these verses are described as younger than
Job. They are not high-born or well bred; they are
boorish in their manners and scrabble about in
desert and marsh for sustenance (30:3-8). They are
'a senseless, a nameless brood' (30:8) whose de-
meanour and conduct towards others have become
so intolerable that they have been driven out of
society. Even so, Job would have thought their
fathers too venerable to be employed as night guards
of his flock and to be left in the company of scaveng-
ing dogs (30:1). But their sons do not show Job even
that much regard! The respect that Job has been
used to is not only being withheld; he is actually
being ridiculed — a great change indeed!

2. 'And now I have become their song' (30:9-15)

30:9-11
And now I have become their song;
    I am a byword to them.
They abhor me; they keep aloof from me;
    they do not hesitate to spit at the sight of me.
Because God has loosed my cord and humbled me,
    they have cast off restraint in my presence.

And the situation has grown even worse! Ribald comment has been set to music and so has become cap-
able of being repeated like a child's rhyme (30:9). But
it is not only words and taunts that Job has to bear.
He is given a wide berth and spat at (30:10). He sees
himself as surrounded and besieged by those who
need no encouragement or assistance to break in upon
him like a hostile foe or a flood. And this is all because
'someone' (Job does not specify that it is God — see
also 30:19-23) has taken away his **'cord'** — that is, his
strength (30:11). The allusion could be to the guy rope
that holds a tent taut, but it could also be to the string

that fires an arrow. We shall opt for the latter, seeing that he has just recalled how his bow was new (see 29:20). The point is that he is now defenceless and vulnerable to attack. Capitalizing on his exposure, dishonouring verbal and physical attacks have been launched against him and in those one who does not need to be identified has been involved.

3. 'And now my soul is poured out within me' (30:16-31)

30:16
And now my soul is poured out within me;
   days of affliction have taken hold of me.

30:20-21,23
I cry to you for help and you do not answer me;
   I stand, and you only look at me.
You have turned cruel to me;
   with the might of your hand you persecute me…
For I know that you will bring me to death
   and to the house appointed for all living.

30:27
My inward parts are in turmoil and never still;
   days of affliction come to meet me.

In this extended account of his **'days of affliction'** (30:27) Job begins and ends with a description of his agonies (30:17-18,24-31). Between these is an accusatory section in which he refers to the one who is responsible for his sufferings (30:19-23). Given what he has said so often, this must be God, but he begins by using the third-person singular to 'identify' him (30:19) and then a second-person singular verb (30:20-23). The fact that Job does not use the term **'God'** (which has been supplied by the translators of the ESV) points in the direction of the spectre with

which he is grappling, this 'God without a name', as
the one who has perpetrated all his calamities.

A succession of word pictures depicts how Job has
been made to feel. His *élan vital* is dissipated by day
and his bones are being devoured by night. He is
caught in a vice between those two pressures, like
one who is compressed by garments that are too tight
for their wearer (30:16-18). He is thrown into mire
and is like the dust and ashes on which he sits
(30:19; cf. 2:8). His cries for help are met with a cold
stare, not a reply (30:20); the hand that lifted him up
has cruelly oppressed him (30:21). He uses a verb
that sounds like 'Satan' and of course the action it
describes is one that is very much in keeping with
Satan's character. Elevated as if on the wind (30:22),
he now finds that it has become a storm that inexorably leads to death (30:23). This is an **'I know'** of a
very different kind from the one in chapter 19.

The contrast between the way in which Job has
responded to those in need and distress and the way
in which he has been treated is powerfully present to
his mind (30:24-31). Not only have his hopes not
materialized, but the exact opposite has been his lot
— evil, not good; darkness, not light. He is given no
help or companionship except for that of wild animals. His skin is blackened and his bones are blaz-
ing. He sings his own funeral dirge.

Day of accounting
(Job 31:1-40)

31:1-4
I have made a covenant with my eyes;
    how then could I gaze at a virgin?
What would be my portion from God above
    and my heritage from the Almighty on high?
Is not calamity for the unrighteous,
    and disaster for the workers of iniquity?
Does he not see all my ways
    and number all my steps?

This chapter begins with the word **'covenant'**, which is an important term for understanding the whole Bible. In the Old Testament it is intimately related to God's relationship with Israel but here Job uses it, and he was not an Israelite.[1] That fact is significant and noteworthy.

This term provides a framework for understanding all that Job goes on to say. Admittedly, the kind of covenant that he refers to is one that he had made with himself, and not with God (let alone a covenant that God had made with him). But it would be completely inadequate on our part to understand this as being no more than a personal resolve, because in what he goes on to say he mentions God Almighty, his creation of human beings and his judgement of the wicked, as well as numerous religious and moral duties. In speaking of a **'covenant with [his] eyes'** (31:1), he is therefore describing his response to God in the world that he has made and shaped and which he governs. For Job 'covenant' means obligations with sanctions attached in the case of disobedience. It is an echo of God's command to Adam, whose sin Job mentions (31:33).

All this shows that covenant-making was not limited to Israel and her unique relationship with the Lord. It was a feature of ancient Near-Eastern societies. This is confirmed by the fact that it was Abimelech, the King of Gerar, who proposed a sworn agreement with Abraham that resulted in a covenant being made between them and their descendants (see Gen. 21:32). Some tension had built up between them and the potential for trouble still existed. A binding agreement was therefore desirable. Covenants could be personal, as well as national, but even when they were between individuals they often included descendants.

Generally, agreements with promises and sanctions attached were associated with a sacrifice that symbolized death. (In Genesis 21 it was an extra gift from Abraham to Abimelech that made the agreement absolutely firm.) They were sealed with an oath and the sanctions were applied to the party that broke the covenant. The oath that was taken was often expressed in the words: 'May God do so to me and more also if I do [or do not])...'

All this supplies the background for Job's thinking at this point. He is aware that he has obligations to God that carry consequences with them for good or ill according to how he responds. What he has just described in his lament amounts to a complaint that the sanctions of the covenant have been put into effect against him in spite of the fact that he has not broken the covenant stipulations. Now he is taking the matter further; he is going to enter a legal protest on that score and demand a verdict. This is the nub of the whole issue.

Satan regards Job's relationship with God as hollow on both sides, so to speak. He is intent on bringing that out into the open by making Job renounce God. The calamities brought upon Job are of the kinds that resemble covenant curses (see Deut. 28:22). The Friends draw the inevitable conclusion, given the limited knowledge they possess — knowledge that Job agrees with, namely that God does bring **'calamity'** on **'the unrighteous and disaster for the workers of iniquity'** (31:3). But Job was not unrighteous — and knew that he had not been. And, what is more, he knew that God knew it too! In this chapter we therefore have the opposite of a covenant-breaker being threatened with judgement, as in the case of Israel by the Old Testament prophets. We have someone protesting his innocence and invoking a judgement on himself if that is not the case.

31:5,7-8
If I have walked with falsehood
   and my foot has hastened to deceit …
if my step has turned aside from the way
   and my heart has gone after my eyes,
   and if any spot has stuck to my hands,
then let me sow, and another eat,
   and let what grows for me be rooted out.

31:35,37
Oh, that I had one to hear me!
   (Here is my signature! Let the Almighty answer me!)
   Oh, that I had the indictment written by my adversary! …
I would give him an account of all my steps;
   like a prince I would approach him.

In this chapter Job draws up a statement of covenant loyalty, in reverse. The words **'If…'** and **'then'**, which recur, point to the heart of it. He lists a number of sins that would be tantamount to covenant-breaking and exposes himself to their just due — but maintains that he has not committed any of them. He has not hidden from God as Adam did (31:33, see ESV footnote), but has lived in the open before him. This lengthy submission becomes his defence, which he signs (31:35). If only the Almighty would submit a charge and sign it! In full possession of the facts on both sides of the case, Job would then stride into the high court of **'God above'** (31:2,28) as confidently as he had done many times in the land of Uz. Is there not a massive degree of overconfidence at work here?

There is a debate about several matters in our text. Job's statement is not as logical in its development, or as complete in its syntax, as pundits would like — for example, the 'if' clause is not always followed by a 'then' clause; the number of sins that are listed is not clear; and the order in which they are mentioned involves some repetition. These critics would do well to remember that this statement was not drawn up in a solicitor's office! In my view, the number of alterations to the text that have been put forward undermines the need for any of them. There are far more important points to consider about this deed of deposition. We shall set them out thematically rather than follow our usual method of making our way through the text progressively.

The range of sins covered

Firstly, the range of sinful actions should be noted. Job moves from lack of integrity in word and deed (31:5-8) to secret immorality (31:9-12), to social injustice (31:13-23), to false trust and idolatry (31:24-28) and, finally, to hatred of adversaries (31:29-30). These areas of human behaviour are as wide as life and living itself, and they resonate with the Decalogue and also the Sermon on the Mount.

They are in keeping with the apostle Paul's teaching that it is not only Jews who are related to the requirements of the law (see Rom. 2:12-14).

The emphasis on the heart

Secondly, the element of inwardness should be noted. Job is aware that more than deeds or words are involved. Desires and attitudes are also covered — for example, the **'eyes'** (31:1) that lead the **'heart'** and the **'foot'** (31:1,5,7,9,26,27); the wave of the hand that disdains the rights of others (31:21; cf. vv. 13-14,16-17) and dismisses their needs (31:19-20); a hand full of gold (31:25) that is kissed by a mouth that respects false gods (31:26-27) and that calls down a curse on one's foes (31:29-30). This concern on Job's part with his 'heart', with the inwardness of the law's demands, is in harmony with our Lord's exposition of the law in the Sermon on the Mount (see Matt. 5:20-48). It is also an exposition in advance of the apostle John's description of the 'world' as 'the desires of the flesh and the desires of the eyes and pride in possessions' (1 John 2:16).

His sense of accountability

Thirdly, Job's ethical outlook is set firmly in the context of creation and judgement. Part of the driving force of Job's 'fearing God and turning away from evil' was his awareness that other human beings were also made by God, and that was as true of the servant as the master (31:13), of the poor and the widowed as of the rich (31:16-20). Such a perspective also made him aware that his neighbour's wife was as sacred as his own (31:9-12), and so was his enemy's life (31:29-30). He was therefore responsible for doing all he could to relieve the needs of others, those with a just grievance (31:13), the hungry (31:16-17), those suffering from the cold (31:19), the downtrodden (31:21) and the stranger (31:32).

But it was not only a shared humanity that motivated Job to such conduct, but also an awareness of a special accountability. He makes several references to the fact that the God who sees all (31:2-40) also does what is right. Job knows that 'what a man sows, he reaps' at the hand of God, whether in this life or not. He refers to God's wrath reaching to Abaddon and also being worked out in following generations (31:12). If Job were to abuse his power, then he knows that he will have to answer to God for it when he **'rises up'** 31:14; cf. 19:25). If that were to happen Job knows he would have to face God in his majesty (31:23), and that would be something that he could not do.

There is one other detail to note that recurs in this chapter, namely the way in which Job specifies the calamities that should befall him if he had committed the sins he lists in spite of his protestation to the contrary. This kind of statement does not appear in similar texts, which usually leave the horrors unmentioned, but of course well understood. Not so in the case of Job! In verses 8,10,14,22,28 and, climactically, in verses 38-40, he brazenly envisages thorns and weeds engulfing his land — something worse than the curse on the ground mentioned in Genesis 3 and not merely akin to it.

The anomaly that Job refers to points in the direction of the fact that God was doing something new with Job. God was not merely responding to evil (of course he was not!), let alone giving in to Satan. God who is Jehovah had his own agenda — and it was good, not evil. To all with eyes to see, Job's undeserved suffering points forward to the Messiah and it lights the path for those who 'take up [their] cross and follow [Christ]' (Matt. 16: 24).

6. Elihu intervenes

(Job 32:1 – 37:24)

There is no need to present an argument for these chapters being a distinct section in the book of Job. That is evident and is admitted on every hand. Two questions do have to be faced, however, in connection with them: namely whether they are part of the original text and, if that is so, how they fit into the narrative.

A later addition?

For some considerable time many Old Testament scholars have regarded these chapters as a later addition to the story. But there have always been those who have taken the opposite view[1] and in some recently published works it is being openly acknowledged that the grounds for their exclusion do not carry weight.[2] An argument has also been advanced in favour of their being broken up and inserted at different places in the book. But that has not commended itself either. For one thing, all the manuscript evidence is against it. There is no version of *Job* extant that lacks these chapters or locates them elsewhere. It is far easier to face the challenge of why these chapters are where they are, and how they relate to what has preceded and to what follows, than to find compelling reasons for any of the proposed rearrangements.

The case that is made for the non-authenticity of these chapters is grounded on data relating to style, vocabulary and content.

With regard to *style*, there is an obvious difference between Elihu's speeches (particularly the first) and those of the Friends, and this comes out even in the English translation. But it is possible to make too much of this subjective claim, as has been done with other parts of the Bible. Might this variation not be deliberate on the part of a skilful author? Could there be another explanation of it? I would suggest that there is, as will become evident from what follows.

As far as *vocabulary* is concerned, the fact that these speeches contain a number of words that do not appear elsewhere in Job (or, indeed, in the Old Testament) and that many of them are Aramaic in origin does not necessitate a later date for them than for the rest of the material.

As regards the *content*, that will be responded to by commenting on the chapters themselves as we go along. But in my opinion the objections on these grounds are not substantial.

Part of the story line?

However, there are some who discount these chapters as a real part of the story line of the book, even though they accept the text of *Job* and work with it as it is. They regard these chapters as an interlude provided by the author so that readers might have some relief after the stormy exchanges between Job and his friends and before the upheaval caused by the Lord's appearing. In their view, therefore, these chapters function in a way that resembles moments of comic relief in Shakespeare's tragedies. What about this suggestion?

Undoubtedly, there is such a change of tempo after chapter 31, but the explanation just offered for it is highly subjective. Without doubt, Elihu's ministry provided a relief *to Job* after the *Sturm und Drang* of the debate. But we have to be careful in saying even that because, as we shall see, his message was no light diversion. To claim, however, that these chapters were inserted for the sake of *the reader* would mean that they can be disconnected from the thread of the narrative without any loss to it, or to Job. That is not so. It must not be done and it should not be even thought of!

We can therefore have no sympathy with such treatment of these chapters, much less with this dismissal of Elihu. Indeed, the author's statements at the beginning of chapter 32 should surely prevent such a notion even being entertained. Apart from the few words at the end of the preceding chapter, the Prologue, the Epilogue and the prefaces to the speeches, these lines are the only pieces of prose in the book. They therefore advertise themselves as the comments of the author/narrator, who regarded them as being integral to the book he was writing. They are therefore most important. Just as the Prologue is necessary in order to make sense of what immediately follows, so this intervening comment is necessary for the rest of the narrative. To fail to make proper use of these verses is the result of prejudice, not of scholarship.

They lay down three facts about Elihu.

1. Elihu has been present during the debate

It is not special pleading to accept this at face value. To do so requires no more than the recollection that Job and the Friends were not having a debate in a closed room. Job was in a public place, even if it was the town refuse tip, and people would have come and gone, but one (Elihu) stayed. To claim that he could not have been present because he was not mentioned along with the Friends is an unwarranted assumption in defiance of the text. Why not accept the author's satisfactory explanation as to why he has been silent — which of course implies that he has been present? (See 32:4-5).

2. Elihu distances himself from the Friends (and from Job)

It has often been claimed that Elihu merely repeats what the Friends had said, but here he is presented as being at odds with them all. He neither endorses all that the Friends have said nor all that Job has said. He is discriminating. It is indeed true that he does speak of suffering having a chastening purpose, as did Eliphaz, but he also says that God has a beneficial design in it, and that is something that Eliphaz did not say, nor did Bildad or Zophar. In addition, Elihu does not address Job in the way that the Friends had done. They said that Job was suffering because he had sinned. Elihu says that Job has sinned because he was suffering. That is a vital difference to bear in mind. Elihu thinks that he has something to say that has not yet been said and is also quite adamant that he is not going to use the Friends' arguments to deal with Job (see 32:14). So why not accept that, and examine what he says to find out what it is? That will be our method.

3. Elihu intervenes at a critical point in the narrative

For the first time for a long while there is silence. Job and the Friends have no more to say. But plainly something more needs to be said. The story cannot be left as it is. The Friends and Job have all said

their piece and Elihu has heard it all. He is, of
course, as unaware of what transpired in God's court
as they all were. But he knows what the Friends have
said, or rather what they have not said, and also
what Job has said and should not have said. It is in
that emergency that he speaks up.

The significance of Elihu's contribution

Two further details about Elihu's ministry should be
noted before we look at anything that he has to say.

First, Elihu speaks four times, which is once more
than Eliphaz and Bildad and twice more than Zophar. This points to his having greater significance in
the unfolding of 'the purpose of the Lord' with regard
to Job (see James 5:11), which is what this book is
all about. It is to Job in particular that Elihu directs
his ministry. Although he refers to the Friends, it is
Job whom he regards as his responsibility. Time and
again Elihu refers to what Job has said and when he
describes his goal it is Job whom he refers to.

Secondly, Elihu pauses after each of his first three
speeches (see the prefatory remarks in 34:1; 35:1;
36:1), but neither Job nor any one of the Friends has
anything to say. Earlier, all of them had been chafing
at the bit, it seems, each waiting for the other to
finish. But now no one wants to take on Elihu. That
is interesting. There must be some explanation for it
and there is one that this commentary will offer.

Elihu's role is absolutely essential to the book.
Without it the rest of the book would not hang together. That is something that should become evident as we proceed.

'Listen to me; let me declare my opinion' (Job 32:1-22)

This chapter divides itself into two parts. First, there are the opening five verses, in which Elihu is introduced by the author of the book, and then we have Elihu's own statements by means of which he introduces his first speech. We shall deal with these in continuity with each other in order to focus on the significance of Elihu in the narrative. He has suffered from bad press and needs to be rehabilitated.

The importance of Elihu is highlighted by the way in which he is identified. In contrast to the Friends, his lineage and place of origin are mentioned. His father's name, Barachel, means 'God blesses' and Buz was a descendant of Abraham's brother (see Gen. 22:21). Elihu is therefore related to the tribe and region from which Abraham came. In view of his patrimony and provenance, it has been suggested that the author is pointing to the trustworthiness and authority of Elihu's message over against that of the Friends.

He burned with anger (32:1-5)

32:1-3
So these three men ceased to answer Job, because he was righteous in his own eyes. Then Elihu the son of Barachel the Buzite, of the family of Ram, burned with anger. He burned with anger at Job because he justified himself rather

than God. He burned with anger also at Job's three friends because they had found no answer, although they had declared Job to be in the wrong.

In verses 2-5 Elihu is described four times as 'burning with anger'. Does this mean that he merits the sobriquet 'the Angry Young Man' by which he is still described? Before an affirmative answer is given to that question several things should be noted. First, reasons are given for his anger against Job and the Friends, and secondly those reasons differ. Neither of them relates to his being personally displeased or neglected, either by Job or by the Friends. His anger is therefore not pique and, as reasons are given for it, it is not blind rage. It should be noted that exactly the same expression, **'burned with anger'**, is used by God himself with regard to the Friends (see 42:7) and something similar is expressed in the Lord's arraignment of Job (see 38:1-2; 40:1-2). The possibility therefore exists that Elihu's anger is in measure akin to the anger of the Lord. This does not mean that Elihu's anger was as pure as God's, only that it was of the same kind. It was neither lacking in self-control nor in moral justification. We could say that God's zeal for his own glory translated itself into Elihu's jealousy for God's glory. (**'Zeal'** and **'jealousy'** are the same word in Hebrew). This is why Elihu is angry; 'indignant' would be a better word to use. It is because right[eous]ness is not being upheld by Job or the Friends.

That ties in with the words **'righteous'**, **'justified'** and **'declared ... to be in the wrong'**, or 'condemned' (32:1,2,3). Job is described as justifying **'himself rather than God'** and the Friends are described as unjustly declaring Job to be in the wrong. It is worth noting at this juncture that these reasons are later validated by God (see 40:2; 42:7). This is partly why Elihu is not mentioned again. When the Lord appears

it is to adjudicate and humble the proud, and Elihu
was not among those. Consequently, there was no
need for him to appear at God's bar.

This analysis of the situation that the author
provides makes clear that Elihu is engaged in a
battle on three fronts. There is Job's battle with God,
and in that Job is at fault. There is also a battle
between the Friends and Job, and in that the Friends
are at fault. They have misrepresented God in declaring Job to be in the wrong. Thirdly, there is also
Elihu's battle over against Job and the Friends in
which he strives to maintain God's honour.

Elihu accuses Job of being guilty in being more
concerned with his own vindication than with God's.
Several times in the debate Job has bordered on this
(see 9:21; 10:7; 12:4; 16:17), but in what he has just
said (chapter 31) it becomes explicit and dominant.
His assuredness of his own integrity has become so
strong, and the extent of his claims so large, that he
is almost claiming to be sinless before God. Job did
not speak like that after Satan's assaults on him, or
for some while after sitting on the ash-heap. Then he
only bemoaned his plight and longed for death. But
in chapter 31 he virtually dares God to find any fault
with him. **'In his own eyes'** (note the allusion to
31:1 in 32:1) he is absolutely righteous. Job should
have continued to bow before the administration of
God, receiving evil from his hand as well as good (see
2:10). Had he done that, he would not have sinned
nor charged God with wrong. Elihu is intent on
addressing that sin. This is why he can speak of
chastisement.

With regard to the Friends, Elihu is concerned
about their condemnation of Job (32:3). That is what
is written in the Hebrew text, but there is an old
Jewish tradition that indicates that scribes thought
the original text had 'they condemned God' and that
the wording was changed to what is in our Bibles out

of reverence. Either way, the Friends' words had the effect of putting God and Job in the wrong by misrepresenting each, albeit in different ways.

At this point we need to refer back to something that was mentioned in the introduction (see page 22) It concerns the double reference of the word **'judgement'**. The term can refer either to the law court or to the throne room, to a place where a verdict is reached or an edict is promulgated. Job and the Friends have been operating only in a law-court setting — that is, a place where guilt is determined and punishment is apportioned. Consistently, the Friends have said, 'Guilty', and Job has said, 'Not guilty,' though at times he has believed what they said in God's name.

Now Elihu does not deny the reality of the law court, but he reminds Job of God's throne room. He speaks of God's administration of his kingdom as well as his adjudication of his subjects. He uses the word 'judgement' in both senses and brings into the discussion the throne room that was depicted in the opening chapters — all unknowing on his part, of course.

'I', 'my' and 'me' (32:6-22)

32:6,8,10
I am young in years,
    and you are aged;
therefore I was timid and afraid
    to declare my opinion to you...
But it is the spirit in man,
    the breath of the Almighty, that makes him understand...
Therefore I say, 'Listen to me;
    let me also declare my opinion.'

32:17-18,20
I also will answer with my share;
   I also will declare my opinion.
For I am full of words;
   the spirit within me constrains me...
I must speak, that I may find relief;
   I must open my lips and answer.

The author's explanation that Elihu had waited silently because of his youth has not deterred people from depicting him as opinionated. In addition to the 'Angry Young Man', he has been designated 'Mr Pompous'. Support for that is derived from the very frequent use of the first-person singular pronoun in the opening section of his address. However, the circumstances in which he spoke should be borne in mind[3] and there are several facts to note in that connection. First, the inference from what Elihu says is that he would not have spoken at all if the Friends had dealt with Job as they should have done. Secondly, he was young and he lived at a time and in a culture where respect for older folk was woven into everyone's upbringing. Thirdly, he was ploughing a furrow between four disputants on two fronts, and was agreeing with neither side. He was in an extremely awkward position, and he knew it, and that could well account for the hesitation and prolixity of his opening remarks. I am more than ready to agree with any reader of the text who thinks that Elihu was somewhat precocious, provided that the reader is also willing to concede the points that have just been made.

But there are some other facts about Elihu that must be noted. The first is his awareness of being inwardly taught and stirred (32:7-9,18-19). He acknowledges that his expectation that the older men would know what to say and how to say it has taken a severe blow and he has been forced to realize that it is not always so. Wisdom comes to man's spirit from the same source that gave him breath (32:8; cf. Gen. 2:7). It is not the same as human opinion or reflection. Towards the end of the chapter he uses the process of fermentation as an analogy for the way in which he has been inwardly stirred by the words that have come to his mind. Secondly, he knows he is account-able to God for what he says (32:21-22) and liable to his judgement if he favours anyone more than God. Thirdly, he expresses a desire to put Job in the right with God once again (see 33:22). This combination of constraint, humility and goodwill is in keeping with a concern for God's glory. It is the hallmark of old-covenant prophets and new-covenant preachers because it was so of the Messiah himself. As Elihu typifies them all, he is not a pre-incarnate appearance of the Mediator.

Elihu – a prophet among the wise men

In what has just been said a view has been expressed of the status and role of Elihu in the history recorded in the narrative. He has been likened more to a prophet than a wise man (in the making), and there-fore by extension is a type of a gospel preacher. This is not an allegorizing of the text in the interests of a favoured point of view. There are three statements in the text that support such an identification. We shall examine them in turn.

33:6-7
Behold, I am towards God as you are;
    I too was pinched off from a piece of clay.
Behold, no fear of me need terrify you;
    my pressure will not be heavy upon you.

There are two lines to verse 6. The second, **'I too was pinched off from a piece of clay'**, indicates that Elihu is as human as Job. (It also confirms the Genesis account of the creation of Adam.) But what about the first line? In the ESV we have, **'Behold, I am towards God as you are'**, a rendering that expresses the theme of a common humanity. But another translation is possible, one that is found in the KJV and the Geneva Bible. It is, 'Behold I am according to *thy wish in God's stead*', and that points to a view about Elihu's role that is no longer generally affirmed. If there was a common view of Elihu in the seventeenth century, it was that he was 'a man sent from God'.

The KJV version could be made less tendentious by dropping the words 'in' and 'stead' which are not necessary to make the point, and just using the word 'for' or 'to'. What we would have then would be: 'I am according to your wish [literally, "mouth"] for [or "with regard to"] God'.

The crunch question concerns the meaning of the word **'mouth'** in the original text. Does it refer to speech? Job had asked God to speak to him by someone who would not terrify him (see 9:34; 13:21). This may well be what is referred to in the next verse (33:7), as an almost identical form of the word is used in 39:27, where it is translated 'command'.

But there is another possibility. In Exodus 12:4 the size of the Passover lamb is to be determined by the number of 'mouths' that it has to feed, and so 'mouth' is a way of designating a human being. This is what gives rise to the ESV rendering and other translations, but in my opinion 33:7 settles the matter in favour of the older translation, 'wish'. However, all that is being argued for at this juncture is that the older rendering should be held in mind as a possibility, both from a textual and contextual point of view. But it is not the only text that is relevant. There are two others.

33:23
If there be for him an angel,
    a mediator, one of the thousand,
    to declare to man what is right for him...

Whoever is referred to here is described in three ways: **'an angel'**, **'a mediator'** and **'one of the thousand'**. The last expression is a metaphor that refers to rarity or worth, as we shall see later. The other two are synonyms. The word rendered **'mediator'** in the ESV should not be thought of in too theological a sense — that is, in relation to covenant (see Heb. 8:6) — because it is used in the Old Testament for human beings generally. In another form of the verb it refers to a scorner; here it designates someone who interprets, and the emphasis in this verse is on someone who speaks, explaining the ways of God.

The crucial term is the word translated **'angel'**. Does this *have* to refer to a supernatural being? Angels do interpret as well as protect and deliver. But in *Job* angels are called 'sons of God' or 'holy ones'. The word (*mal'akh*) can and does refer to a human messenger, as in the name Malachi. This phrase can therefore be translated, 'a messenger [who is] an interpreter, one among a thousand' who declares what is right for man, and we can associate this with the idea of a human spokesman for God presented in 33:6. Could Elihu be referring to himself in this verse? If so (and I think he is) then it is noteworthy that he does not use the first-person singular to do so. He speaks impersonally.

36:2-4
Bear with me a little, and I will show you,
    for I have yet something to say on God's behalf.

I will get my knowledge from afar
    and ascribe righteousness to my Maker.
For truly my words are not false;
    one who is perfect in knowledge is with you.

The opening statement is unambiguous and it settles
the question of how Elihu is to be regarded. He says
that he has **'*yet* something to say on God's behalf'**.
The use of the word **'yet'** includes what he has
already said (chapters 31 – 35) and what he is about
to say (chapter 37). He is claiming to be a messenger
from God and, what is more, one who deals with
righteousness. He claims that his **'words are not
false'** and that God, who is **'perfect in knowledge'**,
is with Job by means of them. His claim to being
stirred inwardly by the Spirit, and being unable to
contain what he has been given to say, is reminiscent
of the great Jeremiah. But, coming immediately
before the LORD as he does in the book, he prefigures
John the Baptist, who paved the way for the Messiah's appearing, and also every gospel preacher.

'Hear my speech, O Job' (Job 33:1-33)

Having introduced himself, Elihu addresses Job by name. He calls on Job to listen to all that he has to say because he is speaking truth sincerely and as a result of the inspiring Spirit of God (33:1-4). Using military terms, but in relation to the world of legal debate (33:5), he calls on Job to answer what he has to say — if he can. After all, Job should not feel threatened by him as they share a common humanity.

'You have spoken in my ears' (33:8-11)

33:8-9
Surely you have spoken in my ears,
   and I have heard the sound of your words.
You say, 'I am pure, without transgression;
   I am clean, and there is no iniquity in me...'

Elihu begins to read the charge sheet against Job and the evidence that he presents is made up of some of Job's own remarks (33:8-11) which show that Job has not dealt justly with God (33:12; see also 34:5-6). He then proceeds to refute Job's allegations and concludes by inviting Job to speak, pausing in order to give him opportunity to do so (33:31-33). But Job remains silent. A reason for this will be suggested below.

It would be useful to turn to 13:23-27 at this point because the statements that Elihu claims to have heard from Job (33:9-11) are probably those that are recorded there. They relate to Job's claim to be pure and also to his accusation that God is unjust. That charge (33:10-11) is quoted from the latter part of 13:24 and also the opening part of 13:27, where Job claims that God has designated him as an enemy and has treated him accordingly. But the claim to purity is not as easily identified. Where had Job said such a thing? Is Elihu guilty of putting words in Job's mouth?

Given that a connection with chapter 13 has been partly established, it is natural to look there for something that amounts to such a claim. The only place in that chapter where Job refers to 'sins and iniquities' is in verses 23 and 26, but the latter is an admission of sin. The only possible source of this claim is in verse 23, where Job had asked, 'How many are my iniquities and my sins? Make me know my transgression and my sin.' At first sight it might seem that the meaning of these words is the exact opposite of **'I am pure, without transgression; I am clean and there is no iniquity in me'** (33:9). But that depends on how the question was voiced, and that of course is beyond our ability to discover. It could have been a rhetorical denial, and two details go some way at least towards supporting that suggestion.

The first is that the sins that Job does admit to in chapter 13 are those of his youth (see 13:26). They are therefore past, not present, sins and, given the way in which Job prayed for his children, is it not likely that he had done so for himself too and had found pardon with regard to them? In verse 26 he is therefore complaining that he is being punished for sin that has been forgiven, and that fits and furthers his charge that God is being unjust, charging for sins twice, as it were.

Secondly, Job's silence when Elihu reminds him of what he has said is eloquent. Is it conceivable that Job, who accused his friends of unfair and cruel treatment, would have remained silent if Elihu had misrepresented him? I think not, and so read his question in 13:23 as being tantamount to a denial of sin, and the request that follows it to a conviction that he had not committed any sins that God could show him. This single section of text could therefore furnish the likely background to both charges that Elihu makes, but there are other statements of Job that also tend in the direction of an assertion of purity, and not just general blamelessness (see 7:20-21; 9:20-21). This is all of a piece with the way in which 'he justified himself' rather than God (32:2) and it means that Elihu was speaking truthfully (see 33:3) and that Job cannot contest the evidence provided by his own words.

God speaks to conceal pride from man (33:12-33)

33:12-14

Behold, in this you are not right. I will answer you,
 for God is greater than man.
Why do you contend against him,
 saying, 'He will answer none of man's words'?
For God speaks in one way,
 and in two, though man does not perceive it.

Elihu's distinctive message appears in this section for the first time and it will be developed later. Having charged Job with speaking lightly of God, he sets out to restore the proper balance. He begins by exalting God with the words: **'God is greater than man'** (33:12). Some have regarded this statement as trite and as being as irrelevant to Job's case as the Friends' thesis, but to view it in this way fails to give proper consideration to the connection between verses 12 and 13, and so to all that follows.

Elihu is not asserting divine transcendence in a way that is removed from the living situation of Job's predicament and protests. On the contrary, he immediately connects God's greatness with Job's summons against him (33:13). By claiming that God has not answered him, Job has shown that he has forgotten how great God is. Elihu's point is that because God is so great it ill becomes human beings like Job to arraign him on account of the exercise of his sovereignty.

But God's 'silence' does not mean that man is treated disdainfully. In fact God is not silent at all. It is just that he refuses to answer at Job's peremptory beck and call — let alone to respond to his accusations. God does speak and, what is more, he has been speaking! The reality is that Job has been deaf and not that God has been dumb! (33:14).

The great truth that Elihu declares is that God **'speaks'** (that is, acts) with a good purpose in view. He is mysterious not only in his greatness, but in his graciousness. Differentiating transcendence from aloofness, but retaining its exalted character, Elihu translates it into the wonder of colossal condescension on God's part.

That is what Job has forgotten and what the Friends have not said. This is the note that causes Job and the Friends to fall silent because it casts such a new light on Job's situation. Elihu proceeds to prove this by describing how God speaks to the afflicted, and why he does so.

God uses two methods to speak to man — that is, to Job. On the one hand, there is revelation by dream (33:15-16), and on the other, there is mortal illness (33:19-21). The Friends had also pointed this out. Eliphaz had referred to a vision and all of them had pointed to Job's sufferings as being God's voice to him, calling him to repent of the sin that had brought such judgement upon him.

Elihu's description of God's direct address to man during his unconscious hours is a feature of the patriarchal period of redemptive history to which this book relates.[4] It stresses the sovereign monergism of divine activity. Examples of this that are particularly significant are of course the creation of woman (Gen. 2:21) and the making of the covenant with Abraham (Gen. 15:12). But God spoke by dreams to those outside the line of redemptive revelation too: for example, Abimelech (Gen. 20:3), Pharaoh's cup-bearer and baker (Gen. 40:5) and Nebuchadnezzar (Dan. 2)

Job had not only referred to terrifying dreams (see 7:13-15) but to imminent death, and Elihu's description of the sufferer could well be a verbal portrait of him (33:19-21). Nagging pain that banishes rest and nauseating revulsion at the sight [or smell] of food — both the most basic and the choicest of fare — combine to make him look like a skeleton already.

So far the Friends might agree with Elihu. But now he goes on to make a totally different point. He says that God's purpose via dream and pain was beneficent. It was not punitive; it was not even purgative. It was preventative. It was **'to turn man** [Job] **aside from his deed and conceal pride from a man'**, and so to keep him **'from the pit'** (33:17,18,22,30).

Related to what lay behind the events recorded in the Prologue, this means that God had his own purpose in allowing Satan to tempt Job, which was to prevent Job from sinning by means of suffering. This might seem a backhanded way of proceeding, so we need to recall that Job's initial responses to his afflictions did express a deeper submission to God than had been the case previously. The Lord followed the same path with regard to Paul (see 2 Cor. 12:7).

33:23-24
If there be for him an angel,
  a mediator, one of the thousand,
  to declare to man what is right for him,
and he is merciful to him, and says,
  'Deliver him from going down into the pit;
  I have found a ransom...'

Piety does not automatically cancel out pride, and pride can temporarily overcome piety. Even such pain as makes life unbearable and death inevitable does not automatically produce humility before God. So what does? It is a messenger, **'one of [a] thousand'**. Numbers are metaphorical in this speech, as in 5:19. God speaks in more than one way (33:14) and he acts more than twice (33:29). This means that he speaks and acts in a thousand and one ways. But this messenger is 'one of [a] thousand' and that metaphor describes his worth and rarity (see Eccles. 7:28).

It is the ministry of such a messenger that is described in verses 23 and 24, and that helps in identifying who is referred to by the third-person singular pronouns in those verses. Who is the **'he'** in each case? There are rapid changes of subject here.[5] The following is a suggested paraphrase:

> ... to declare to [a] man what is right for him, then [God] is merciful to [man] and says, 'Deliver him from going down into the pit; I have found a ransom; let [man's] flesh return to the days of his youthful vigour'; then [man] prays to God and [God] accepts [man]; [man] sees his face with a shout of joy and [God] restores to man his righteousness. [Man] sings before men and says, 'I sinned and perverted what was right and it was not repaid to me. [God] has redeemed my soul from going down into the pit and my life shall look upon the light.'

Elihu was such an interpreter of the ways of God with men. He pointed out to Job **'what [was] right for him'** and the way to blessing from God's 'severe mercy' that was intended for him (33:32). Consequently, Job was delivered from the jaws of the pit into which he was expecting to fall and restored to a right relationship with God again, as the Epilogue records.

33:26-28
… then man prays to God, and he accepts him;
   he sees his face with a shout of joy,
and he restores to man his righteousness.
   He sings before men and says:
'I sinned and perverted what was right,
   and it was not repaid to me.
He has redeemed my soul from going down into the pit,
   and my life shall look upon the light.'

Verses 26 and 27 record the response of the one who has been delivered and restored. He prays and shouts; he sings and shouts. These terms are associated with both worship and conquest. Supplication for mercy brings a sight of God's favour, and that generates a shout of joy, which includes the realization that one has been spared the judgement due and has been shown undeserved mercy.

But is it only Elihu that is to be seen here? What about the Angel of the LORD, as well as that greater one who *actually* pays the ransom price to effect such deliverance, and also those whom he sends to make known the good news of reconciliation with God? Such a rich concentration of redemptive themes is not unusual in the Old Testament.

'Job answers like wicked men' (Job 34:1 – 35:16)

Although Elihu includes the Friends in these speeches (see 34:2-4,34-35;⁶ 35:4⁷), it is Job that he really has in view. This is seen by the fact that when he does address the Friends, he is pressing them to agree with him in his estimation of Job. This has led some commentators to see Elihu as being no different from the Friends and to argue that he emphasizes the justice and power of God over against Job's sins, just as they had.

But Elihu and the Friends deal with sin and suffering from diverse perspectives. While there can be no doubt that Elihu deals severely with Job in the light of the justice and power of God, he does so because Job had impugned God, explicitly as well as by necessary consequence. But that was done during and because of his affliction, and not prior to it (not that his words were any the less grievous on that account!). Whenever the Friends took Job to task for his sins, they were thinking of sins that Job had committed prior to his being afflicted by way of punishment. This was a supposition which they could not validate, whereas Elihu is highlighting sins that he can and does prove. What is more, they are sins that Job cannot and does not contest.

'Far be it from God that he should do wickedness'
(34:1-15)

34:2,7-8
Hear my words, you wise men,
    and give ear to me, you who know...
What man is like Job,
    who drinks up scoffing like water,
who travels in company with evildoers
    and walks with wicked men?

34:10,12
Therefore, hear me, you men of understanding:
    far be it from God that he should do wickedness,
    and from the Almighty that he should do wrong...
Of a truth, God will not do wickedly,
    and the Almighty will not pervert justice.

This part of Elihu's second speech is divisible into
two parts, as is obvious from the repetition of verse 2
in verse 10. In the first (34:1-9), he presents his
evidence against Job and in the second his charge
(34:10-15). This is his standard method of proceeding
and he is certain that his case will carry weight with
everyone who can differentiate between tastes
(34:3-4; cf. 12:11). To such, Job's words will not have
passed unnoticed.

Job has spoken in such an outrageous way that
Elihu can point out — just as Job did with regard to
his wife (see 2:9-10) — that he is indistinguishable
from the wicked. This does not mean that Job *is*
wicked, only that his speech makes it appear that he
is.[8] Elihu here borrows a metaphor from Eliphaz,
namely, that of a thirsty man gulping down **'water'**
(see 15:16), but he makes a significant alteration as
he does so. Eliphaz had said that it was 'injustice'
that Job swallowed like water; Elihu uses the word
'scoffing' in order to specify the kind of injustice that

Job was guilty of (34:7). It was 'scoffing', or derision.
Job was asserting that he was in the right and God
was treating him as if he were in the wrong. God was
punishing him as if he were not innocent (34:5-6).
Such talk is the language of the wicked (34:8), as is
denying that there is any benefit to be gained in
serving God (34:9).

That is the evidence that Elihu presents against
Job and he responds to it by way of an all-out rejection of the faintest notion that God could be unjust,
calling, as he does so, on the Friends to agree with
him. Bildad had said, 'Does God pervert justice? Or
does the Almighty pervert the right?' (see 8:3), and
here Elihu seems to be saying exactly the same
thing. But there are two vital differences to be borne
in mind. First, there is the matter that has already
been referred to about how sin and suffering are to
be correlated. Secondly, there is also the fact that in
what he says Bildad is thinking only of judgement in
terms of verdict, and that is made clear by the fact
that he goes on to speak about sin and punishment.
Elihu is not denying that verdict is a part of God's
justice, but he also wants to emphasize that *edict* is
part of it too. After asserting that God will judge
(34:11-12), he speaks of God's government of the
earth and of mankind (34:13,17) — all under the
heading of God's not doing wickedly or perverting
justice. As man's **'breath'** and **'spirit'** come from
God, he could terminate life instead of sustaining it,
and in an instant all would perish (34:14-15). He is
the Creator and Ruler, and all are dependent on him.

'For his eyes are on the ways of men' (34:16-33)

34:17-19,21
Shall one who hates justice govern?
   Will you condemn him who is righteous and mighty,

who says to a king, 'Worthless one'
and to nobles, 'Wicked man',
who shows no partiality to princes,
nor regards the rich more than the poor,
for they are all the work of his hands? ...
For his eyes are on the ways of a man,
and he sees all his steps.

At this point Elihu begins to reason with Job. He uses a singular verb in order to address him directly. Borrowing an analogy from the realm of human affairs, he says that if people do not tolerate injustice in a human judge (34:17), how dare they [in other words, Job] censure the one who is righteous and mighty — namely God? In the ancient world kings or their equivalent combined power and authority. There was no separation between the judicial and executive branches of government, and tyrants could reign. But God is no stronger than he is just. It is therefore preposterous to think of God (with all that that word connotes) being anything less than absolutely impartial in his rule. Kings and nobles, rich and poor are all treated alike (if they are wicked) because they are all his subjects. God removes them in a moment and without any notice or help because they are all his creatures (34:19-20).

Elihu has something else to say about God's just administration of affairs and people in his world. It is that God rules on this most solid basis because he is omniscient (34:21). No physical darkness can conceal man's ways from him and he does not need to conduct a painstaking investigation in order to ensure that a proper moral basis exists for a judgement to be made (34:22-23). The God who exalts also abases (Ps. 75:7). God sees immediately and he acts invincibly, whether by night or day, whether secretly or publicly (34:25-27). He does this in answer to the cry of the downtrodden and the afflicted (34:28) in order to prevent a tyrant from continuing to reign by means of craft to the detriment of the people (34:30).

34:29
When he is quiet, who can condemn?
  When he hides his face, who can behold him,
    whether it be a nation or a man?

Verse 29 is marked as a parenthetical statement in the ESV and that is helpful. It indicates that during a period marked by God's 'silence and inactivity' — that is, between a cry for help and an intervention by way of answer — it is not permissible for either a nation or an individual (34:28) to censure God, as Job has done. Job's afflicted condition is therefore a case in point.

34:31-32
For has anyone said to God,
  'I have borne punishment; I will not offend any more;
teach me what I do not see;
  if I have done iniquity, I will do it no more'?

What God does and when he does it is his prerogative to decide and so, having censured Job for his impudence, Elihu now points the way forward for him. He tells Job what he ought to say to God, namely that he should admit his guilt,[9] resolve not to be wayward in future and ask God to show him what he is ignorant of, even the sin he has committed.[10] Elihu calls for the penitent submission to God that he had mentioned earlier(see 33:27).

'Job speaks without knowledge' (34:34-37)

34:35-36
Job speaks without knowledge;
  his words are without insight.

Would that Job were tried to the end,
  because he answers like wicked men.

Elihu concludes this speech with the same sort of
appeal as he began it, perhaps including a wider
group of observers, or even city elders, and not just
the Friends. He is confident that everyone who has
the faintest glimmer of understanding will agree that
Job (he now names him twice) has shown colossal
ignorance and used the most intemperate language
against God. Elihu longs that Job should be thoroughly examined because he has spoken so im-
piously of God. But if Elihu can only say this, who is
going to do it? [11]

'God does not hear an empty cry' (35:1-16)

35:2-4
Do you think this to be just?
  Do you say, 'It is my right before God',
that you ask, 'What advantage have I?
  How am I better off than if I had sinned?'
I will answer you
  and your friends with you.

In this third speech Elihu follows his usual method.
He refers to something Job has said (35:2-3) and he
then responds to it. In doing the latter he does not
once address the Friends, but he believes that what
he has to say to Job is also applicable to them
(35:4).[12] Elihu uses the second person singular with
reference to Job (35:2-8) and still has him in mind
(35:14) although he goes on to speak more impersonally (35:9-15). The conclusion of this speech is stated
as a fact for the whole court to hear, as it were, and it
refers to Job by name (35:16).

Although Elihu begins by reasoning with Job (35:2), there is a note of reproof in what he says. (Repentance does, after all, begin with the understanding!) Elihu therefore reminds Job that he has not only maintained his own righteousness in serving God, but that he has also denied that there is any benefit to be gained from doing so. He declares that such thinking is not in accord with what is **'just'**, with the way that God rules the world.

God rules the world by having it in his control and carrying out his will in it. He is above the earth as the skies and clouds are higher than those who live on it. Man (in this case, Job) is therefore to look up and not lift himself up. Elihu asserts that God's nature is neither altered by man's (i.e. Job's) sinfulness or by man's righteousness (35:6-7). Just as the clouds are beyond man's reach, so God's blessedness can neither be diminished by Job's wickedness nor augmented by his righteousness. Wickedness and righteousness affect man's character, not God's (35:8). Although God's dealings with man do relate to man's dealings with him, God remains unchanged in himself. By this assertion of God's immutability and impassibility, Elihu does not mean that God is morally indifferent or ambivalent. After all, he is counselling Job in God's name to cease fighting with God and to submit to him.

35:13-14,16
Surely God does not hear an empty cry,
    nor does the Almighty regard it.
How much less when you say that you do not see him,
    that the case is before him, and you are waiting for him! ...
Job opens his mouth in empty talk;
    he multiplies words without knowledge.

Elihu then comments on the way that those who are oppressed by evil people are not answered by God

(35:9). This seems to be unrelated to Job and also to what Elihu has just been saying. But after indicating that the reason for God's inactivity is the superficiality of the cry for help that such people raise heaven-wards, Elihu says, **'How much less ... you** [Job]**!'** (35:14). Elihu is therefore preparing the way for confronting Job and not letting him off the hook.

What is it that Elihu calls upon Job to face? It is that he is so wrong to construe God's silence as if it were indifference or hostility. Job has said that he does not see God and that God does not take notice of him. But God does not always respond when people call on him with an **'empty cry'**, and Job has been using empty talk about God. **'Beasts of the earth'** (35:11) that teach that God cares for them (see 12:7-8) also squeal in a trap, but that is not prayer — neither is the clamorous sound of Job's words.

What is appropriate and acceptable to God from someone in need is a song of praise that God is not far away when his people are in the dark (see 1:21; 2:10). Such knowledge is true wisdom, and Job is no longer showing that he possesses it. This is the point of Elihu's ministry and its function in the book as we have it. Elihu's charges against Job relate to how he has conducted himself *during* his suffering, and not prior to it. He has sinned. There all four speakers agree. But three of them say that his suffering is brought about by sin; the other says that sin is brought about by his suffering.

'Behold, God is great'
(Job 36:1 – 37:24)

If Elihu's introduction to his first speech were to be excluded from the reckoning, this last speech of his would be the longest. It certainly sums up his whole message and ministry. Its theme is the incomparable greatness of God (see 36:5,22; 37:22-23) and its aim is to bring Job to a realization of his own smallness, but included in this is an emphasis that a benevolent God is purposefully active in Job's suffering (see 36:8-11).

Some regard these truths as being at such variance with each other that they claim that there is a serious tension in Elihu's teaching about God. The fact that Elihu deals with the justice and power of God in his second and third speeches does not entail any dissonance, let alone conflict with a God of goodness and graciousness. To think like this is merely a variation on an old theme which receives its fullest and most fallacious presentation in the notion that it is a God of love that is presented in the New Testament and a God of petty malignity in the Old. Not only does this destroy the unity of the Bible, it undermines the atoning work of Christ and, by extension, the authenticity and vitality of the church. Elihu's ministry is in the name of a God of both 'kindness' and 'severity' (see Rom.11:22). There is no other God in either Testament, and Elihu is seeking in his name to bring Job to a better mind. In that ministry he is paving the way for the appearing of the LORD.

'I have yet something to say on God's behalf' (36:1-4)

36:2,4
Bear with me a little, and I will show you,
for I have yet something to say on God's behalf...
For truly my words are not false;
one who is perfect in knowledge is with you.

Knowing that he has more to say **'on God's behalf'**, or 'for God' — that is, in keeping with God's righteousness — he appeals for attentiveness to the true things that he has to say (36:1-4).

But to whom is he referring when he says, **'... one who is perfect in knowledge is with you'**? The first thing to say is that Elihu does not have to be referring to himself by these words because he also describes God in this way (see 37:16). He could therefore mean that God was present with Job seeing that true words from and about him were being spoken. If this sounds like special pleading, it should be remembered that the word **'perfect'** does not mean 'omniscient' any more than it means sinless (see 1:1). If Elihu were therefore referring to himself by this expression he would only have been claiming a greater (i.e. a fuller) knowledge of God's ways with Job than the Friends possessed. This is entirely in keeping with his awareness that he was speaking for God (see 33:23).

What are those words of 'perfect knowledge'? They relate to God's greatness and goodness in relation both to human beings (see 36:1-25) and the natural elements (36:26 – 37:24) of the world that mankind inhabits. A chapter division would therefore be better located between these two discussions than where it is in our English versions, and that is how we shall divide our consideration of what he says.

'Behold God is mighty and does not despise any' (36:5-25)

36:5,7-10
Behold, God is mighty, and does not despise any;
    he is mighty in strength of understanding...
He does not withdraw his eyes from the righteous...
And if they are bound in chains
    and caught in the cords of affliction,
then he declares to them their work
    and their transgressions, that they are behaving arrogantly.
He opens their ears to instruction
    and commands that they return from iniquity.

Though God is great in power, he does not regard anyone with disdain (36:5). Human beings are not his playthings. He does not exercise his great power in an arbitrary manner; much less is he tyrannical. His powerful activity is in perfect accord with his knowledge of the moral and spiritual character of his creatures and subjects. He who knows (better than any) the difference between good and evil can best identify the wicked and the righteous. He does not treat the former as if they were the latter, or vice versa. He brings a deserved death on the wicked but he remembers and he exalts the righteous, who are often afflicted by them.

These affirmations (36:6-7) have been pointed to as proof that Elihu advocates the same argument as the Friends. But this is not correct, as is evident from the verses that follow them. Verses 6 and 7 state general principles or truths; verses 8-12 present an exception to them. Elihu thinks not only in terms of general principles, as the Friends do, but of exceptions as well. There is no room for exceptions in the world view of the Friends. To them Job's affliction must be judgement on the wicked. Elihu says it is the affliction of the righteous. It is a type of bondage (see comments on 42:10). Job's case is the exception to the rule, but it is not a contradiction of it, because Job must demonstrate his righteousness by heeding God's word to him in the midst of his troubles (36:12).

36:15-16
He delivers the afflicted by their affliction
   and opens their ear by adversity.
He also allured you out of distress
   into a broad place where there was no cramping,
   and what was set on your table was full of fatness.

And what does God say, and how does he say it? Here Elihu reverts to the theme of his first speech (see 33:12-33). God declares to the afflicted **'their work'** — that is, their **'transgressions'**, which are born of arrogance (36:9; cf. 33:17). And how does he do that? It is by a human messenger like Elihu, who commands and comforts, who calls for repentance and promises restoration to the penitent (36:10-11).

This is the difference between the **'godless'** and the righteous. The former do not seek help from God in their trouble. Instead they rage against God (36:13) and those of their number who are young become dissolute (36:13-14). But God is teaching Job ('opening his ear') by means of adversity and Elihu's accompanying ministry (36:15), and God is wooing ('alluring') him from distress and confinement into peace and plenty (36:16). He will sit at table again with family and guests surrounding him (see 42:11).

36:17-18, 21-22
But you are full of the judgement on the wicked;
   judgement and justice seize you.

Beware lest wrath entice you into scoffing,
   and let not the greatness of the ransom turn you aside…
Take care; do not turn to iniquity,
   for this you have chosen rather than affliction.
Behold, God is exalted in his power;
   who is a teacher like him?

But at present Job is **'full of the judgement on the wicked'** (36:17). What do these words mean? This verse and those that immediately follow present considerable difficulties. But this much is clear: Elihu is addressing Job in the light of God's disciplinary dealings. The notes of wooing and warning found in the earlier verses should continue to be borne in mind with regard to verses 17-20. This is evident from verse 21: **'Take care; do not turn to iniquity, for this you have chosen rather than** [submit to] **affliction'**, as he had done at the beginning (see 1:20-21; 2:10).

Using this thread of thought, the following explanation is offered of verses 17-20:

> 1. Verse 17 has been rendered 'full of the judgement *of* the wicked' (ASV). If the text is construed in this way, Elihu is referring to the fact that Job has been judging God in the same sort of way that the wicked do. This is something that Elihu has said before (see 34:35-37). It is a serious sin and it cannot be overlooked.
> 2. There are two problems with verse 18. First, it contains in its first line the word that is translated 'allure' in verse 16. This time, however, it is used in a bad sense, meaning 'incitement to evil', and not to what is good — that is, returning to God. It means turning against him with an 'anger' that is born of self-sufficiency.[13] Job had done that too.

Secondly, the word **'ransom'** appears in the second line of this verse. Elihu had used this in 33:24, and there it means the price of deliverance for an afflicted person who has sinned. The same meaning (i.e. price) should be carried over into this verse, but now related to the costliness of the repentance that is the prelude to restoration. Elihu is warning Job not to let such a cost hinder his turning to God.

3. Verses 19 and 20 direct him not to trust even in any cry for help, and certainly not to long for sudden death. Again, Job has done both.

This twofold address continues into verses 22-25, as is obvious. Because God is so great how can anyone (Job in particular, of course) presume to instruct, let alone correct, him? The appropriate response is so different. It is not merely to submit to the work of his hand, but to sing about it — that is, to praise him, to 'bless the name of the LORD', as Job had done (see 1:21). Even so, God's works exceed man's understanding and ability to express them because he is so great (see 26:14).

'Behold, God is great, and we know him not' (36: 26 – 37:24)

36:26
Behold, God is great, and we know him not;
   the number of his years is unsearchable.

God's greatness is such that no limits that can be set to his age (36:26), and that relates to his wisdom rather than to his eternity. Wisdom and age were closely associated in the ancient Near East and Elihu recognized this, even though he was forced to conclude that they did not always go together (see

32:7-9). But God is God; he always knows why he is doing what he is doing, and his works are beyond human comprehension (see 36:29; 37:5). Man can neither circumscribe nor encapsulate him.

The descriptions of the processes of nature that follow demonstrate this. They are not merely displays of divine power, but are aspects of God's wise administration or providence (see 36:31; 37:7,12-13).

First, Elihu describes the processes of evaporation and precipitation (36:26-28) as being God's activity. **'He'** (that is, God) draws water upward and then it is let down from the skies as **'his'** mist or rain. This is for **'mankind abundantly'**, and human beings could not survive without it. God sustains and provides for the life he creates.

Secondly, Elihu turns from the gentle rain to the thunderstorm (36:29 – 37:5). He records its awe-inspiring build-up, the thunder from **'his** [i.e. God's] **pavilion'** that crashes on human ears and the forked lightning that always strikes wherever God may hurl it. These are indeed 'acts of God' which manifest his displeasure as well as his beneficence.

Thirdly, the snow and ice, and a blasting freezing wind that accompanies them, come from God too (37:6,9). These prevent animals and people from going about whatever business they may engage in, good or bad. This is all at his directing and in pursuance of his purpose, which may be of correction, or just for the land, or out of his love and mercy for people, and that is what Job needs to hear.

37:14-15,18
Hear this, O Job;
   stop and consider the wondrous works of God.
Do you know how God lays his command upon them
   and causes the lightning of his cloud to shine? ...
Can you, like him, spread out the skies,
   hard as a cast-metal mirror?

Elihu has reviewed these **'wondrous works of God'** with a view to Job's benefit. He therefore calls upon Job personally to consider them and confronts him with the limitations of his knowledge and of his power by means of the two questions: **'Do you know...?'** and **'Can you...?'** (37:14-20) When a wind blows from the desert, Job's body temperature rises. The air is stifling and it is difficult to do anything (37:18), let alone spread the steely blue sky. With a degree of sarcasm Elihu then asks Job for instruction as to how he and others might enter a complaint against God in his court, when even at midday (see 37:17-18) man's understanding is so darkened. What could be said to God, who does not need to be told that someone wishes to speak with him, and by someone who is so easily overawed by his presence?

37:22-23
Out of the north comes golden splendour;
 God is clothed with awesome majesty.
The Almighty — we cannot find him;
 he is great in power;
 justice and abundant righteousness he will not violate.

Even as Elihu describes the activity of God in a thunderstorm he trembles and becomes agitated (37:1). But he now becomes aware of something more awesome than a storm brewing up (37:21). It is the light of God that floods the landscape after the storm has passed and the clouds have cleared. God's majestic presence draws near. The Almighty, who cannot be found by human effort, wisdom or righteousness, condescends to disclose himself, and he does so in the interest of maintaining justice and showing saving righteousness. He is to be feared by any who are proud and confident — Job included (37:23-24).

The word **'Behold'** is one of Elihu's favourite words. He uses it twelve times in his addresses (see

32:11,19; 33:2,6,7,10,12,29; 36:5,22,26,30.) It is an important term in what he says. To omit it from a translation, as the NIV does, is a serious omission. It is not superfluous but significant. Its meaning is obvious, but the way Elihu uses it is what is important. Once it is used to call Job to look at himself; five times it is used to make Job aware of who (or what) Elihu really is, and the remaining six occurrences focus on God. This term sets up a triangle of relationships between Elihu, Job and God that points to the nature and purpose of Elihu's ministry, which is to bring Job to God. Its omission from the second and third speeches is noteworthy because that is where Elihu reasons with Job. It is in his first and last speeches that he calls Job to stand to attention and to focus 'eyes front' on God.

7. The LORD speaks

(Job 38:1 – 42:6)

Chapters 38 – 42 record the intervention of the LORD
and the restoration of Job. The latter is largely described in the last eleven verses of the book and they
are in prose, not verse. They are therefore left for
consideration by themselves and at this point we
shall simply note that they bring the narrative of Job
to a most fitting conclusion.

The remainder of these chapters consists of the
LORD's two speeches to Job and his two replies. The
same pattern of speech and reply is therefore continued from the previous chapters, and that contributes
to the wonderful harmony of the book. However, this
personal encounter and verbal exchange is so special
that it is vital to appreciate its significance before we
look at any of its details. We shall therefore focus our
attention on the ways by which the author signals
that the end of the narrative is to be understood in
the light of the beginning. There are two matters to
note.

The reappearance of the divine name

God is referred to as 'LORD' in these chapters and
also in the prose section at the end of the book. That
is the name used for God in the opening two chapters. **'The LORD'** stands for the covenant Redeemer,

the 'I AM THAT I AM'. Job may be the chief human actor in the drama, so to speak, but Jehovah is the chief agent in the history that this book records. The narrative is related to the message of his sovereign, redeeming grace towards his people — and that is the theme of the whole Bible. Whatever else must be acknowledged in these chapters, the grace of the LORD is paramount.

The duplication of speeches and replies

38:1,3
Then the LORD answered Job out of the whirlwind and said:

'... Dress for action like a man;
   I will question you, and you make it known to me...'

40:6-7
Then the LORD answered Job out of the whirlwind and said:

'Dress for action like a man;
   I will question you, and you make it known to me...'

The fact that the LORD speaks *twice* is also a reminder of the beginning. Just as his two speeches about Job to Satan had set in motion the trial of Job in which he stood up so magnificently, so now there are two speeches which bring him to a better frame of mind. This 'doubling' feature leads up to the statement in 42:10 that is so important.

These literary features recapitulate the opening prose section and they indicate that the author wants the climactic end of the narrative to be connected with its staggering beginning.

Looking more closely at these chapters, we need to note three recurring phrases. They are as follows:

1. The LORD addresses Job out of the whirlwind (38:1; 40:6)

Job has been wanting God to speak to him. At last he does. But it does not take place as or when Job requested it. Elihu was the answer to his demand that God would appear and declare him to be in the right. The LORD neither hurried nor humbled himself to do what Job demanded. He appeared in his own time and way — and that was not as Job's equal! He came in his majesty, by way of a theophanic manifestation, akin to what happened on Mount Sinai. That was heralded at the end of Elihu's last speech and he withdrew to leave Job alone before the LORD.

2. The LORD summons Job to prepare for verbal combat (38:3; 40:7)

'Dress for action [literally "Gird up your loins"] **like a man,'** means more than just 'Stand on your feet' (cf. Ezek. 2:1). Each word has an association with a contest: for example, the word for **'man'** is the word for a warrior; **'loins'** are the upper thighs that contribute strength to posture; and **'gird'** refers to the act of tying a belt around robes which had been pulled up because they would otherwise impede freedom of movement (see Exod. 12:11; 1 Kings 18:46). Here is a call to arms, or to a wrestling bout, but the combat is to take place in a court of law. This is a trial by ordeal, as in the case of a wife suspected of adultery (see Num. 5:11-31) or of opposition to Moses and Aaron (Num. 16; 17). Anyone who removed his opponent's belt in a wrestling match effectively disabled him and won the bout. God is going to wrestle with Job as the Angel of the LORD did with Jacob (Gen. 32:24).

3. The LORD calls Job to instruct him

'**I will question you, and you make it known to me**' (38:3; 40:7) are words that are full of irony and warning. The LORD feigns to take the part of a disciple or student and invites Job to be his teacher, and in effect his ruler. This is no more than a taking of Job at his word and a turning of the tables on him. It is the nature of the ordeal — not physical, hand-to-hand combat, but a verbal battle about who knows where wisdom lies, about who has the right to rule and who knows best (see 38:2; 40:2,8). God does not appear in order to provide Job with an explanation of his suffering, but with an examination of his thinking and attitude.

The LORD sets about this by means of a most fearful interrogation of some seventy questions. We shall see that the first of these deals with Job's ignorance (38:2) and the second with his impudence (40:2). This progression endorses the admonitory aspects of Elihu's ministry and these are registered in Job's two responses (40:4-5; 42:2-6), the second of which reaches the bottom line of spiritual reality and humility. The first is an admission of frailty; the second is a confession of sin.

Given this progression in the narrative, our consideration must proceed in sequence, just as in the case of the opening two chapters of the book. We shall therefore consider each speech and reply as a unit, but make some further division within each speech of the LORD because of their length. Formerly Job was the one who had most to say. Now that is not so.

'Shall a fault-finder contend with the Almighty?'
(Job 38:1 – 40:2)

The LORD's first speech proceeds from 38:1 – 40:2. We have already commented on 38:1 and 3 and now focus on the remainder of the passage.

38:2
Who is this that darkens counsel by words without
    knowledge?

Elihu had charged Job with speaking without knowledge and insight (see 34:35) and here the LORD endorses that judgement. He describes Job as one who **'darkens counsel by words without knowledge'**, charging him with having confused matters rather than clarifying them. This is the opposite of wisdom.

What follows is a most fearful interrogation. Job is battered from pillar to post and to a degree beyond anything that he has had to endure from the Friends. A barrage of questions assails his ears about himself in relation to his environment — about the earth and the sea (38:4-21), the skies (38:22-38) and, finally, the land animals and birds (38:39 – 39:30). It is this transition from the inanimate to the animate that provides the explanation for the division in our exposition at this point.

The form of some of these questions is impersonal: for example, 'Who founded and measured the earth?'

(38:4-5); 'Who shut in the sea?' (38:8); and 'Which is the way to...?' (38:19). But there are others that are personal, such as, **'Where were you...?** (38:4), **'Have you commanded...?'** (38:12), **'Can you...?'** (38:31,34,39) and **'Do you know...?'**(38:33; 39:1). Most of them are left without answers, but not all. There are first-person singular declarations (38:4,9,23; 39:6) which spell out the answer to all the others. God the LORD is the one who has the knowledge and power to act.

Job is being put in his place by means of rhetorical and direct questions because he has not given God his proper place. He is interrogated about his environment so that he might become aware of his own great ignorance about it, and therefore his unfitness to rule over it. And if that is so with regard to the world around him, then what about the world above him, with God, who is the Creator, Sustainer and Ruler of all, and also the world 'below' him?

The earth and the sea (38:4-21)

38:4,8-9

Where were you when I laid the foundation of the earth?
    Tell me, if you have understanding...
Or who shut in the sea with its doors
    when it burst out from the womb,
when I made clouds its garment
    and thick darkness its swaddling band...?

Like a massive edifice, the foundations of the earth were laid and its dimensions were determined, and all according to plan. Who was the builder? Job was nowhere in sight, nor was anyone else either. Only the angels witnessed the cornerstone being laid, and they were the ones who rejoiced (38: 4-7).[1]

Like an infant in the womb (see Ps. 139:13), the sea was 'knitted together' and then allowed to burst

out in all its surging power, but still confined in a
place assigned to it. Who did that? (38:8-11). Where
was Job then? Clearly, space is not under Job's
control and neither is time at his beck and call
(38:12). The sources of morning light and its spread-
ing distribution over the earth are beyond Job's
ability to discover and re-enact. Each day is a new
work of God, stamped with his insignia and adorned
with his splendour (38:14). It is like a day before the
Fall, for the wicked hide from the light and for a
while their shameful activity is suspended (38:13,15).

38:16,18-19,21
Have you entered into the springs of the sea,
    or walked in the recesses of the deep? ...
Have you comprehended the expanse of the earth?
    Declare, if you know all this.
Where is the way to the dwelling of light,
    and where is the place of darkness...?
You know, for you were born then,
    and the number of your days is great!

The mention of wickedness in God's world, together
with impending judgement, leads to a connection
between the sea (**'the deep'**) and darkness, the
darkness of death (38:16-17). Again, this is within
the scope of God's knowledge and rule. (This note
perhaps paves the way for what follows in the second
speech.)

Job is therefore being made aware that he knows
so little about God's world (38:18) and does so little in
it, and that is because he has arrived in it so late
(38:21). Heavy sarcasm pervades this piece, but it is
only a reply to Job in the same coin as he has spoken
both to and about God. More importantly, God is here
being the LORD — that is, the Redeemer. He is seeking to recover someone who has wandered from him.

The skies (38:22-38)

38:22
Have you entered the storehouses of the snow,
    or have you seen the storehouses of the hail…?

Elihu had referred to the wonders of precipitation and here the LORD does the same. God has direct access to the warehouses where the natural elements are stored. They are his, and he uses them in accord with his good pleasure. Snow and hail, winds, torrential rain and ice are all his servants, just as the stars are. They all do his bidding. He uses some for judgement, like the hail (see Josh. 10:11), and others so that an uninhabited desert may bloom. He cares for the land he has made, and not only the creatures he has put in it. He is a bountiful provider and a wise administrator.

38:31,33
Can you bind the chains of the Pleiades
    or loose the cords of Orion? …
Do you know the ordinances of the heavens?
    Can you establish their rule on earth?

But it is not only the natural elements that are in his employ. So too are the heavenly constellations (38:31-33). 'Bound', they are suspended invisibly in space; 'loosed', they complete their circuits. But who appoints them these courses and tasks? They may rule, but who rules them? Is it Job? If it is, then perhaps he can govern. But stars are not at his beck and call, and neither are clouds (38:34-35). The rain is not his to direct, to soften hard soil so that it is made workable; lightning is not at his command. Exactly the same is true of wisdom (38:36).[2] God places it where he wills and uses it as he chooses —

and at the moment Job has been showing that he
lacks it.

The animals (38:39 – 39:30)

38:39-41
Can you hunt the prey for the lion,
    or satisfy the appetite of the young lions,
when they crouch in their dens
    or lie in wait in the thicket?
Who provides for the raven its prey,
    when its young ones cry to God for help,
    and wander about for lack of food?

39:26-27
Is it by your understanding that the hawk soars
    and spreads his wings towards the south?
Is it at your command that the eagle mounts up
    and makes his nest on high?

The LORD continues, and turns Job's attention from
the inanimate to the animate world. Land animals are
those that are selected, but they are all wild. They are
therefore outside man's care and control. But the God
who made them is sovereign over their movements
and instincts, and he provides for their needs. The
point that is being stressed is not man's superiority
over them (as in Genesis 1) but their direct depend-
ence on the God who created and sustains them. Man
is just a vicegerent in God's world, over which he has
not abdicated his sovereignty.

First, the king of the beasts is mentioned, or
perhaps it is the lioness (38:39-40). Does Job (i.e.
man) need to find food for them and their young?
They know where to place their dens for maximum
protection so as to take advantage of their prey. They
know how to hunt themselves and satisfy the hunger

of their cubs. And the same is also true even of ravens and their young, whose cry for food is personified as a cry to God (38:41) and is satisfied.

Secondly, the **'mountain goats'** (i.e. the ibex) and the hind are presented (39:1-4). They live out in the open, on rocky cliffs, and do not seek shelter or provision from human beings. They reproduce without human help, and the young are soon able to sustain themselves. Job is asked if he can put a timescale to all this. The implication is that not only is there one who can, but that he has done so, and he cares for mother and young without looking for human charity.

Thirdly, much the same is true of the wild ass (39:5-8). It roams free by God's behest and is not reined in by any man. Personified, it disdains city life and the shout of a cart driver to his burdened animal. It enjoys its freedom, and God provides what it needs even in uninhabited and inhospitable regions.

Thirdly, the **'wild ox'** is brought forward (39:9-12). This creature is massive and dangerous (Num. 23:22; 24:8). This is not the same as a bull. It would be extremely useful to a cart driver or a ploughman! But there is no hope of that. Sarcastically, Job is asked whether the ox would behave like a domesticated animal (39:9) or offer its services for daily tasks. Its phenomenal strength would be dangerous — but only to man and not to God, its maker and provider. A new note is struck here in the reference to creatures that present some kind of threat to man, and this will be developed later.

Fourthly, there is **'the ostrich'** (39:13 -18), which seems to be wholly lacking in maternal instinct. She seems not to care for her young, leaving her eggs where they are so vulnerable. But even this is in accord with divine provision (39:17) and her treatment of her eggs, though risky, is not ridiculous. But she is odd! Her great wings that flap do not enable her to fly! Yet she can outrun a horse that is spurred on by a rider! She is one of God's creatures too. He is sovereign over what seems to man to be senseless.

Fifthly, the war-horse itself is described (39:19-25). Job is reminded specifically that he has not given it its strength or splendour. Its flowing mane is not man-made and it prances like a locust and paws the ground as it snorts at the sound and smell of the battle. Fearlessly, it rushes over the ground and into the fray in spite of the weapons of war, and not because it is emboldened by man. God has made it so.

Finally, birds of prey are introduced, namely the hawk and the eagle (39:26,27). These do not migrate to the south, or return to nest beyond human reach at Job's command. They do not soar high and see far below because Job has given such power to their wings and such clarity to their eyes. Their young are fed from those humans slain in battle. Their behaviour (as also in the other cases cited) displays an innate **'understanding'** — the very thing that Job does not possess (see 38:4). God's plan for all things includes even death.

There is a conclusion to this speech that answers to its introduction. First, Job is described as lacking in wisdom and knowledge (see 38:2). Now he is described as one who nevertheless disputes with the LORD (40:2). God has thrown down his gauntlet and it is time for the foolish fault-finder to speak and to substantiate his accusation against the LORD.

'I lay my hand on my mouth'
(Job 40:3-5)

For one who does have knowledge to invite someone who has just been charged with ignorance to become his teacher is heavy irony indeed (38:2,3). But those are the terms of the debate to which the LORD God summons Job. It is therefore striking that Job's reply is so brief, but it is significant that he speaks at all. After all, he had not replied to Elihu although the latter had spoken to him of God's good purposes in affliction. But now Job is confronted by the LORD and the power of his word and of his grace, and it is as impossible for him to continue to be silent as it was for Satan not to reply when the LORD spoke to him. But what does Job say?

40:4-5
Behold, I am of small account; what shall I answer you?
　I lay my hand on my mouth.
I have spoken once, and I will not answer;
　twice, but will proceed no further.

First, he acknowledges that he is **'of small account'** (40:4) and he prefaces this admission with the word **'Behold'**. Job has been looking at himself as God's word has cut him down to size. Prior to the LORD's appearing, he was confident in his righteousness, claiming that God had 'stripped from [him his] glory and taken the crown from [his] head' (see 19:9; cf. 29:20). But that notion has been dispelled, and by his use of the word 'Behold' he now draws the LORD's attention to that fact.

In addition he says that he is 'light' (translated **'of small account'**; 'unworthy', NIV). The Hebrew word for 'glory' is connected with a verb that means 'to be heavy'. By using the word **'light'**, Job is therefore renouncing his previous claim to glory and his assertion that he would approach God 'as a prince' if God would only grant him an audience (see 31:37). He is acknowledging that he now has a much lower opinion of himself. But he needs to go lower still, and it is only God's word that can abase him.

Thirdly, he acknowledges that he had spoken before a number of times,[3] but he expresses the determination not to do so again. To resolve not to repeat a grievous mistake is progress. To 'lay one's hand upon one's mouth' is an emphatic way of expressing a resolve to be silent (see 21:5; 29:9). It can express a sense of reverence and shame, and here both are present to a degree. This amounts to the recovery of some wisdom, although he needs to go further still, much further! (That is why the LORD speaks once more, and this time Job's reply is more appropriate.)

Although Job does say something to the LORD by way of reply to his first speech, it is important to remember that, in reality, he refuses to reply to his challenge. He does not pick up the gauntlet that the LORD has thrown down. He says something about himself which was true, but he says nothing about God. He has acknowledged his own insignificance, but has not exalted the LORD's knowledge and wisdom. He is aware that he should not have spoken, but does not repent of his pride in having repeatedly done so. Job is therefore only sobered but not humbled. He is not yet worshipping the LORD as he did at the beginning (see 1:20; 2:10). The interrogation is therefore resumed and taken further and deeper.

'Who can stand before me?'
(Job 40:6 – 41:34)

40:8 (NIV)
Would you discredit my justice?
  Would you condemn me to justify yourself?

The all-important question that Job is now asked is: **'Would you discredit my justice?'** This translation is preferable because it contains the word **'justice'**, and that is what Job must acknowledge, namely the justice of God's rule.[4] To bring this about the LORD, who has invited Job to teach him what he does not know (see 38:4), now gives him an opportunity to rule the world instead of him! (40:10-14).

Having made a bid to 'approach' God 'like a prince' (see 31:37), Job is now told to dress as he had when he was a judge (40:10). If he can rule the world — and it is significant that it is the world of the proud and the wicked that is in view (40:12) — then the LORD will acknowledge that he has a right to rule and also the might to deliver himself. But can he?

40:9
Have you an arm like God,
  and can you thunder with a voice like his?

Merely to raise this question is of course to answer it. To be able to rule Job has to have **'an arm like God'** (40:9). In this verse **'arm'** is not just a synonym for strength, which it is in other places. It is parallel to

God's **'voice'**, because his arm accomplishes what his word declares. Can Job speak like God, so that what he says is done? Can he abase the proud and imprison the wicked by his mere say-so?

It is such a world of pride and wickedness that the LORD describes by speaking of Behemoth and Leviathan. They are the very apotheosis of evil. At this point it would be useful to refer to the section in the introduction that deals with mythology (see pages 33-36) because the question that has to be faced is whether these creatures are just ordinary, or whether they have any relevance to a supernatural realm, and if so what that may be. Such questions must be answered by patient investigation of this context, and not just verbal connections with extra-biblical literature.

We begin by noting three basic matters about Behemoth and Leviathan:

1. They are God's creatures (40:15,19; 41:33). This fact must be remembered because these beasts appear as divine beings in Egyptian and Canaanite mythology. There is no condoning of such a world view in these speeches. What we have is the same distinction between God and all else that was noted in the opening chapters. Mythological allusions may be employed, but monotheism is never even questioned.

2. They are not like the creatures mentioned in the LORD's first speech. Those animals were creatures of land and air. Behemoth and Leviathan are found on land and in water (see 40:21-24; 41:31). They are amphibious. The sea is associated with the deep and with evil.

3. But most important is the fact that these animals are not just independent of man. They are hostile to him.

We shall now examine what is said about each and do so from the standpoint of whether Job can rule them.

'Behold, Behemoth' (40:15-24)

40:15,19
Behold, Behemoth,
   which I made as I made you;
   he eats grass like an ox...
He is the first of the works of God;
   let him who made him bring near his sword!

'Behemoth' is a plural noun in Hebrew and it means 'cattle'. In its singular form (*behemah*) it is used to designate a beast or an animal. In the plural, it is also used metaphorically for the land and empire of Egypt, an enemy of Israel (Isa. 30:6). What does it stand for here?

First, let us notice the details that are natural. Behemoth **'eats grass like an ox'** (40:15), but it is stronger by far. It is herbivorous and has often been identified with the hippopotamus. It lives in the wild and it lies in the water (40:20-23) and is as unstressed in the one habitat as in the other. Even if the water[5] becomes turbulent, this creature knows no agitation, as a land animal would. It cannot drown. It also resists capture by man (40:24), and the same is said about Leviathan (see 41:1-7).

The LORD is here confronting Job with something that actually threatens his existence, and not only with something that can exist without him, as in the previous speech. And Leviathan is worse in this respect than Behemoth.

But secondly, are there details in the text that indicate that there is something more than what is natural here? There are in fact several.

1. It should be noted that all the verbs in this section are in the singular number, but Behemoth is a plural noun. It is therefore a plural of excellence.

2. This creature is described as **'the first of the works of God'** (40:19). In what sense is **'first'** used? Was Behemoth the first creature to be made? No, its 'primacy' consists in something else.

3. **'Behold, his strength...'** (40:16) is the answer to this question. Behemoth is **'power'** from head to tail; its frame, muscles and limbs are all impressively described by way of allusion to hard metals. Even its stumpy tail can be stiffened to good effect!

4. The only existing power that can overcome it is a **'sword'** that is wielded by its Maker (40:19). It lies almost submerged in water (40:24) and man cannot capture it.

Behemoth is therefore a creature of God that does not submit to man (who was given lordship over the animals), but only to its Maker. This is significant. It opens up the possibility that something that is more than what is natural is in view here, something that threatens man, the crown of God's creative handiwork.

And also Leviathan (41:1-34)

The transition to Leviathan is made with immediate ease and with the same point under consideration. Leviathan is a creature that God has made and placed in that sea on which ships sail and where it 'plays' (see Ps.104:25-26). But here Leviathan is not to be played with (41:5). Is there something that is more than what is natural in this depiction too?

We need to remember that Job has also referred to Leviathan in terms that are ominous, and not innocuous (see 3:8). In his mental-spiritual struggle with evil, as he laments his existence, he refers to those who 'rouse up Leviathan' so that sun and moon, the 'rulers' of day and night (see Gen. 1:14-19), are swallowed up. This is an allusion to Canaanite mythology which Job is only using for poetic effect to express the intensity of his desire to have the day of his birth obliterated. But what does the reference to Leviathan connote here in chapter 41?

Again we begin with the natural identification of this creature. It is the crocodile that is most usually favoured because of the remarkable description of that creature's anatomy in the text (41:12-34). It exceeds all that is said about Behemoth. The picture therefore worsens. Leviathan wears armour like a warrior — only much more of it. The **'doors of his face'** (i.e. its jaws, 41:14) spell terror. Its back has so many shields on it, all of which interlock so perfectly (41:15-17). Its nostrils squirt spray that becomes translucent in the light, and the narrow slits of its eyes are like the first light (41:18). Spray from its mouth looks like fire in the sunshine (41:19). Its neck is formidable; its skin is uniform, and it is fierce (**'his heart is hard'**, 41:24). It inspires fear and it resists weapons. When it walks, its underparts leave tracks in mud; when it swims it causes water to seethe. It leaves its mark on earth and its wake in the water (41:30-32).

But is there something more here besides a creature that is untamed by man? It is readily admitted that the natural identification of Leviathan (and Behemoth) could satisfy the purpose for which they are introduced, namely to humble Job. But are there more details to consider? I would suggest that there are and note them now so that they may be pondered.

1. The more fearful beast (41:1-7)

41:1-2
Can you draw out Leviathan with a fish-hook
    or press down his tongue with a cord?
Can you put a rope in his nose
    or pierce his jaw with a hook?

The LORD tells Job to 'behold' Behemoth (40:15,16,23) and concludes his description of it with just one question to him (40:24). But he asks him seven questions about Leviathan, almost all directed to Job specifically, and calculated to make him aware that not only is there a world that is beyond his control, but that there is one which is hostile to him. Leviathan is therefore more terrifying than Behemoth. Leviathan cannot be caught as one would catch a fish (41:1-2); it will neither plead for mercy nor promise service (41:3-4); it will not become a child's toy or a trader's wares (41:5-6). Its skin is impermeable to harpoons and spears (41:7). It cannot be penetrated. This is far more than is said about Behemoth.

2. The greater assault (41:8-11)

41:8,10
Lay your hands on him,
    remember the battle — you will not do it again! ...
No one is so fierce that he dares to stir him up.
    Who then is he who can stand before me?

Job is therefore invited to use his hands to catch this creature which fishing spears cannot subdue (41:8). Some battle would ensue! Job would not forget it. Of course Job would not do anything so foolish (41:9-10). But he has been guilty of greater folly. Job has claimed to stand before God himself! (41:10). There is a strong contrast expressed in this verse. If

Leviathan is not to be roused, what price God? No human being in his senses would launch an assault barehanded on Leviathan. But Job has been high-handed in his treatment of God, who is not indebted to anyone and therefore not obligated to any (41:11; cf. Rom. 11:33-36). Behemoth and Leviathan are merely creatures of the Creator!

3. The real clue (41:33-34)

41:33-34
On earth is not his like,
   a creature without fear.
He sees everything that is high;
   he is king over all the sons of pride.

The final two verses of the LORD's speech are in the nature of a summary comment about Leviathan. They describe it in relation to mighty people (41:25) and all the other animals (41:33); to all that is high and exalted. It has no equal among beasts or humans. Leviathan is fearless and formidable and laughs playfully at everything that opposes it (41:29). It **'sees** [looks down on] **everything that is high; he is king over all the sons of pride'** (41:34).

Having been careful not to allow Handel's *Messiah* to determine the interpretation of Job 19:25, we had better not let Luther's words, 'Strong mail of craft and power he weareth in this hour; on earth is not his equal', exert too strong an influence on our thinking with regard to this verse! But it is difficult to restrict this depiction to what is only natural, and that is not only because of the way in which the presence and power of 'super-nature' were attested in ancient Near-Eastern mythologies. In Egyptian art, for example, the hippopotamus and the crocodile were often represented together.

It seems to me that the connection between Job and the book of Revelation is more important and significant than that between Job and ancient Near-Eastern literature. There are echoes of Job 40 – 41 in Revelation 12 – 13, where two beasts are described as being in league with the dragon and Satan. 'Leviathan' was translated by the word 'dragon' in the Greek (pre-Christian) translation of the Old Testament. One of the beasts was terrestrial and the other aquatic and they are both connected with the dragon/Satan. All of these made war on the Saviour and on the saints — just as happened to Job. The possibility therefore arises that the amphibious Behemoth, itself a plural noun, is further described and divided, so to speak, into the two beasts of Revelation 13. Whether that is far-fetched or not, the expression 'Who is like ...?' in Revelation 13:4 is an echo of **'On earth there is not his like'** (41:33).

Job is therefore being told that there is fierce evil in God's world that opposes God's people. *To that extent* his suffering is explained, but he must realize that, as it is only the LORD who can rule creatures which present such 'hideous strength' and are clothed with 'strong mail of craft and power', he must bow low before the LORD. That is his wisdom and piety.

'I despise myself and repent in dust and ashes'
(Job 42:1-6)

There has been so much disputing in the book of Job. First, Satan disputes with the LORD in his court over Job's piety, and all the subsequently recorded events and words are to be related to that disagreement, albeit in different ways. Job then disputes with God; the Friends dispute with him and he with them, before Elihu takes issue with them all, again for different reasons. Finally, the LORD intervenes and, significantly, does not dispute with Elihu but he does take up the cudgels against Job and the Friends. Will the war ever subside? Will peace ever return?

To be accurate, the clamour did begin to subside when Job was able to refute the basic thesis of the Friends and they began to withdraw. Its decibel level was then reduced even further as a result of Elihu's intervention and ministry because no one answered him. At last, and then only by way of response to the LORD's first address, Job declared 'no contest' and resolved to remain silent. But silence is not peace or harmony. *Shalom* has not yet been established.

In order to bring about such restoration the LORD speaks again to Job and this time a significant and desirable change occurs. Job agrees with the LORD and prostrates himself before him. He confesses that God is right(eous) and that he himself is in the wrong, totally and utterly. He is using **'dust and ashes'** language once more, as in chapters 1 and 2.

This is what marks the return to a true and growing harmony, which is described in the Epilogue. Restoration is therefore inward before it is outward, and spiritual before it is physical and social.

We shall use this theme of 'agreement' in order to make our way through these verses, and that of 'restoration' with regard to the concluding section of the book (42:7-17). Repentance (and, indeed, faith) consists in agreeing with God, having reflected on what he says. It is an unreserved and intelligent 'Amen' that God delights to hear and to which he responds with abundant blessing, as Elihu had promised (see 33:23-30).

Job agrees with the LORD about himself (42:2).

42:2
I know that you can do all things,
    and that no purpose of yours can be thwarted.

He uses the term **'I know'**, which recalls his joyful confession recorded in 19:25-27. It is not sullen capitulation but glad submission. Job gave up in his first reply; he gives in with these words and he glorifies God. Just as he had said to his wife that they should receive evil as well as good from the LORD's hand, so now that is in effect what he is doing. He acknowledges the LORD's power and purpose towards him in all his dealings, his sufferings included. With a mind renewed, he is finding that God's will is 'good and acceptable and perfect' (see Rom. 12:2).

Job agrees with the LORD's view of himself (42:3-6)

42:3-4
'Who is this that hides counsel without knowledge?'

Therefore I have uttered what I did not understand,
   things too wonderful for me, which I did not know.
'Hear and I will speak;
   I will question you, and you make it known to me.'

In verses 3-4 Job acknowledges the truth of what the
LORD had said about him. He does this in two ways.
   First, he makes use of words that the LORD has
spoken and he makes comments in the light of them
(42:3). Secondly, he quotes some of his own words to
God that God had turned back on him (43:4).
   In verse 3 he quotes the LORD's opening words to
him (see 38:2). By doing so without any comment he
is acknowledging that they apply to him. He is the
one who, lacking all knowledge, has presumed to
advise God. How could he be so foolish? Only because
he was without 'understanding' and the matters he
spoke about were too 'exalted' for him to know (42:3).
He is here confessing that there is something within
him that prevents him from knowing what is above
him. This is not a denial of his spiritual integrity, but
an acknowledgment that he has thought too highly of
himself and his own understanding.
   In verse 4 Job is quoting both himself and God. He
had asked — and in a most peremptory spirit — that
God would speak to him on his own level, or vice
versa (see 13:22). But when the LORD appeared and
spoke to Job he quoted Job and with a holy sarcasm
invited Job to do what he had said! (See 38:3; 40:7).
   Now Job is putting things the right way around,
and he is doing so with a humble spirit. He is saying
that it is the LORD who knows why he does what he
does, and that he is therefore the one who should
speak and to whom he will listen.

42:5
I had heard of you by the hearing of the ear,
   but now my eye sees you...

In verse 5 Job explains that his previous outbursts were linked with a knowledge of God that was less than that which he now possesses. He contrasts **'hearing'** with 'seeing' in order to describe this, and that is a strong but not an absolute contrast. In understanding what it means (and does not mean) two facts need to be borne in mind.

The first is that Job's previous knowledge by hearing was not just notional or theoretical. It had a profound and far-reaching impact on his life (see the opening chapter of *Job*). The second is, of course, that the enlargement of Job's knowledge is related to a theophany, a revelatory intervention of the LORD. It is a larger and louder disclosure of the LORD in his graciousness that corresponds to his confession that he would see God as his Kinsman-Redeemer (19:25-27).

42:6
… therefore I despise myself,
  and repent in dust and ashes.

In verse 6 Job expresses the immediate effects of this personal encounter with God. This is an important statement, but three difficulties have to be faced in considering it. The first is textual and the others concern translation. We shall consider these in turn and in that way comment on this important statement.

1. 'Myself'?

There is nothing in the Hebrew text that corresponds to the word **'myself'**. The verb **'despise'**[6] has no object, and so the question has therefore been raised as to who it is that Job is despising. Is it himself, or is it God? Some have advocated the latter view.[7] On this matter it is helpful to note that Job has used exactly the same verb without an object before. In 7:16 he had said (literally), 'I despise' before continuing with

the words: 'I would not live for ever.' At that point he
was resenting strongly what he believed were God's
dealings with him. But he later makes it clear that it
is '[his] life', and not God, that he is despising (see
9:21).

Applying this to verse 6 means that Job himself is
in some sense the object of the rejection that he
expresses. The reason for this is not far to seek. It is
implicit in the word **'therefore'** which precedes the
verb. He despises himself for the way in which he has
spoken (42:3). The very suggestion that Job was
despising God is unnecessary and destructive of any
harmony in the book, and therefore of any spiritual
benefit to be derived from it. People may talk about
the dignity of human defiance of God, but it is just
another name for blasphemy and hopeless despair.

2. 'Repent'?

The other two matters concern the word **'repent'**.
Should this be understood as a confession of sin or
an expression of hope? There are those who, although
they reject the idea that Job is despising God, are
concerned to argue that Job is not confessing and
repudiating any sin by his use of this word. In support of this view they point to the fact that his sufferings were not due to his sin and also that ignorance
is not the same as iniquity. But weren't Job's accusations against God and misrepresentations of him
sinful? And doesn't the same apply to his overconfi-
dent assertions of his blamelessness? To fail to see
this is superficial and undercuts Elihu's role in the
narrative. It is true that the LORD does not accuse Job
of being a sinner in so many words. But he does
accuse Job by implication of foolishness (see 38:2)
and explicitly of finding fault with him (see 40:2).
What does that amount to, if not sin? Therefore Job

has something to confess and renounce before God, and that means repentance is appropriate.

But the word for 'repent' can also be translated 'comfort oneself',[8] and that is included as an alternative reading in the ESV. Rendering it that way means that the idea that Job was not confessing sin can be adopted and the verb 'repent' treated as meaning no more than an acknowledgment of limited understanding. This also belittles the enormity of Job's accusation against God.

But everything hangs on whether Job has sinned or not. If he has, then repentance is required and self-deprecation is fitting. The mention of **'dust and ashes'** points in this direction. These words should not be connected with Abraham praying for Sodom and Gomorrah (see Gen. 18:27). The differing contexts must be taken into consideration. At this point Job is not praying for the Friends but for himself. Job is not just confessing frailty before God. He sees the rubbish heap on which he is sitting to be an appropriate place for him to be because of his arrogance as well as his ignorance.

Once again he is worshipping Jehovah. Job has triumphed over Satan and God is glorified. We are back to the beginning — almost!

8. The Epilogue

(Job 42:7-17)

In the previous chapters of this commentary the term 'narrative' has been frequently used. That is only proper because *Job* does tell a story. It has a beginning and an end, and there is a thread of continuity between them. Even though much of it is in the form of poetry, that does not cancel out the historicity of the narrative; it enshrines it.

The focus of the story is on a part of Job's life. It is not a complete biography in the usual sense of that designation, although it should be noted that Job's birth (1:21), his youth (13:26; 31:18), his 'prime' (29:4) and his death in old age at the very close of the account (42:17) are all referred to. The story is therefore time-space history but, as with the case of the record of the Lord's life and ministry in the Gospels (see Luke 1:1-4; John 20:30-31), selectivity is employed in the interests of the history of God's redemptive self-revelation.

It has been the aim of this commentary to keep pace with the narrative from both the human and divine perspectives, and now that we come to the end of the book we must continue to do the same.

From a literary point of view this section corresponds to the opening chapters of the book, the Prologue. Like them it is in prose and is presented as a piece of continuous narrative. We shall therefore work our way through these verses as we did with those two chapters. But the divine layer of the history must not be overlooked for, just as the events in the Prologue introduced the theme of the 'steadfastness of Job', so those of the Epilogue record 'the purpose [literally "the end"] of the Lord', and they show that 'The Lord is compassionate and merciful' (see James 5:11-12).

Viewed from this twofold perspective, it becomes obvious that the expression 'Happy ever after' is hopelessly unsuitable as a description of these verses. For one thing, it is borrowed (or transferred) from the world of the fairy tale, and that hardly befits a book of sacred history. It is also used as a crowning indignity to indicate how untrustworthy the story line of Job is and how unsatisfactory is its content as an answer to the problem of apparently undeserved suffering. The use of it indicates the prejudiced mindset of many who take it upon themselves to comment on the Word of God.

This commentary has sought to demonstrate that the point of the book is not to answer the problem of suffering but to consider, as the New Testament says, 'the purpose of the Lord' with regard to Job, and so to encourage all Christian sufferers. It is not a fairy story, or a fable, but an epic of believing bravery, just like the heroes of faith listed in Hebrews 11, who 'by faith' obtained something better and 'of whom the world was not worthy'. As such, Job is a remarkable and an enduring success, and the Epilogue enhances that rather than diminishes it.

'The LORD turned the captivity of Job'
(Job 42:7-17)

42:10 (KJV). And the LORD turned the captivity of Job, when he prayed for his friends: also the LORD gave Job twice as much as he had before.

Having rejected the notion that these verses are non-historical and non-theological, we turn our attention to the question of how they should be understood. In my view the opening words of verse 10 provide such a key, but only when they are properly translated. Since the end of the nineteenth century they have been rendered as 'made [Job] prosperous again' (NIV) or **'restored the fortunes of Job'** (ESV). Older translations (and the ASV) give a more literal translation: 'The LORD turned the captivity of Job.'

It is essential to retain this older rendering, because it provides the key to understanding these verses, and we shall use it as gratefully as we adopted the statement of James, the Lord's brother, as the key to the whole book. But before we do this, the question as to why recent translations avoid the older rendering should be reflected on.

The answer, of course, is not that the older rendering was unknown. It is noted and commented on by writers on *Job*, and its accuracy as a translation of the Hebrew has been acknowledged. In general it can be said that the change is the result of the way in which theology is no longer given the entrée into the world of Old Testament study that it had previously enjoyed.[1]

But a particular reason is advanced for setting aside the older translation and this is something that we must take note of. It is that in all the other uses of this expression in the Old Testament (see Deut. 30:3; Ps. 126:1; Jer. 30:3,18; 31:23) the reference is to the bondage of the nation of Israel to an alien power that occupies its land. It is only in Job 42:10 that it is used of an individual. To that the only answer is: 'So what?' Was Job not hedged about by the LORD, as the promised land was later? And was Job not 'invaded' by an alien power? Why not recognize that what was frequently the case with Israel in the Old Testament is here the case with Job, the only difference being that Job had not sinned and his being 'occupied' and plundered was not due to God's judgement? The statement that 'The LORD turned the captivity of Job' makes clear that Job's sufferings were a kind of bondage and his restoration was a kind of deliverance or redemption.

This expression creates another link between Job and Israel because it describes spiritual blessing being manifested in material ways that express the LORD's kindness towards his believing people (see Deut. 28:1-14). Job 42:7-17 fits into that framework with ease and the events it records are typical of a return from bondage and exile and of an anticipation of heaven. This older translation must therefore be preserved. It is absolutely vital for a theological understanding of 'the coming of the Lord' (James 5:8).

Job's restoration, which has begun in his reconciliation to the LORD, is now demonstrated outwardly in two stages.

His restoration to a ministry for the LORD (42:7-9)

42:7-8. After the LORD had spoken these words to Job, the LORD said to Eliphaz the Temanite: 'My anger burns against you and against your two friends, for you have not spoken of me what is right, as my servant Job has. Now therefore take seven bulls and seven rams and go to my servant Job and offer up a burnt offering for yourselves. And my servant Job shall pray for you, for I will accept his prayer not to deal with you according to your folly. For you have not spoken of me what is right, as my servant Job has.'

Although it is the Friends that are addressed by the LORD in these verses, the focus is still on Job. Four times he is described as the LORD's servant (42:7-8) and he is differentiated from the Friends in terms of his having said what was right about the LORD. So God the LORD reverses their standing respectively. It is they who are charged with folly and threatened with punishment, and not Job.

However, the LORD graciously provides them with a means of averting his anger. It involves their repentance because they have to go to Job, who is still afflicted, and seek his priestly ministry. They are to go to him with sacrifices that are costly and numerous, and he will pray for them in connection with the sacrifices being offered. That the Friends did this is an indication that they were good men. That Job prayed for them to be forgiven while he himself was still afflicted makes him a wonderful type of the Lord Jesus, the Christ of God, the Lord's Suffering Servant and the High Priest of his sinful people. It also displays how wrong Satan was in his view of Job and of God.

But what does 'speaking what is right about the LORD' mean? The Friends are said not to have done this, whereas the opposite is declared about Job. Several suggestions have been made. Many of these involve very fine distinctions indeed and some are based on a tenuous psychological reading of the characters involved.

The simplest and clearest explanation is related to what Job has just said. He has confessed his limited understanding and outspokenness; they have not.[2] The Friends presumed to know what was right about Job's case and said so in God's name. They said that he had been afflicted because God was punishing him for sins that he had committed before any of the losses that he had sustained. That was **'not ... right'**. But they did not admit it and withdraw their diagnosis. They had misrepresented God, and so were exposed to his holy displeasure. Job had also maligned God, but he had acknowledged his ignorance and confessed his arrogance.

His restoration to family and community (42:10-17)

42:10,12,17. And the LORD restored the fortunes of Job when he had prayed for his friends. And the LORD gave Job twice as much as he had before... And the LORD blessed the latter days of Job more than his beginning... And Job died, an old man, and full of days.

This account of the LORD's dealings with Job is a public demonstration of the sincerity of his piety and also of the LORD's delight in him. There is no mention of his being healed, although it clearly happened, and no record of his asking for such a blessing. He was healed as he was praying to the LORD for the Friends. His healing was a kind of transfiguration in communion with the LORD and as such is a type of the resurrection of the body and conformity to the Lord Jesus Christ.

Attention is focussed on his restoration to society and to family. Kinsmen return (**'brothers and sisters'** can include cousins) and close friends too. They express sympathy on account of his horrendous trials and provide some monetary compensation and a ring, which symbolizes honour (42:11; cf. Gen. 24:22,30,47). His livestock is doubled (this refers to a full measure of something — see Isa. 40:2) and his children too, for his former sons and daughters are not regarded as non-existent. Though no mention is made of Job's wife by name, no other is mentioned either. We presume she survived with him and enjoyed the LORD's blessing too. Their daughters are honoured by the LORD with beauty and by Job with suitable names[3] and, surprisingly, with an inheritance along with their brothers. His remaining lifespan is double the 'threescore years and ten' and three further generations surround him. His **'latter days'** are long and full of the LORD's blessing, a depiction of eternity in Old Testament terms.

But they are only an anticipation. Death, the last enemy, did intervene, but it was not in the form in which Job had either feared or fought it. It came in the midst of a life of bliss and ushered Job away in, and into peace (see Ps. 37:37).

Job 42:17 is the writer's epitaph for him. Although he was not a Hebrew or an Israelite, it is identical with that of the patriarchs Abraham and Isaac (see Gen. 25:8; 35:29), with the prophet-psalmist-king David (1 Chr. 28) and with the priest Jehoiada (2 Chr. 24:15). Job is therefore most worthy to be included in the annals of the Old and New Testament people of God, not only as a believer, but also as a 'messianic' figure, a type of that 'Kinsman-Redeemer' through whose sufferings at the hands of both God and Satan all who trust in him are saved, and are safe for evermore.

Select bibliography

Commentaries

Andersen, Francis I. *Job — An Introduction and Commentary,* Tyndale Old Testament Commentaries (Leicester: IVP, 1976)

Hartley, John E. *The Book of Job,* New International Commentary on the Old Testament (Grand Rapids, MI: Wm. B. Eerdmans Publishing, 1988)

Kline, Meredith G. *Job,* The Wycliffe Bible Commentary (Moody Press, 1962)

Thomas, Derek. *The Storm Breaks — Job Simply Explained,* Welwyn Commentary Series (Darlington: Evangelical Press, 1995)

Other writings

Calvin, John. *Sermons on Job* (Edinburgh: Banner of Truth Trust, 1993)

Carson, D. A. *How Long, O Lord? — Reflections on Suffering and Evil* (Leicester: IVP, 1990), especially pp.153-78.

Caryl, Joseph. *Sermons on Job,* volumes 1-12 (Grand Rapids MI: Dust and Ashes Publications and Reformation Heritage Books, 2001)

Fyall, Robert S. *Now my Eyes have seen YOU — Images of creation and evil in the book of Job,* New Studies in Biblical Theology (Leicester and Downers Grove, ILL.: Apollos, IVP, 2002)

Green, William H. *Conflict and Triumph — The Argument of the Book of Job Unfolded* (Edinburgh: Banner of Truth Trust, 1999)

Kline, Meredith G. 'Trial By Ordeal' in *Through Christ's Word: A Festschrift for Dr Philip E. Hughes*, eds. W. R. Godfrey and Jesse L. Boyd III (Presbyterian and Reformed Publishing, 1985)

Newell, R. Lynne. 'Job: Repentant or Rebellious', *Westminster Theological Journal*, 46 (1984), pp.298-316

Payne, J. Barton. 'Inspiration in the Words of Job', *Festschrift for O. T. Allis*, ed J. H. Skilton (Presbyterian and Reformed Publishing, 1974)

Waters, Larry J. 'The Authenticity of the Elihu Speeches in Job 32-37', *Bibliotheca Sacra* 156 (January-March 1999), pp.28-41

'Elihu's Theology and his View of Suffering', *Bibliotheca Sacra*, 156 (April-June), pp.143-59

Zuck, Roy B. (ed.). *Sitting With Job — Selected Studies in the Book of Job* (Baker Book House, 1992)

Notes

Author's preface
1. See N. A. Francisco, 'Job in World Literature', *Review and Expositor* 68 (1971), pp.521-33.
2. Thomas Carlyle, *On Heroes and Hero-Worship*, Centenary edition, p.49.
3. The NIV translation of Job is also recommended.
4. In my view the commentary by J. H. Hartley in the *NICOT* series (Grand Rapids, MI: Wm. B. Eerdmans Publishing, 1988) is particularly valuable.
5. This book has now been republished by the Banner of Truth Trust under the title *Conflict and Triumph*.

Introductory matters
1. In addition to commentaries and journal articles there have been novels, plays and poems. Examples will be given later.
2. James Barr's 1971 lecture 'The Book of Job and its Modern Interpreters', given at the John Rylands Library, seeks to consider the book as a whole but refers to the fact that rearrangements of the material, and even supplements to it, exist 'at least in the back of our minds' (*Bulletin of the John Rylands Library,* 54, p.30).
3. See *Sitting With Job*, a most useful collection of pieces of writing on *Job* edited by Roy B. Zuck (Baker Book House, 1992).
4. Psalm titles are different. They are part of the Hebrew text.
5. See R. K. Harrison, *Introduction to the Old Testament* (Eerdmans, 1969); Dillard and Longman III, *Introduction to the Old Testament* (Zondervan, 1994).
6. It should, however, be remembered on this latter point that such additions are of a very minor kind, whereas what is being posited with regard to *Job* is something on a large scale.
7. Although it is true that the Greek translation of the book is much shorter than the Hebrew text, this is generally attributed to difficulties which the translators experienced with its vocabulary, and not to the existence of a different text from which they

worked. The only departure from our text is in a scroll from Qumran, but that is in a fragmentary condition.

8. R. H. Pfeiffer wrote in 1948, 'It is thus clear that the critics have suggested every possibility: the prologue, the epilogue, or both (in part or *in toto*) were written by the author of the book, or by someone before him, or someone after him' (*Introduction to the Old Testament*, Harper, New York).

9. With regard to *style*, the prose sections (chapters 1 – 2 and 42:7-17) are regarded either as the original narrative, which was divided to make room for the debates, or as a subsequently written framework fitted around them. With regard to *theme*, the striking contrast between the portrayal of Job in the prose and poetic sections has strengthened the idea that two stories have been conflated. In addition, the 'wisdom poem' (chapter 28) and the Elihu portion (chapters 32 – 37) are regarded as each having a different provenance and it is claimed that chapters 24 – 27 are seriously disarranged. What we know as *Job* is therefore seen as the result of several revisions over an unspecified period of years. See my answers/comments on these matters at the appropriate places in the text.

10. See Pfeiffer, *Introduction to the Old Testament*: 'As in the case of the other problems raised by parts of the Old Testament, the evidence available is not conclusive. It is impossible to prove convincingly that the poet either wrote or did not write the folk tale.'

11. *Baba Bathra,* 14b.

12. *Baba Bathra,* 15a (other names were also mentioned by the rabbis).

13. This word of French origin, which literally means 'kind', has come to be widely used in biblical studies to refer to the different sorts of literature — e.g. poetry or prose, narrative or prophecy, etc.

14. See 1 Kings 3; 10; Matt. 12:42.

15. The eighteenth-century German philosopher G. W. F. Hegel claimed that ideas develop according to a movement from the simple to the complex, using the technical terms 'thesis', 'antithesis' and 'synthesis' to describe the development. It was this theory that Julius Wellhausen used to recast the history of Hebrew religion and the composition of the Old Testament. For him it was impossible that monotheism could precede henotheism (adherence to one particular god out of several), and of course both had to be preceded by polytheism.

16. Piety does not always lead to prosperity in Proverbs.

17. See *The Protests of the Eloquent Peasant — A Dispute over Suicide* (Egyptian) and the *Poem of the Righteous Sufferer — A*

Dialogue about Human Misery (Babylonian). These and others are to be found in J. Pritchard, *Ancient Near Eastern Texts*, 3rd ed. (Princeton: Princeton University Press, 1969). See also J. Gray, 'The Book of Job in the Context of Near Eastern Literature', *Zeitschrift für die alttestamentliche Wissenschaft*, 82 (1970), 251-69.

18. See W. J. Whedbee, 'The Comedy of Job', *Semeia* 7, Missoula, 1977.

19. See Barr, 'The Book of Job and its Modern Interpreters'.

20. Archibald McLeish, *J. B. A Play in Verse* (London, 1959).

21. K. J. Dell, *The Book of Job as Sceptical Literature* (Berlin, New York: De Gruyter,1991).

22. Most noticeably, *ribh,* which means 'lawsuit'.

23. H. Richter, *Studien zu Hiob* (Berlin: Evangelische Verlagsanstalt, 1959).

24. Zuck (ed.), *Sitting with Job.*

25. S. H. Scholnick, 'The Meaning of Justice in the Book of Job', Zuck (ed.), *Sitting with Job,* pp. 349-58. See also *Journal of Biblical Literature* 101 (1982) pp.521-9. Her dissertation (unpublished) is entitled *Lawsuit Drama in the Book of Job* (Brandeis, 1975).

26. Another seminal article is M. B. Dick, 'The Legal Metaphor in Job 31', Zuck (ed.), *Sitting with Job,* pp.321-44.

27. Meredith Kline, 'Commentary on Job', *Wycliffe One Volume Commentary on the Bible,* Moody Press. See also Meredith Kline, 'Trial By Ordeal', W. R. Godfrey and Jesse L. Boyd III, eds., *Festschrift for Dr Philip E. Hughes,* P&R, 1985.

28. Pfeiffer, *Introduction to the Old Testament,* p.683f.

29. Ezekiel therefore knew of Job around 600 BC.

30. S. Schreiner, *Where Shall Wisdom be Found? Calvin's Exegesis of Job from Medieval and Modern Perspectives* (University of Chicago Press, 1994).

31. See the work of E. Dhorme and M. H. Pope, *The Anchor Bible,* 1965.

32. Like Robert Gordis, who wrote *The Book of God and Man*; Samuel Terrien, who wrote *Job: Poet of Existence*; Norman Habel's commentary, and Edwin Good, *In Turns of Tempest.*

33. She refers to the work of Robert Gordis, Samuel Terrien, Norman Habel and Edwin Good among the commentaries; also to Carl Jung, H. G. Wells, Archibald MacLeish, Elie Wiesel and Franz Kafka.

34. Schreiner, *Where Shall Wisdom be Found?*, p.158.

35. *Ibid.,* p.163.

36. John Calvin did not write a commentary on Job, but preached 157 sermons on it in 1554. These are published by the Banner of Truth Trust in facsimile form

37. Joseph Caryl was a seventeenth-century English Puritan who preached through *Job*. His sermons are now available in twelve volumes from Reformation Heritage Books, Grand Rapids.

38. See works by W. H. Green, built on by Meredith Kline, Derek Thomas and Robert Fyall in the bibliography.

39. Hartley, *The Book of Job*, pp.12-15.

40. Schreiner, *Where Shall Wisdom be Found?*, p.19.

41. Barton Payne uses the terms 'inspired' and 'non-normative' to express this distinction in 'Inspiration in the Words of Job', *Festschrift for O. T. Allis*, ed. J. H. Skilton (Presbyterian and Reformed Publishing Co.,1974).

42. The same truth is stated in Psalm 9:15-16. Paul may possibly also be alluding to Job 4:8 in Gal. 6:7; to Job 4:9 in 2 Thess. 2:8 and to Job 41:11 (in English versions) in Rom. 11:35.

43. For example, 3:8; 7:12; 41:1.

44. See R. Laird Harris, 'The Doctrine of God in the Book of Job' and Elmer B Smick, 'Another Look at the Mythological Elements in the Book of Job', both in Zuck (ed.), *Sitting with Job*.

45. Elmer B Smick, 'Mythology and the Book of Job' and 'Another Look at the Mythological Elements in the Book of Job', both in Zuck (ed.), *Sitting with Job*.

46. Robert S. Fyall, *Now my Eyes have seen YOU. Images of creation and evil in the book of Job*, New Studies in Biblical Theology (Leicester: Apollos, IVP, 2002) p.26.

47. Fyall takes a mythological view of these creatures, a view that was common in pre-sixteenth-century exegesis, but also sees them in relation to the theology of the Prologue.

Chapter 1 — The Prologue

1. This rendering is to be preferred, rather than 'man', 'mankind' or 'others', as in the ESV, which in Hosea 6:7 renders the same Hebrew word as 'like Adam'. See Benjamin B. Warfield, 'Hosea VI.7: Adam or Man?' in *Selected Shorter Writings*, vol. 1, ed. John E. Meeter, Presbyterian and Reformed Publishing Co., 1976.

2. A good example of this is 1 Kings 21:10,13 with regard to Naboth.

3. See 1 Sam. 25:14; or Gen. 47:7,10; 24:60 respectively.

4. In the cultures of Assyria and Persia, the ruler employed a secret service which was called 'the eyes and ears of the king'. These men travelled throughout the empire and reported on the loyalty, or otherwise, of the subjects.

5. By means of this difference in type translators indicate which of two words is used in the Hebrew text for God. 'Lord' means 'master', 'owner' or 'ruler' and it translates *'adhonai'*. 'LORD' represents the divine, ineffable name (see Exod. 3:13-15; 6:2-3).

6. I am aware that to use the term 'Jehovah', as I do in this commentary, is to buck the scholarly trend which employs the term 'Jahweh / Yahweh'. But it cannot be guaranteed that 'Yahweh' was the correct vocalization, and the age-old rendering of this name as 'Jehovah', with vowels borrowed from *'Elohim'* (God) conveys much more to the Christian — for example, its use in corporate praise. (See R. Laird Harris, 'The Pronunciation of the Tetragam' in *The Law and the Prophets: Old Testament Studies in Honor of O. T. Allis,* ed. John H. Skilton, Presbyterian and Reformed Publishing Co., 1974.) Using 'Jehovah' will also enable the reader to think of the 'God and Father of our Lord Jesus Christ' in reading *Job* and the other Old Testament books, and that is not at all improper.

7. It is often pointed out that what is recorded about Satan in the New Testament should not be read back into Job 1 – 2. While that is fair enough from the point of view of exegetical method, and I would agree with it, it should also be pointed out that what is said about 'the Satan' in these chapters sets the mould for all that follows in the Bible. There is development between the Testaments but not disagreement, and that is the basis on which we shall proceed in this commentary. We shall therefore use the proper name, and justify doing so by the same reason as the use of the name Jehovah.

8. Folly is not silliness or stupidity. It is moral perversity (see the book of Proverbs)

9. The suddenness of their 'intervention' should be borne in mind when Elihu is referred to.

Chapter 2 — The debate between Job and the Friends (I)

1. A marker for the interrogative does not always appear in Hebrew. Voice inflection would be used for this purpose and this has to be deduced from the context. There are markers for 'Why?' in verses 11,12 and 20, but none in verses 16 or 23 — a continuation of verses 12 and 20 respectively.

2. This understanding reflects the valuable study of Jeremiah 4 and Job 3 by M. Fishbane in *Vetus Testamentum* 21 1977 and reviewed by Hartley in his commentary.

3. But he cannot be totally absolved because he becomes more explicit later (see 5:4).

4. Are there not many who still think like that, and proceed in their counselling and ministering on that basis? (See also John 9:1-3).

5. The words of 5:17 have become so familiar to Christian people by the fact that they are quoted in Heb. 12:5. But it is significant that Heb. 12:6 adds Ps. 94:12; 119:67,75 to Job 5:17. That extra quotation brings out the emphasis on adoption and the love of God in the light of the gospel revelation This is a note that Elihu will strike.

6. The word for 'godless' or 'profane' is used of the apostate in Israel (see Isa. 9:17).

7. This 'lack' is something that needs to be borne in mind in connection with other speeches, Elihu's in particular.

8. See Ezek.18:26; 33:12-14.

9. Just as the apostle Paul takes 5:13 out of its immediate setting in order to preach gospel grace in 1 Cor. 3:19, so these promises can be used to the same end in the wider canonical setting.

10. The word translated as 'god' here means image or sword.

11. Interestingly, H. H. Rowley, in his *New Century Bible*, refers to Ps. 51:5 at this point, whereas Francis Andersen sees no need to do so. J. H. Hartley recognizes the possibility that some kind of reference to ritual impurity may be involved and, by extension, to sins that will be committed. But chapter 1 has already referred to a ritual associated with sin and cleansing.

12. This would set Job in the post-Flood era.

13. Sheol at its darkest is where the dead are without God; at its brightest it is where God goes to deliver his people (Ps. 16:10).

14. The reference is to a myth of a heavenly man that became current in later rabbinic literature. The vocabulary here shows similarity with that of Proverbs 8:25-33 and there are echoes of it in Job 38 – 39.

15. Again this description is true — but not of Job! It can therefore properly be used in preaching about divine judgement on the wicked.

16. In the Hebrew 'God' is not named in verses 7-8, but he is in verse 11.

17. See G. Vos, *The Eschatology of the Old Testament* (Presbyterian and Reformed Publishing Co., 2001), pp.21-5.

18. *Ibid.*

19. Many commentators find problems associated with these sentiments in the mouth of Job, but these are based on a failure to understand the reality of the situation that Job now perceives and to appreciate the certainty of divine judgement.

Chapter 4 — Job continues his discourse
1. See the section in the introduction on 'The reality of human perception' (pp.30-32).
2. In Solomon's day silver and gold were brought to him (see 1 Kings 10:11; 2 Chr. 9:13-14).

Chapter 5 — Job's final defence
1. See also 41:4.

Chapter 6 — Elihu intervenes
1. See survey of opinion in Larry J. Waters, 'The Authenticity of the Elihu Narratives,' *Bibliotheca Sacra* 156, January-March 1999), pp.28-41.
2. See Hartley, *The Book of Job* and Francis I. Andersen, *Job. An Introduction and Commentary,* Tyndale Old Testament Commentaries (Leicester: IVP, 1976).
3. Those who read chapter 32 aloud in a church service should not place so much emphasis on 'I' as is often done, so as not to intensify this notion about Elihu that certainly needs to be tempered — if not actually laid to rest.
4. I see no reason for denying that God can and may use, or, indeed, that he has used this way of speaking to individuals who are quite outside the pale of the church to direct them to find a Bible, or to hear the gospel so that they might be saved. See Hywel R. Jones, *Do People Have to Hear the Gospel in order to be Saved?* (Day One Publications).
5. Such changes of subject are common in Hebrew poetry, and the Psalter in particular.
6. Perhaps this includes bystanders as well as the Friends.
7. Perhaps it is not Eliphaz, Bildad and Zophar who are described here. See comment at the appropriate place.
8. See Job's words in 9:20-22; 10:3-7; 13:18-19; 16:13-17.
9. The verb 'bear' lacks a complement but it is often used in connection with guilt.
10. This does not mean the sin for which he was afflicted. That is what the Friends said. Elihu is speaking of the sin Job has committed during his suffering.
11. See 35:16; 38:2-3.
12. It is difficult to see how the three Friends need to hear this speech of Elihu. They had exalted God, and not demeaned him. Perhaps Elihu is here thinking of Job's 'new-found friends' — namely, those referred to in 34:8.
13. This Hebrew word means 'plenty' or 'sufficiency'. The ESV construes the latter as leading to 'scoffing' (see 34:7,8).

Chapter 7 — The LORD speaks

1. As in the case of the Genesis account of creation, there is much here that is of a polemical nature. Ancient cosmogonies depicted the sea and the earth as being produced by battles between various gods. But there is nothing of that sort here, or indeed anywhere else in the Old Testament. Although terms and names (e.g. Leviathan) are borrowed, the conceptual picture is of God's sovereign, monergistic activity.

2. There are rare words here and opinion differs as to whether types of clouds are referred to, or birds (the 'ibis' and the 'rooster') that announce changes in the weather, or man's internal organs (the kidneys and the mind).

3. A metaphorical use of numbers has been noted before in 33:14,29. See also Amos 1; 2, where this occurs frequently.

4. The ESV obscures this point by allowing the second part of verse 8 to interpret the first, instead of noting and reproducing the difference between justice and righteousness. God's justice is an expression of his righteousness, but the two terms are not always interchangeable.

5. The Hebrew word for Jordan means 'a river'.

6. There are two possibilities with regard to identifying this verb. They differ in a single consonant and in some forms they are identical. The one means 'to despise' and the other, 'to melt away'.

7. For a thorough refutation of this view (and more) see B. Lynne Newell, 'Job: Repentant or Rebellious', *Westminster Theological Journal,* 46 (1984), pp.298-316.

8. In another form of the verb it means to comfort someone else (see 42:11).

Chapter 8 — The Epilogue

1. See comments by Schreiner in the introduction (pp.26-7).

2. The Hebrew expression that is translated **'of me'** can also bear the meaning '*to* me' and so what is in view is the Friends' silence, on the one hand, and Job's admission, on the other.

3. Jemimah means 'turtle dove' (see S. of S. 2:14); Keziah is the plant 'cassia', which was used in perfumery (see Ps. 45:7); and Keren-happuch means 'horn [equivalent to "bottle"] of eye-paint'.